BBC

DOCTOR WHO

SUPREMACY OF THE CYBERMEN

"With a lightning-fast pace, an epic scope, and a script that takes full advantage of what makes each modern Doctor fun and compelling, *Doctor Who: Supremacy of the Cybermen* is the series in its purest and most entertaining form!"
NEWSARAMA

"Manages to capture each Doctor and his companions so perfectly!"
THE GEEK GIRL PROJECT

" About as good as it gets... Confident, pacy and fun!"
MYM BUZZ

"A pretty much perfect and exciting mini series!"
THE DOCTOR WHO COMPANION

"If you are a fan of Doctor Who, this is one of the comics you cannot afford to miss. It captures the spirit of the show that we all know and love!"
OUTRIGHT GEEKERY

"*Doctor Who: Supremacy of the Cybermen* is a surefire ride!"
FANGIRL NATION

"Writers George Mann and Cavan Scott deliver an exciting story throughout – accompanied by stunning, colorful artwork from Ivan Rodriguez and Walter Geovanni... The stories instantly come alive!"
BLOGTOR WHO

TITAN COMICS

SENIOR COMICS EDITOR
Andrew James

ASSISTANT EDITORS
Jessica Burton, Amoona Saohin

SENIOR DESIGNER
Andrew Leung

TITAN COMICS EDITORIAL
Tom Williams

PRODUCTION SUPERVISORS
Jackie Flook, Maria Pearson

PRODUCTION ASSISTANT
Peter James

PRODUCTION MANAGER
Obi Onuora

ART DIRECTOR
Oz Browne

SENIOR SALES MANAGER
Steve Tothill

HEAD OF RIGHTS
Jenny Boyce

PRESS OFFICER
Will O'Mullane

COMICS BRAND MANAGER
Chris Thompson

DIRECT SALES & MARKETING MANAGER
Ricky Claydon

COMMERCIAL MANAGER
Michelle Fairlamb

PUBLISHING MANAGER
Darryl Tothill

PUBLISHING DIRECTOR
Chris Teather

OPERATIONS DIRECTOR
Leigh Baulch

EXECUTIVE DIRECTOR
Vivian Cheung

PUBLISHER
Nick Landau

FOR RIGHTS INFORMATION, CONTACT
jenny.boyce@titanemail.com

Special thanks to Steven Moffat, Brian Minchin, Matt Nicholls, James Dudley, Edward Russell, Derek Ritchie, Scott Handcock, Kirsty Mullan, Kate Bush, Julia Nocciolino, Ed Casey, Marcus Wilson and Richard Cookson for their invaluable assistance.

BBC WORLDWIDE

DIRECTOR OF EDITORIAL GOVERNANCE
Nicolas Brett

DIRECTOR OF CONSUMER PRODUCTS AND PUBLISHING
Andrew Moultrie

HEAD OF UK PUBLISHING
Chris Kerwin

PUBLISHER
Mandy Thwaites

PUBLISHING CO-ORDINATOR
Eva Abramik

DOCTOR WHO: SUPREMACY
OF THE CYBERMEN
HB ISBN: 9781785856846
SB ISBN: 9781785856853
FP ISBN: 9781785861895

Published by Titan Comics, a division of
Titan Publishing Group, Ltd. 144 Southwark Street,
London, SE1 0UP.

A CIP catalogue record for this title is available from
the British Library. First edition: January 2017

10 9 8 7 6 5 4 3 2 1

Printed in China.

Titan Comics does not read or accept unsolicited
DOCTOR WHO submissions of ideas, stories or artwork.

BBC

DOCTOR WHO

SUPREMACY OF THE CYBERMEN

**WRITERS: CAVAN SCOTT
& GEORGE MANN**

**ARTISTS: IVAN RODRIGUEZ
& WALTER GEOVANNI**
WITH ALESSANDRO VITTI & TAZIO BETTIN

COLORIST: NICOLA RIGHI
WITH ENRICA EREN ANGIOLINI

**LETTERS:
RICHARD STARKINGS &
COMICRAFT'S JIMMY BETANCOURT**

TITAN
COMICS

BBC

www.titan-comics.com

BBC

DOCTOR WHO

SUPREMACY OF THE CYBERMEN

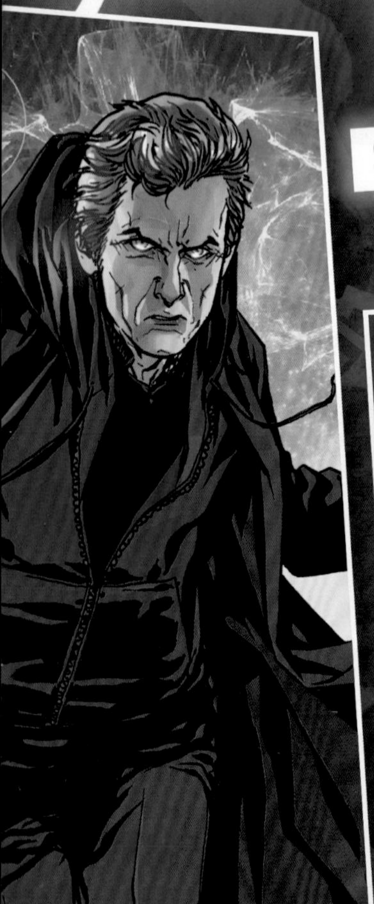

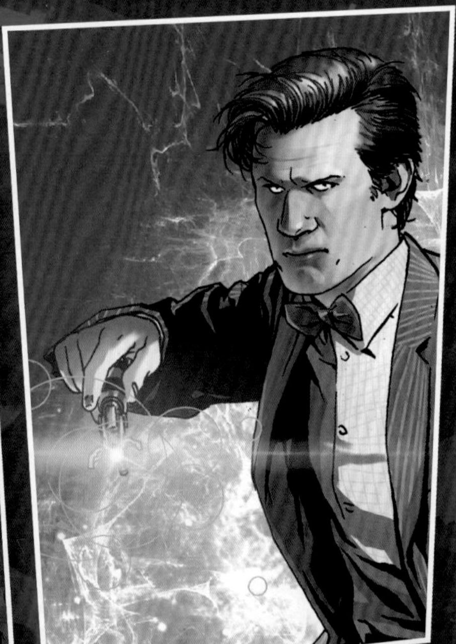

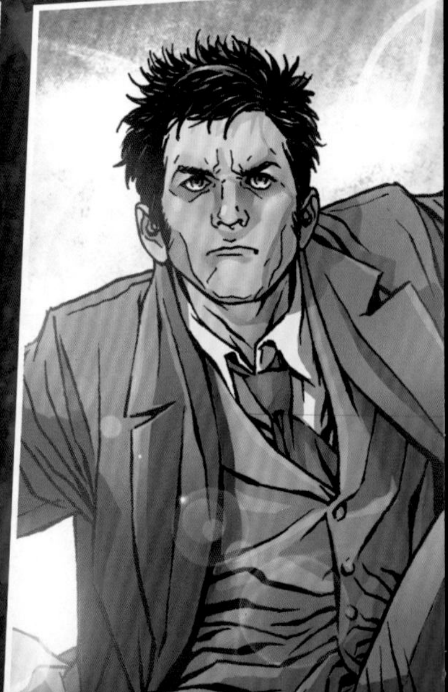

TWELFTH DOCTOR

Never cruel or cowardly, the Doctor champions the oppressed across time and space. His Twelfth incarnation has loosened up a little of late. Of course, having spent an eternity in a Time Lord prison recently, his outlook can still be...*cloudy* from time to time.

ELEVENTH DOCTOR

The Doctor's Eleventh incarnation is a gangly boy professor with an old, old soul. He most recently encountered the Cybermen as part of the alliance of enemies that moved against him in the Pandorica at Stonehenge – shortly before he rebooted the universe...

TENTH DOCTOR

Cloaking his post-Time War guilt in a happy-go-lucky guise, the Tenth Doctor has frequently battled with the Cybermen of a parallel universe, along with those which have made it to his native dimension. Most recently, he and Jackson Lake put paid to a Cyber-King in 1851.

PREVIOUSLY...

The Twelfth Doctor struggled through four billion years of torture to reach Gallifrey, his home world, which now resides at the end of the universe.

One man was not pleased to see the Doctor return: Lord High President Rassilon, responsible for the Doctor's imprisonment and ordeal. Responsible for the death of his companion, Clara.

Rassilon, whom the Doctor subsequently ousted in a bloodless coup, exiling him from Gallifrey to what was left of the cosmos.

But the Doctor's 'mercy' will have repurcussions that will echo back through all of his past lives.

At the end of the universe, Gallifrey is not all that remains...!

NINTH DOCTOR

Newly regenerated from an incarnation he will not talk about, the Ninth Doctor has not yet re-encountered the Cybermen in his new body – though he is still scarred by his memories of fighting them in previous bodies, and of the fronts that opened up against them in the Time War.

THE COMPANIONS

GABBY GONZALEZ

CINDY WU

ALICE OBIEFUNE

ROSE TYLER

CAPTAIN JACK

JACKIE TYLER

DOCTOR WHO

DOCTOR WHO EVENT TEASERS
WRITTEN BY
GEORGE MANN & CAVAN SCOTT

ART BY

FIRST DOCTOR
DAN BOULTWOOD

SECOND DOCTOR
ANDREW PEPOY & JASON MILLET

THIRD DOCTOR
MIKE COLLINS

FOURTH DOCTOR
BLAIR SHEDD

FIFTH DOCTOR
SIMONE DI MEO & ARIANNA FLOREAN

SIXTH DOCTOR
STEPHEN BYRNE

SEVENTH DOCTOR
SIMON MYERS

EIGHTH DOCTOR
LEE SULLIVAN & LUIS GUERRERO

WAR DOCTOR
RACHAEL STOTT & MARCIO MENYS

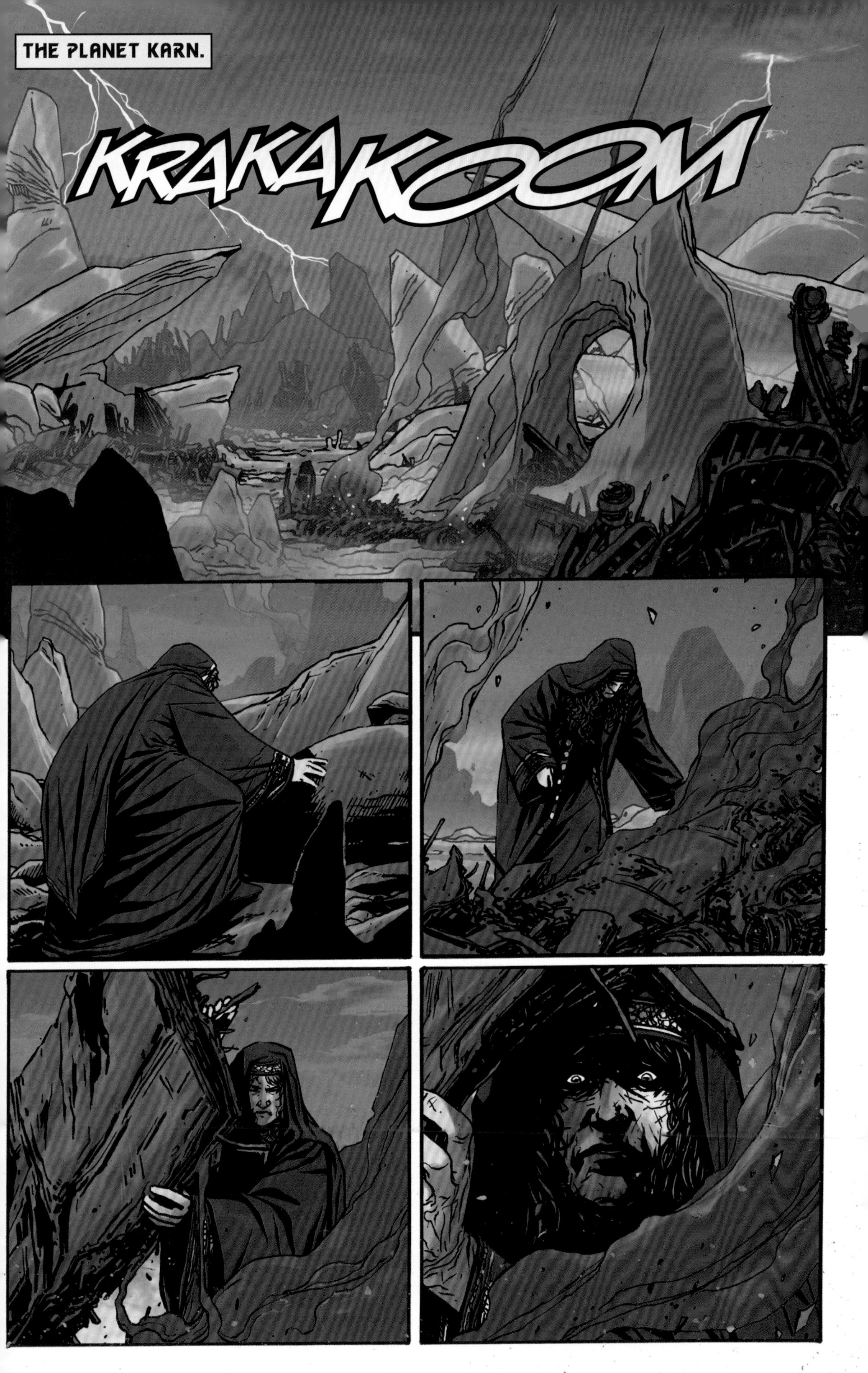
THE PLANET KARN.
KRAKAKOOM

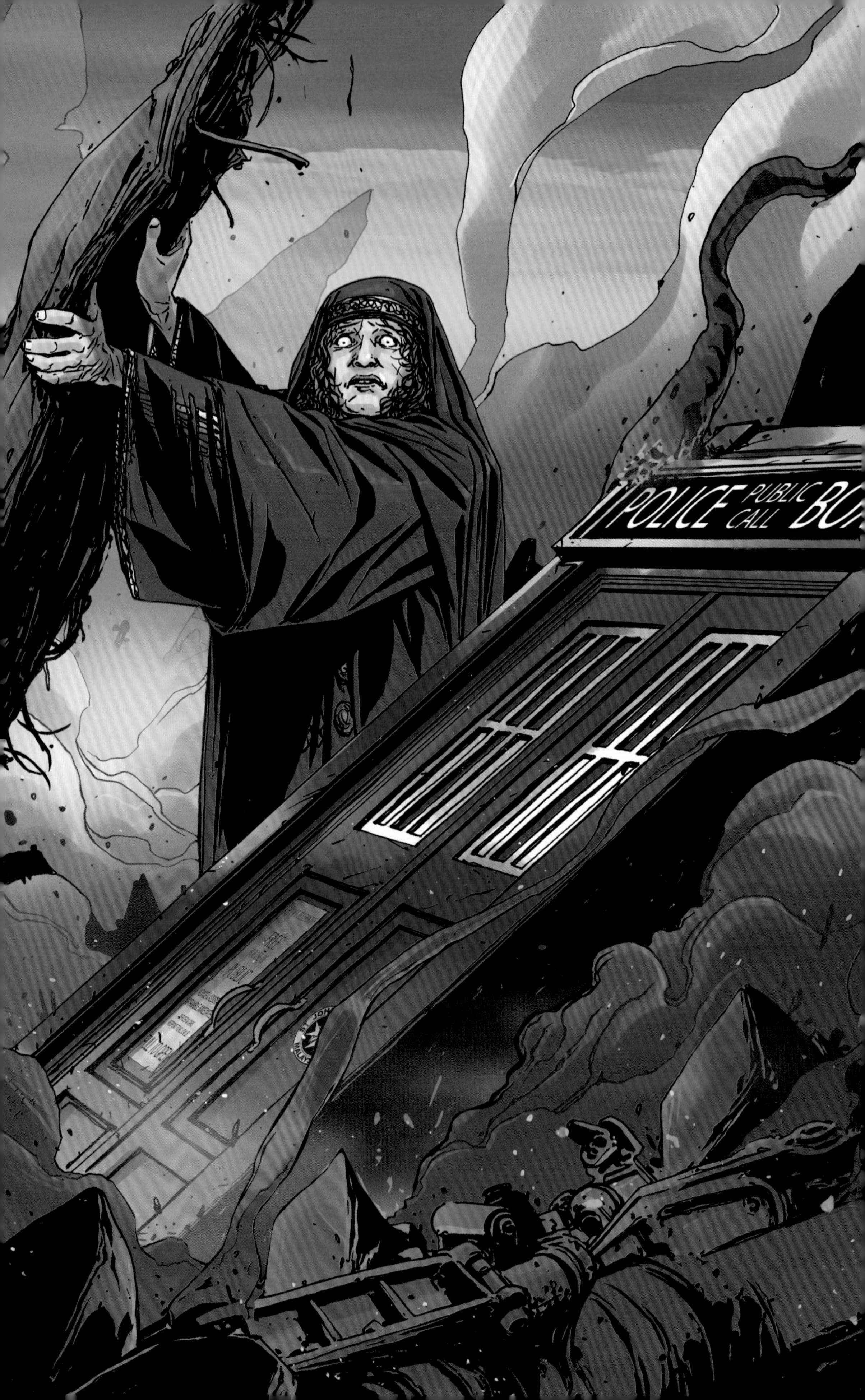
POLICE PUBLIC CALL BO

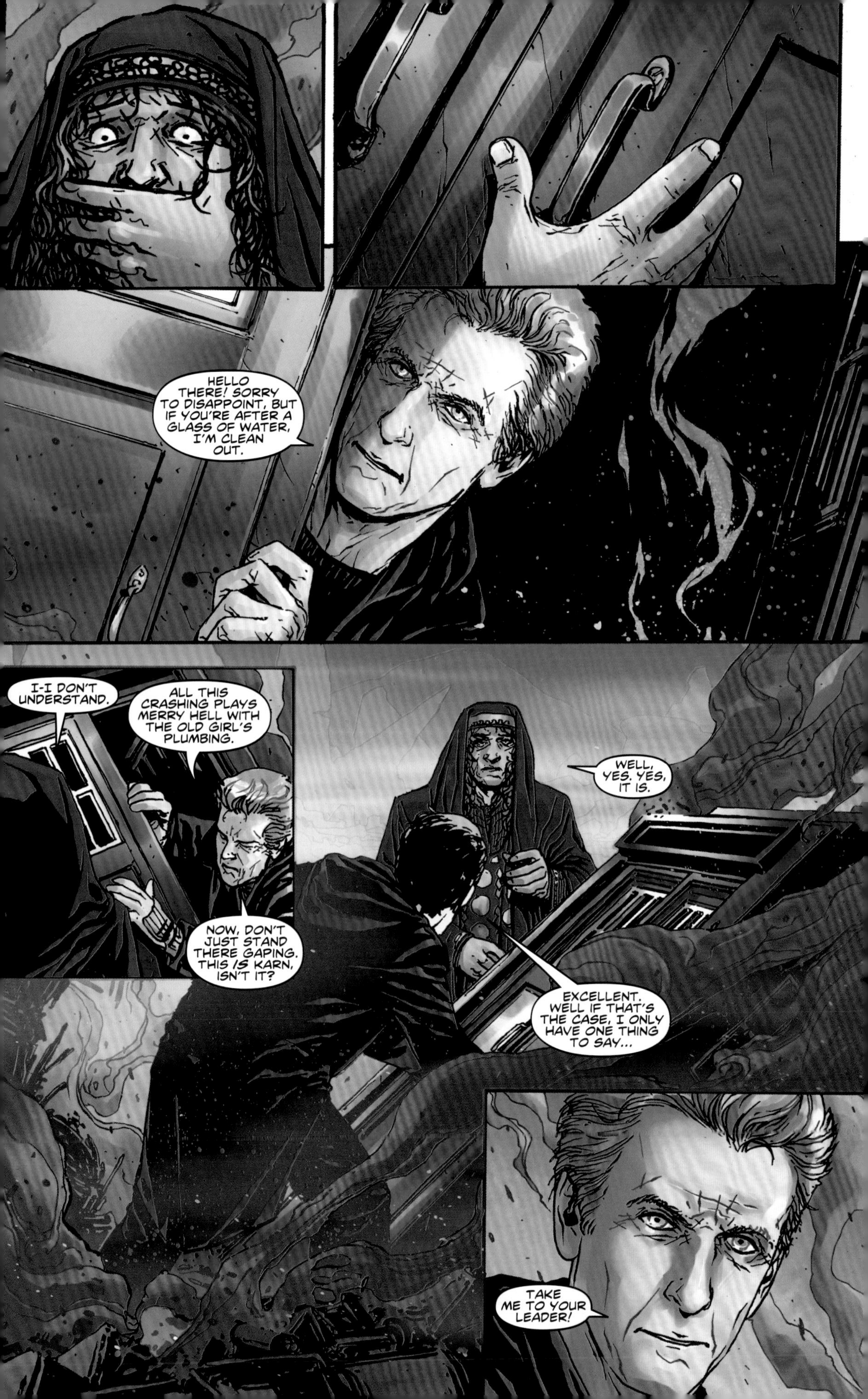
HELLO THERE! SORRY TO DISAPPOINT, BUT IF YOU'RE AFTER A GLASS OF WATER, I'M CLEAN OUT.
I-I DON'T UNDERSTAND.
ALL THIS CRASHING PLAYS MERRY HELL WITH THE OLD GIRL'S PLUMBING.
NOW, DON'T JUST STAND THERE GAPING. THIS *IS* KARN, ISN'T IT?
WELL, YES. YES, IT IS.
EXCELLENT. WELL IF THAT'S THE CASE, I ONLY HAVE ONE THING TO SAY...
TAKE ME TO YOUR LEADER!

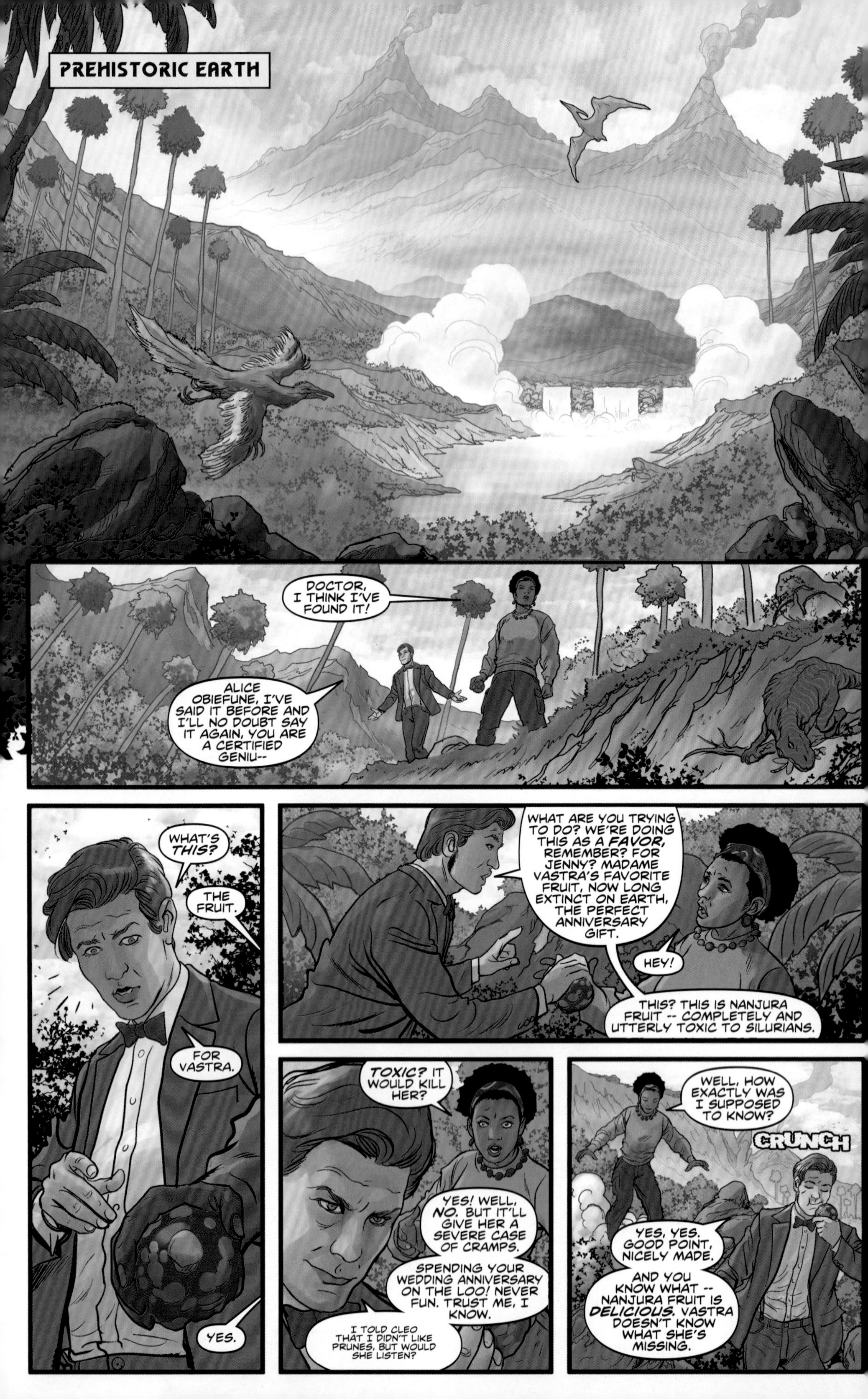
PREHISTORIC EARTH
DOCTOR, I THINK I'VE FOUND IT!
ALICE OBIEFUNE, I'VE SAID IT BEFORE AND I'LL NO DOUBT SAY IT AGAIN, YOU ARE A CERTIFIED GENIU--
WHAT'S THIS?
THE FRUIT.
FOR VASTRA.
YES.
WHAT ARE YOU TRYING TO DO? WE'RE DOING THIS AS A FAVOR, REMEMBER? FOR JENNY? MADAME VASTRA'S FAVORITE FRUIT, NOW LONG EXTINCT ON EARTH, THE PERFECT ANNIVERSARY GIFT.
HEY!
THIS? THIS IS NANJURA FRUIT -- COMPLETELY AND UTTERLY TOXIC TO SILURIANS.
TOXIC? IT WOULD KILL HER?
YES! WELL, NO. BUT IT'LL GIVE HER A SEVERE CASE OF CRAMPS.
SPENDING YOUR WEDDING ANNIVERSARY ON THE LOO! NEVER FUN. TRUST ME, I KNOW.
I TOLD CLEO THAT I DIDN'T LIKE PRUNES, BUT WOULD SHE LISTEN?
WELL, HOW EXACTLY WAS I SUPPOSED TO KNOW?
CRUNCH
YES, YES. GOOD POINT, NICELY MADE.
AND YOU KNOW WHAT -- NANJURA FRUIT IS DELICIOUS. VASTRA DOESN'T KNOW WHAT SHE'S MISSING.

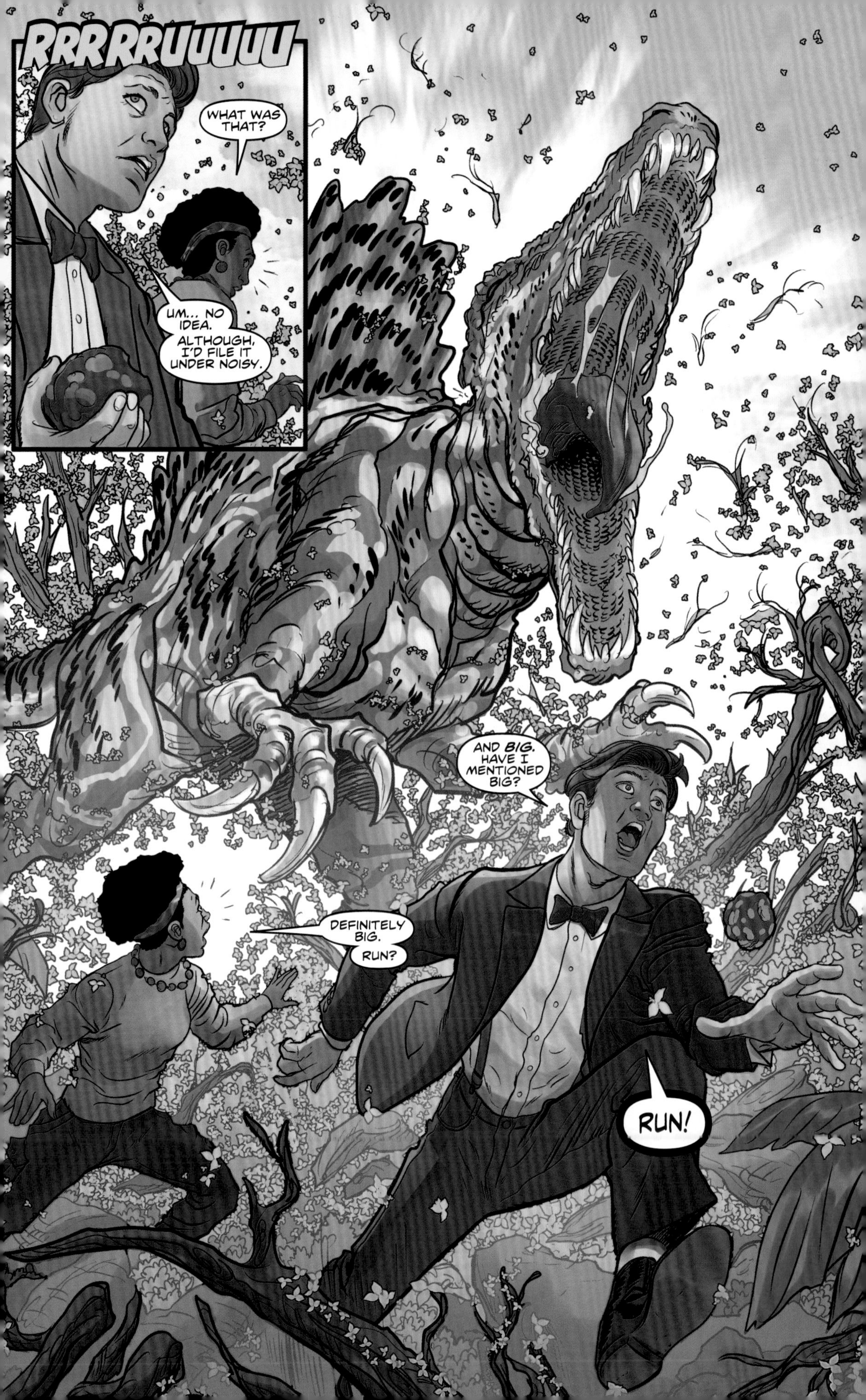
RRRRRUUUUU
WHAT WAS THAT?
UM... NO IDEA.
ALTHOUGH, I'D FILE IT UNDER NOISY.
AND BIG. HAVE I MENTIONED BIG?
DEFINITELY BIG.
RUN?
RUN!

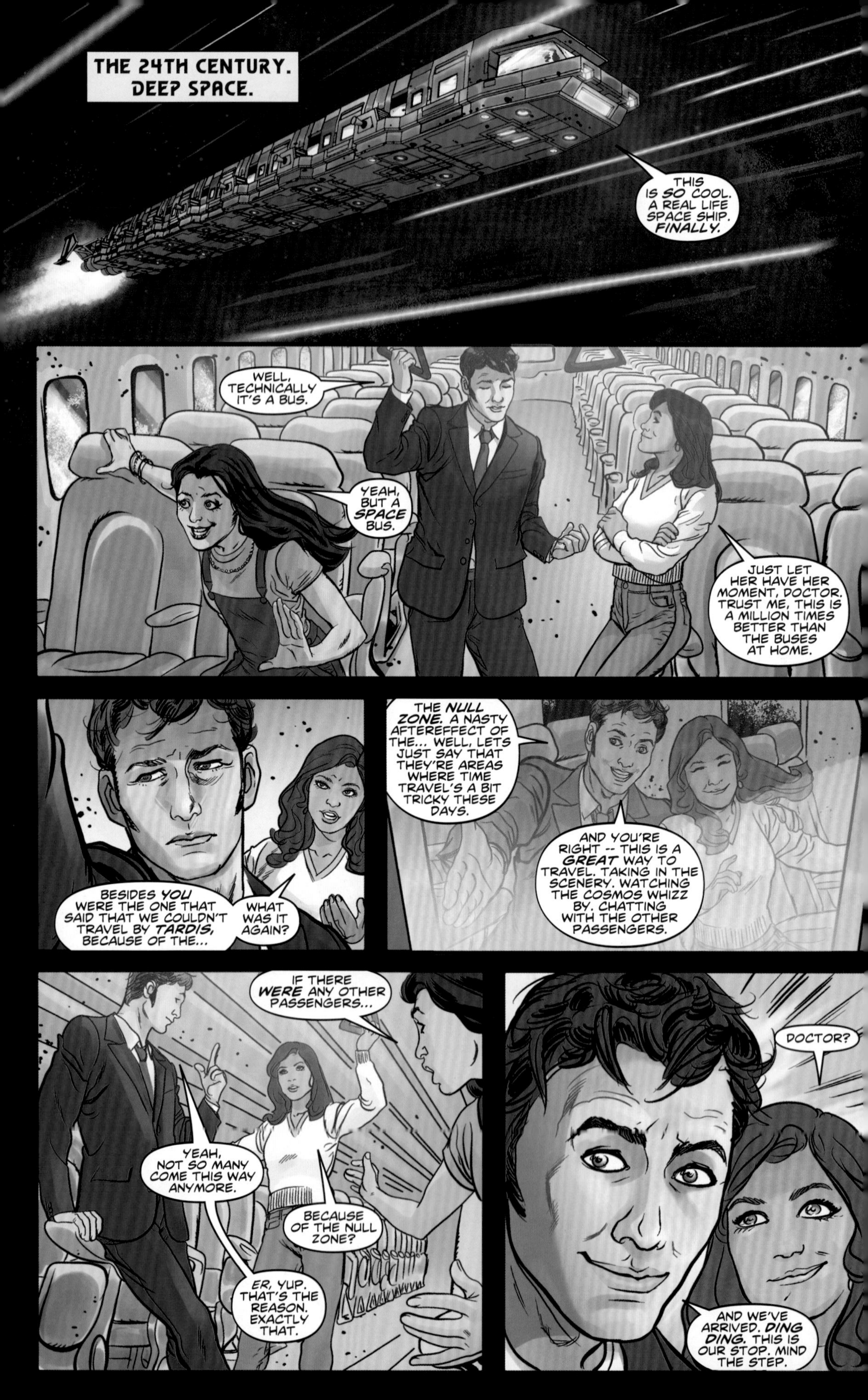
THE 24TH CENTURY. DEEP SPACE.
THIS IS SO COOL. A REAL LIFE SPACE SHIP. FINALLY.
WELL, TECHNICALLY IT'S A BUS.
YEAH, BUT A SPACE BUS.
JUST LET HER HAVE HER MOMENT, DOCTOR. TRUST ME, THIS IS A MILLION TIMES BETTER THAN THE BUSES AT HOME.
BESIDES YOU WERE THE ONE THAT SAID THAT WE COULDN'T TRAVEL BY TARDIS, BECAUSE OF THE...
WHAT WAS IT AGAIN?
THE NULL ZONE. A NASTY AFTEREFFECT OF THE... WELL, LETS JUST SAY THAT THEY'RE AREAS WHERE TIME TRAVEL'S A BIT TRICKY THESE DAYS.
AND YOU'RE RIGHT -- THIS IS A GREAT WAY TO TRAVEL. TAKING IN THE SCENERY. WATCHING THE COSMOS WHIZZ BY. CHATTING WITH THE OTHER PASSENGERS.
IF THERE WERE ANY OTHER PASSENGERS...
YEAH, NOT SO MANY COME THIS WAY ANYMORE.
BECAUSE OF THE NULL ZONE?
ER, YUP. THAT'S THE REASON, EXACTLY THAT.
DOCTOR?
AND WE'VE ARRIVED. DING DING. THIS IS OUR STOP. MIND THE STEP.

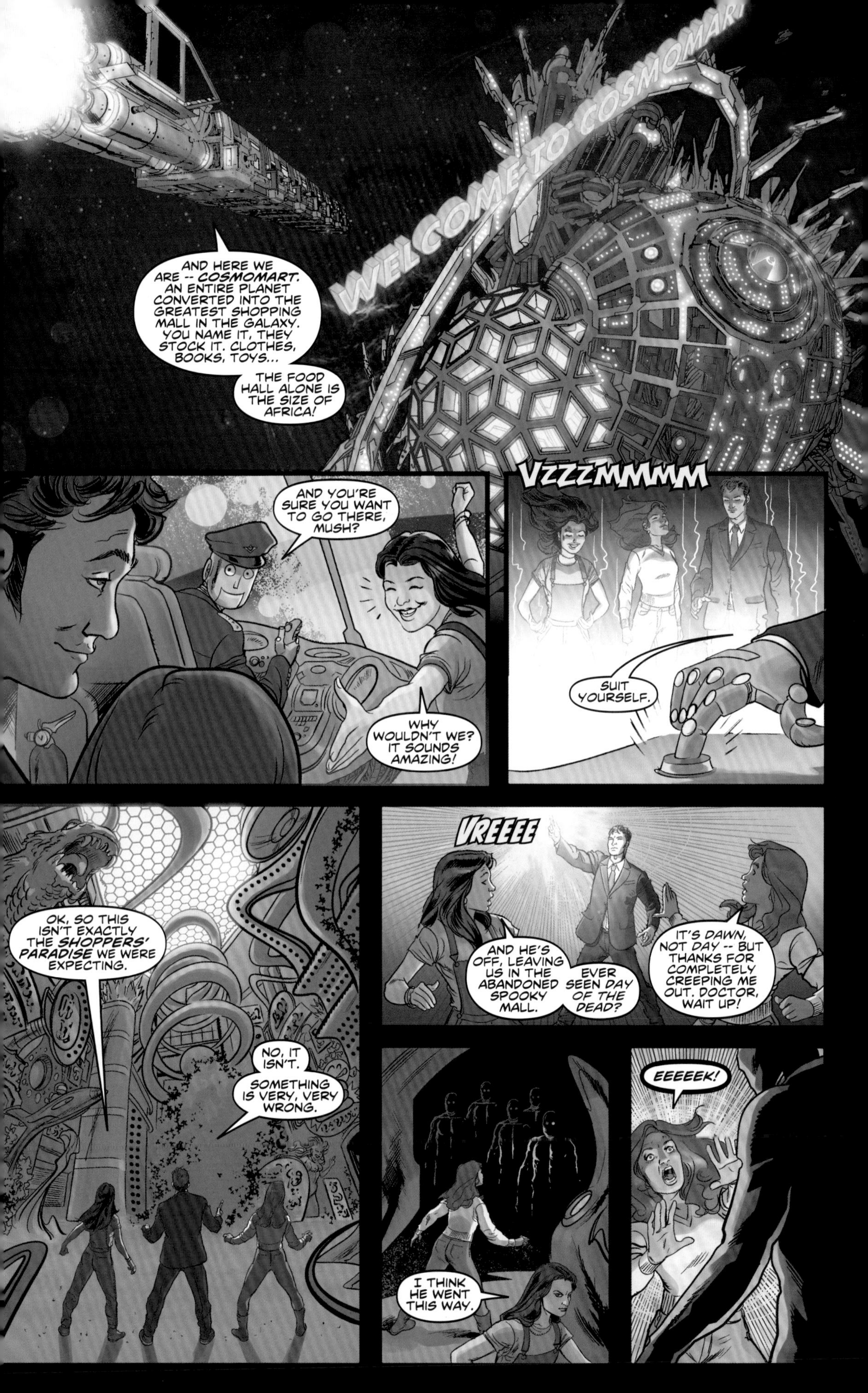
WELCOME-TO-COSMOMART
AND HERE WE ARE -- COSMOMART. AN ENTIRE PLANET CONVERTED INTO THE GREATEST SHOPPING MALL IN THE GALAXY. YOU NAME IT, THEY STOCK IT. CLOTHES, BOOKS, TOYS...
THE FOOD HALL ALONE IS THE SIZE OF AFRICA!
AND YOU'RE SURE YOU WANT TO GO THERE, MUSH?
WHY WOULDN'T WE? IT SOUNDS AMAZING!
VZZZMMMM
SUIT YOURSELF.
OK, SO THIS ISN'T EXACTLY THE SHOPPERS' PARADISE WE WERE EXPECTING.
NO, IT ISN'T.
SOMETHING IS VERY, VERY WRONG.
VREEEE
AND HE'S OFF, LEAVING US IN THE ABANDONED SPOOKY MALL.
EVER SEEN DAY OF THE DEAD?
IT'S DAWN, NOT DAY -- BUT THANKS FOR COMPLETELY CREEPING ME OUT. DOCTOR, WAIT UP!
I THINK HE WENT THIS WAY.
EEEEEK!

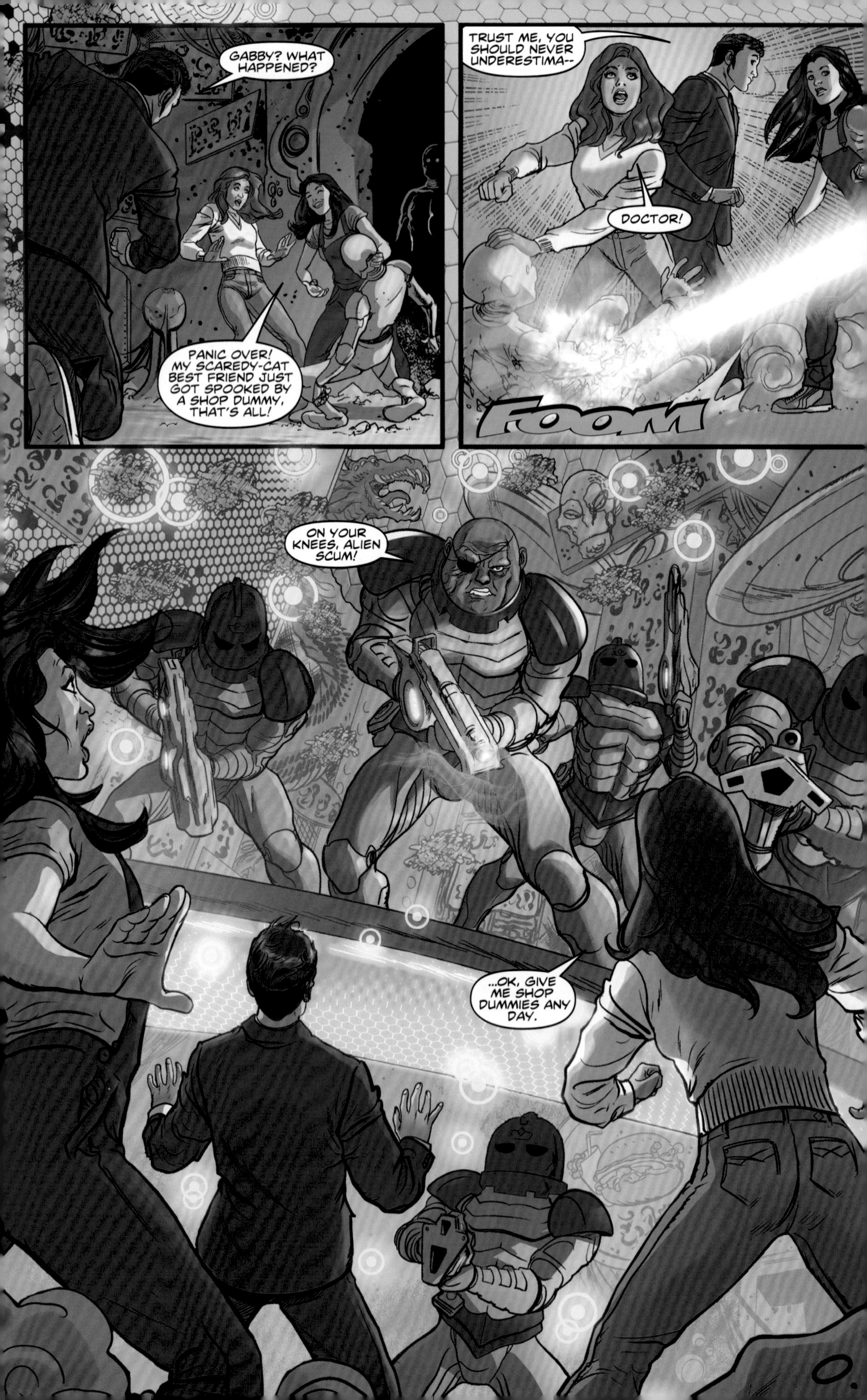
GABBY? WHAT HAPPENED?
PANIC OVER! MY SCAREDY-CAT BEST FRIEND JUST GOT SPOOKED BY A SHOP DUMMY, THAT'S ALL!
TRUST ME, YOU SHOULD NEVER UNDERESTIMA--
DOCTOR!
FOOM
ON YOUR KNEES, ALIEN SCUM!
...OK, GIVE ME SHOP DUMMIES ANY DAY.

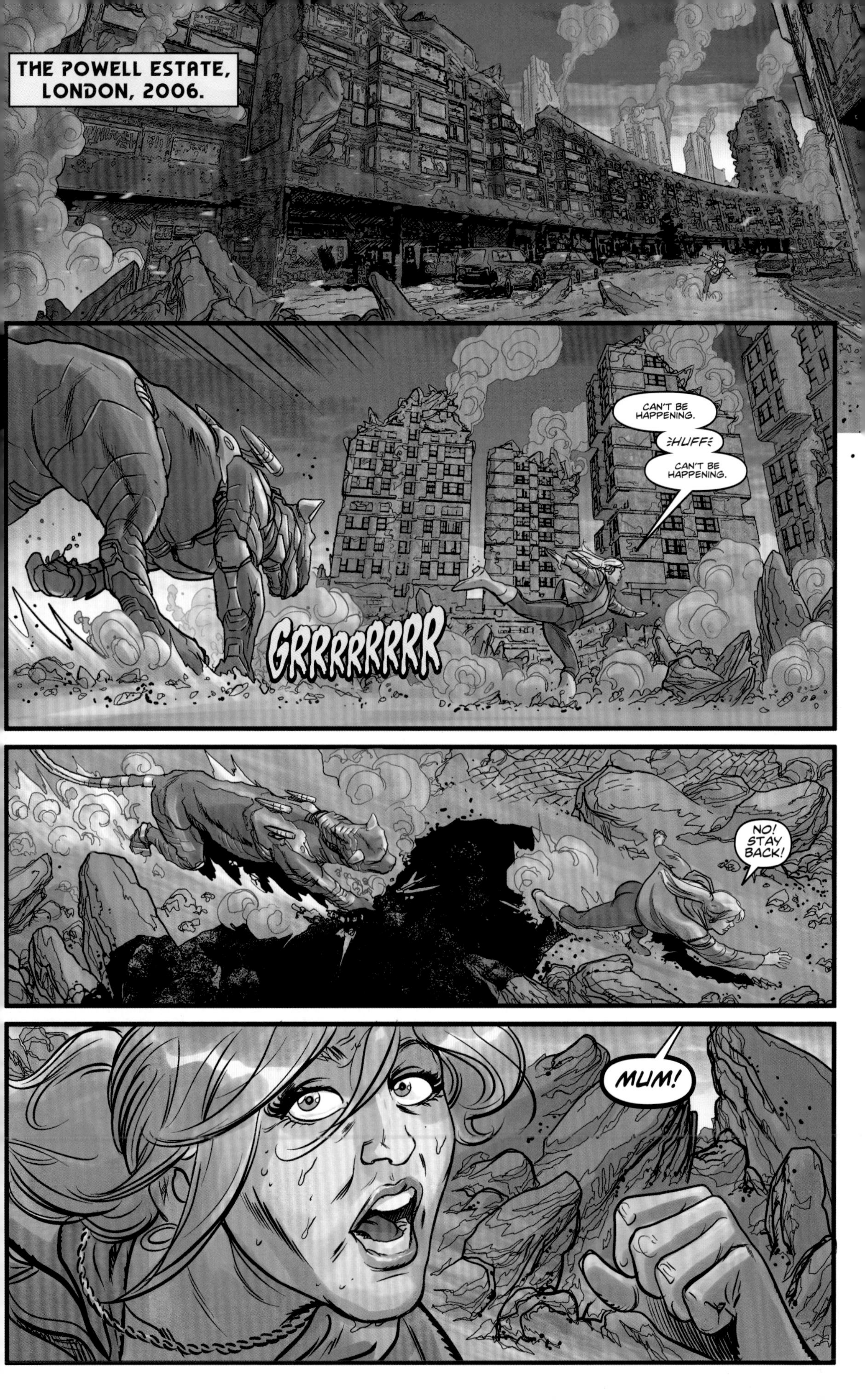
THE POWELL ESTATE, LONDON, 2006.
CAN'T BE HAPPENING.
HUFF
CAN'T BE HAPPENING.
GRRRRRRRR
NO! STAY BACK!
MUM!

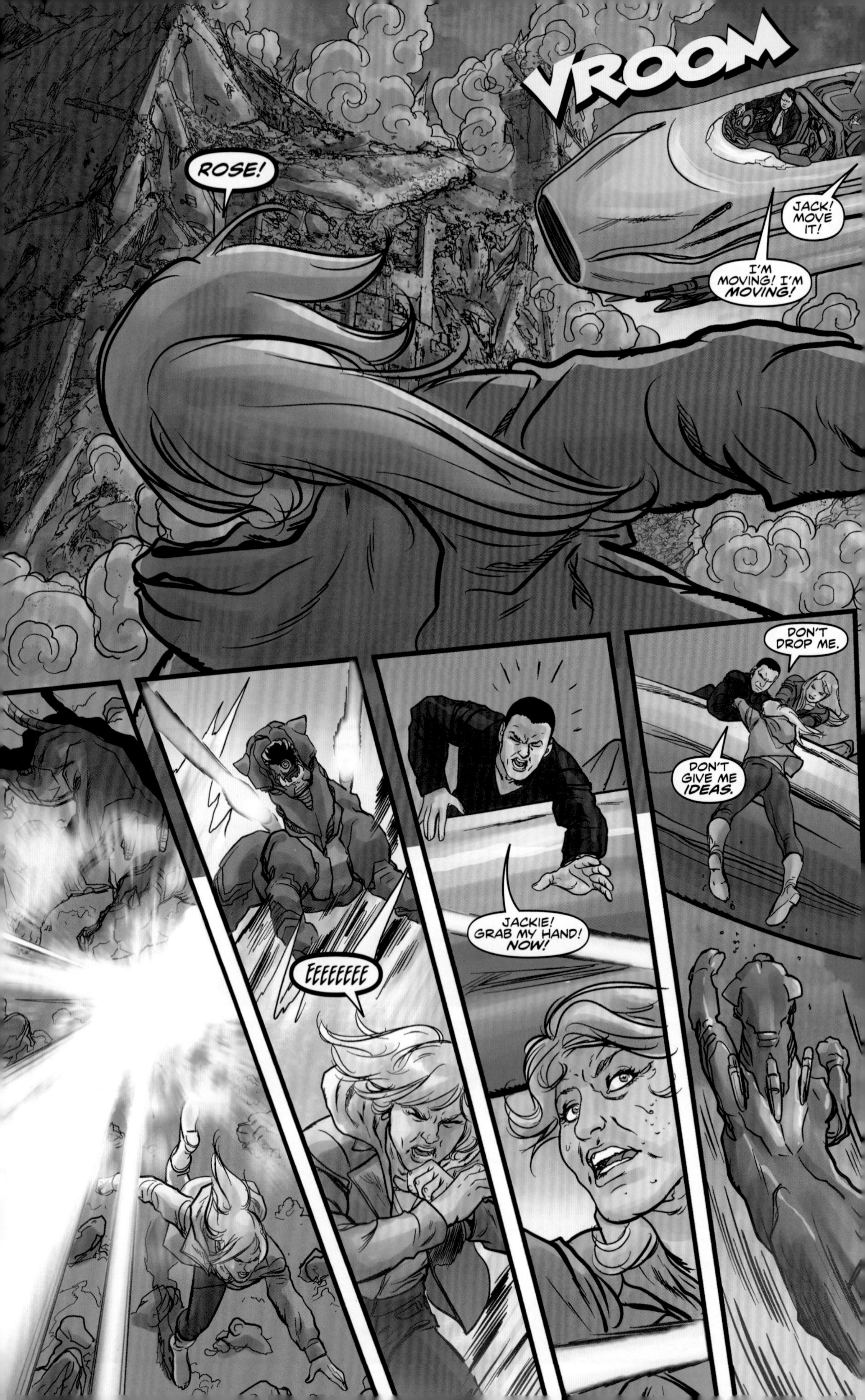
VROOM
ROSE!
JACK! MOVE IT!
I'M MOVING! I'M MOVING!
EEEEEEEE
JACKIE! GRAB MY HAND! NOW!
DON'T DROP ME.
DON'T GIVE ME IDEAS.

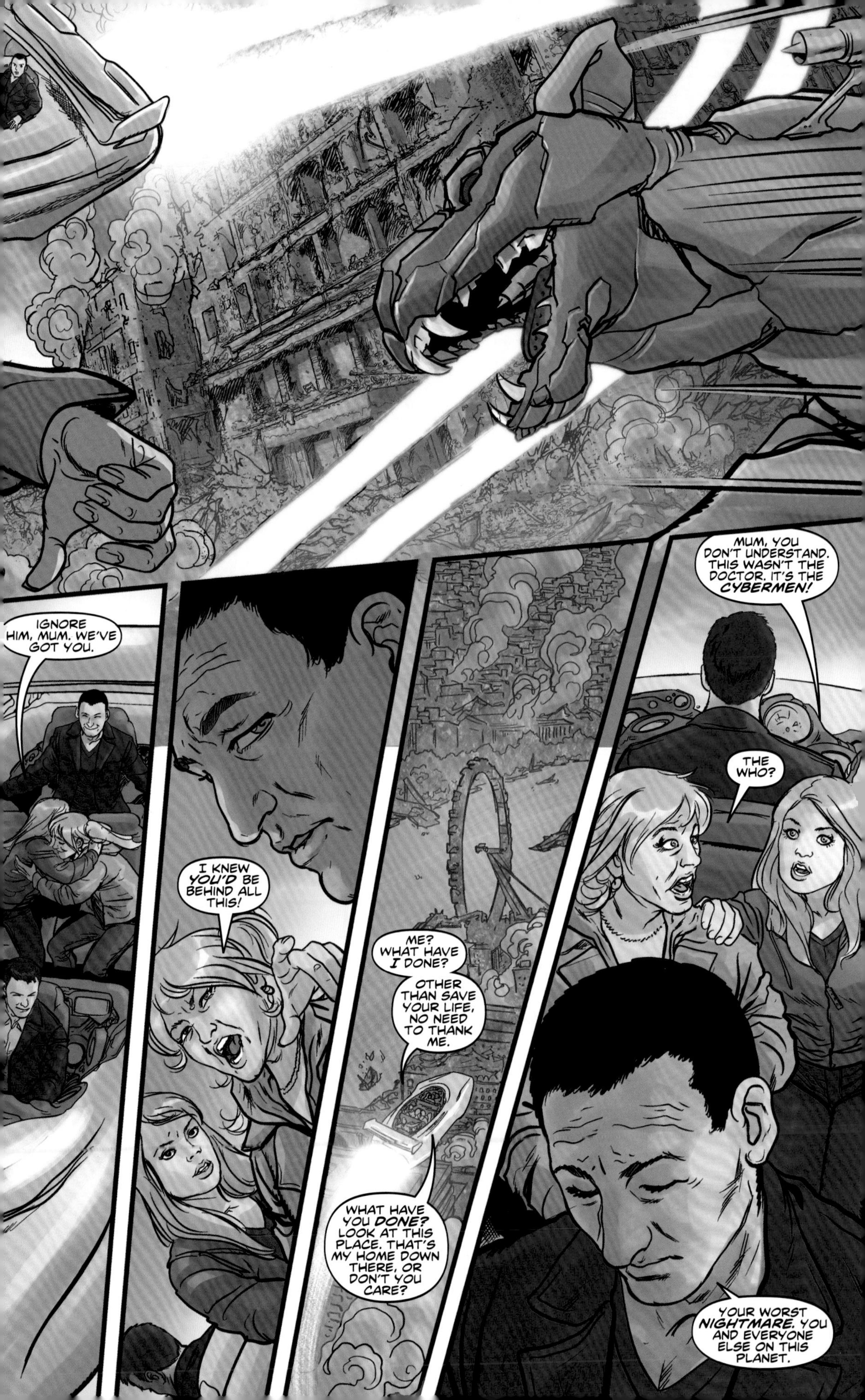
IGNORE HIM, MUM. WE'VE GOT YOU.
I KNEW YOU'D BE BEHIND ALL THIS!
ME? WHAT HAVE I DONE?
OTHER THAN SAVE YOUR LIFE, NO NEED TO THANK ME.
WHAT HAVE YOU DONE? LOOK AT THIS PLACE. THAT'S MY HOME DOWN THERE, OR DON'T YOU CARE?
MUM, YOU DON'T UNDERSTAND. THIS WASN'T THE DOCTOR. IT'S THE CYBERMEN!
THE WHO?
YOUR WORST NIGHTMARE. YOU AND EVERYONE ELSE ON THIS PLANET.

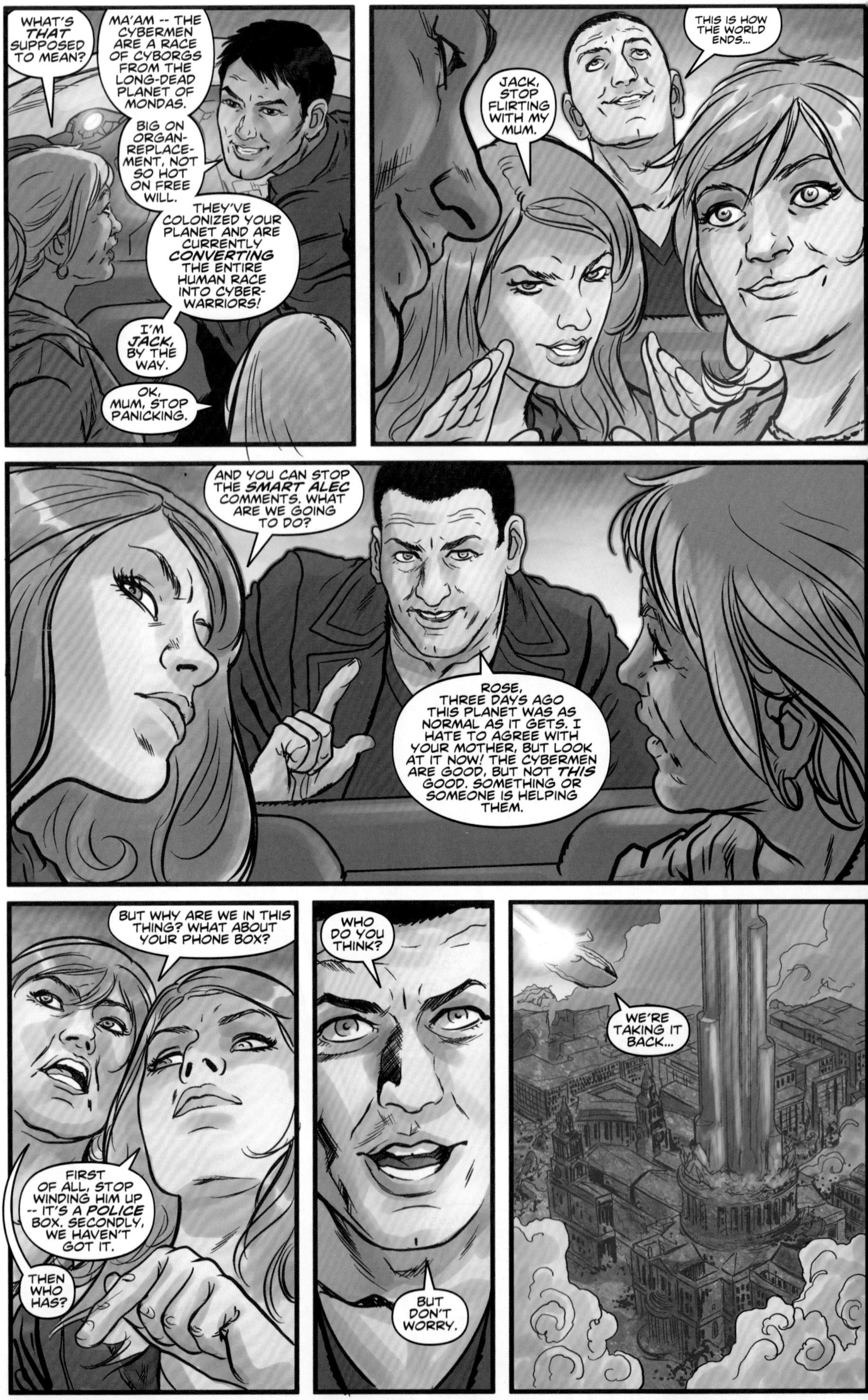
WHAT'S THAT SUPPOSED TO MEAN?
MA'AM -- THE CYBERMEN ARE A RACE OF CYBORGS FROM THE LONG-DEAD PLANET OF MONDAS.
BIG ON ORGAN-REPLACE-MENT, NOT SO HOT ON FREE WILL.
THEY'VE COLONIZED YOUR PLANET AND ARE CURRENTLY CONVERTING THE ENTIRE HUMAN RACE INTO CYBER-WARRIORS!
I'M JACK, BY THE WAY.
OK, MUM, STOP PANICKING.
THIS IS HOW THE WORLD ENDS...
JACK, STOP FLIRTING WITH MY MUM.
AND YOU CAN STOP THE SMART ALEC COMMENTS. WHAT ARE WE GOING TO DO?
ROSE, THREE DAYS AGO THIS PLANET WAS AS NORMAL AS IT GETS. I HATE TO AGREE WITH YOUR MOTHER, BUT LOOK AT IT NOW! THE CYBERMEN ARE GOOD, BUT NOT THIS GOOD. SOMETHING OR SOMEONE IS HELPING THEM.
BUT WHY ARE WE IN THIS THING? WHAT ABOUT YOUR PHONE BOX?
FIRST OF ALL, STOP WINDING HIM UP -- IT'S A POLICE BOX. SECONDLY, WE HAVEN'T GOT IT.
THEN WHO HAS?
WHO DO YOU THINK?
BUT DON'T WORRY.
WE'RE TAKING IT BACK...

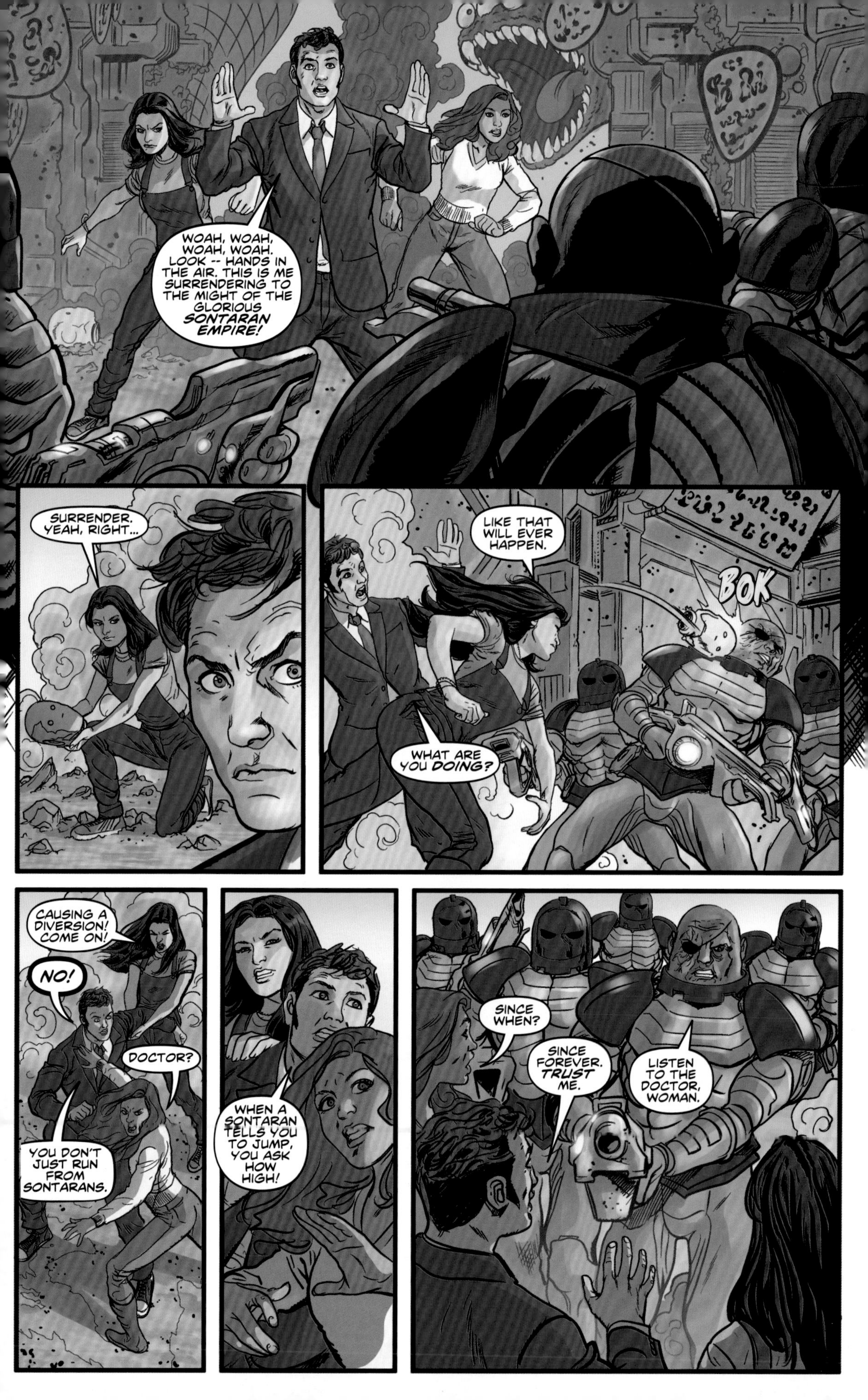
WOAH, WOAH, WOAH, WOAH. LOOK -- HANDS IN THE AIR. THIS IS ME SURRENDERING TO THE MIGHT OF THE GLORIOUS SONTARAN EMPIRE!
SURRENDER. YEAH, RIGHT...
LIKE THAT WILL EVER HAPPEN.
BOK
WHAT ARE YOU DOING?
CAUSING A DIVERSION! COME ON!
NO!
DOCTOR?
YOU DON'T JUST RUN FROM SONTARANS.
WHEN A SONTARAN TELLS YOU TO JUMP, YOU ASK HOW HIGH!
SINCE WHEN?
SINCE FOREVER. TRUST ME.
LISTEN TO THE DOCTOR, WOMAN.

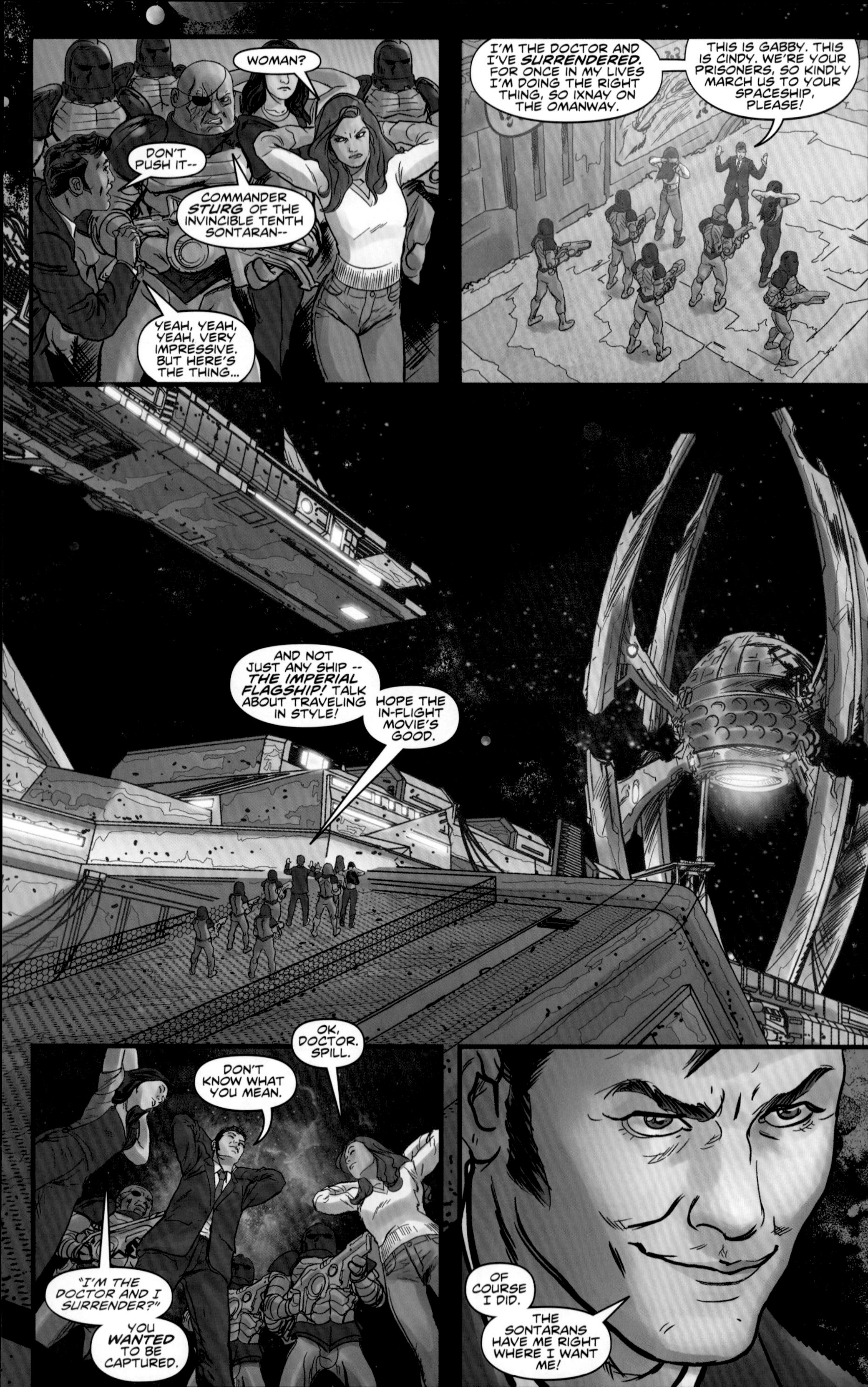
WOMAN?
DON'T PUSH IT--
COMMANDER STURG OF THE INVINCIBLE TENTH SONTARAN--
YEAH, YEAH, YEAH, VERY IMPRESSIVE. BUT HERE'S THE THING...
I'M THE DOCTOR AND I'VE SURRENDERED. FOR ONCE IN MY LIVES I'M DOING THE RIGHT THING, SO IXNAY ON THE OMANWAY.
THIS IS GABBY. THIS IS CINDY. WE'RE YOUR PRISONERS, SO KINDLY MARCH US TO YOUR SPACESHIP, PLEASE!
AND NOT JUST ANY SHIP -- THE IMPERIAL FLAGSHIP! TALK ABOUT TRAVELING IN STYLE!
HOPE THE IN-FLIGHT MOVIE'S GOOD.
OK, DOCTOR. SPILL.
DON'T KNOW WHAT YOU MEAN.
"I'M THE DOCTOR AND I SURRENDER?"
YOU WANTED TO BE CAPTURED.
OF COURSE I DID.
THE SONTARANS HAVE ME RIGHT WHERE I WANT ME!

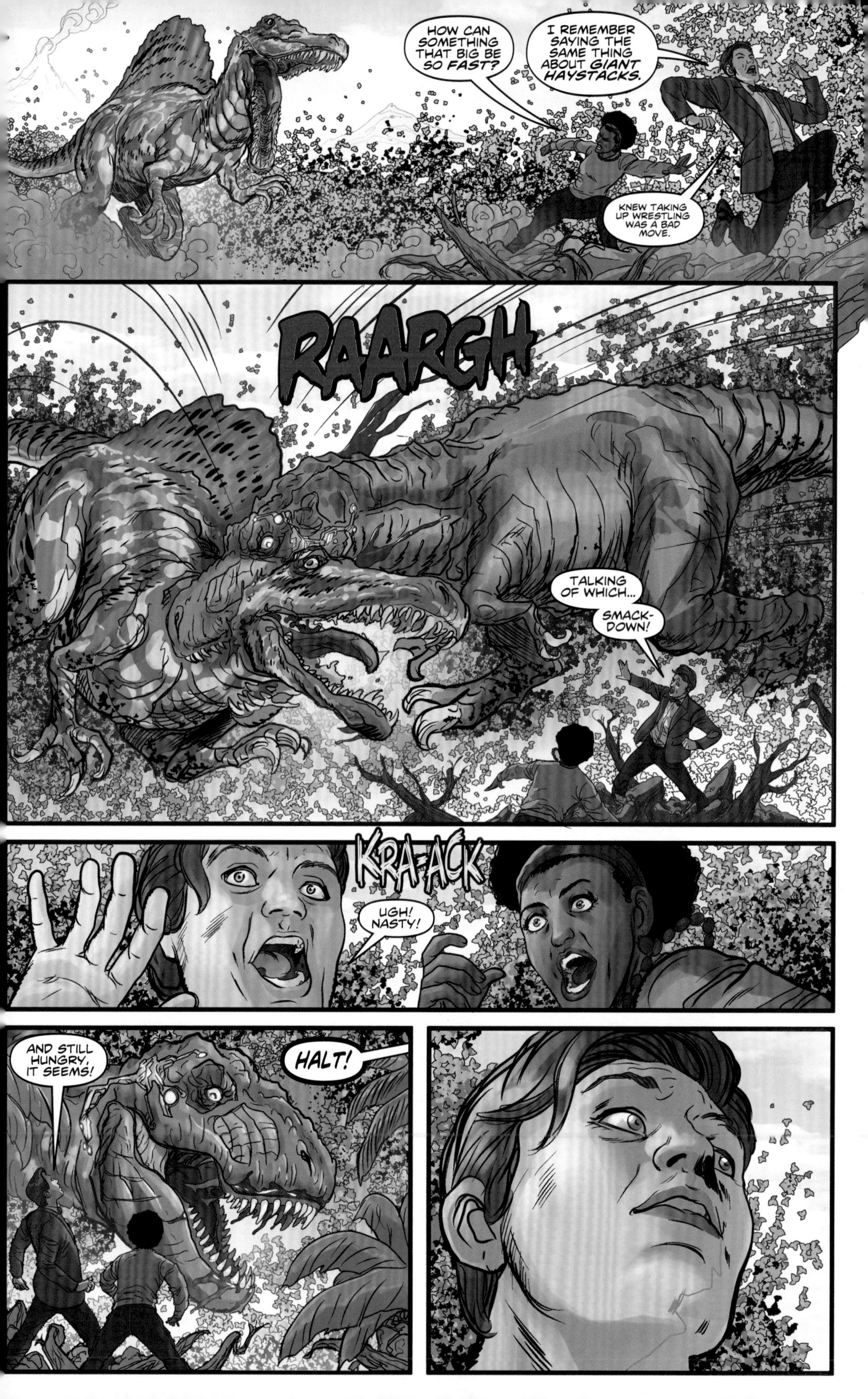
HOW CAN SOMETHING THAT BIG BE SO FAST?
I REMEMBER SAYING THE SAME THING ABOUT GIANT HAYSTACKS.
KNEW TAKING UP WRESTLING WAS A BAD MOVE.
RAARGH
TALKING OF WHICH...
SMACK-DOWN!
KRA-ACK
UGH! NASTY!
AND STILL HUNGRY, IT SEEMS!
HALT!

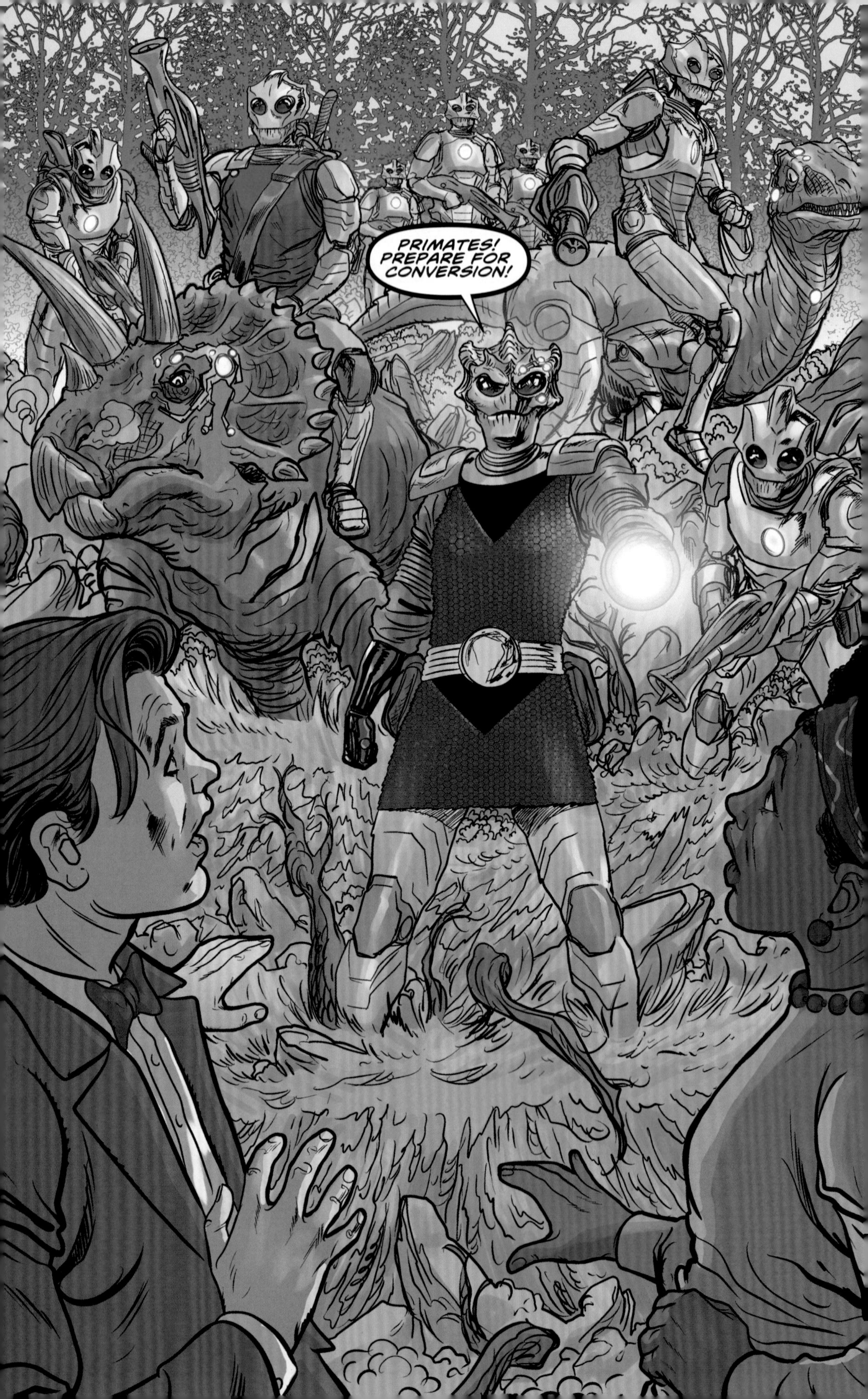
PRIMATES! PREPARE FOR CONVERSION!

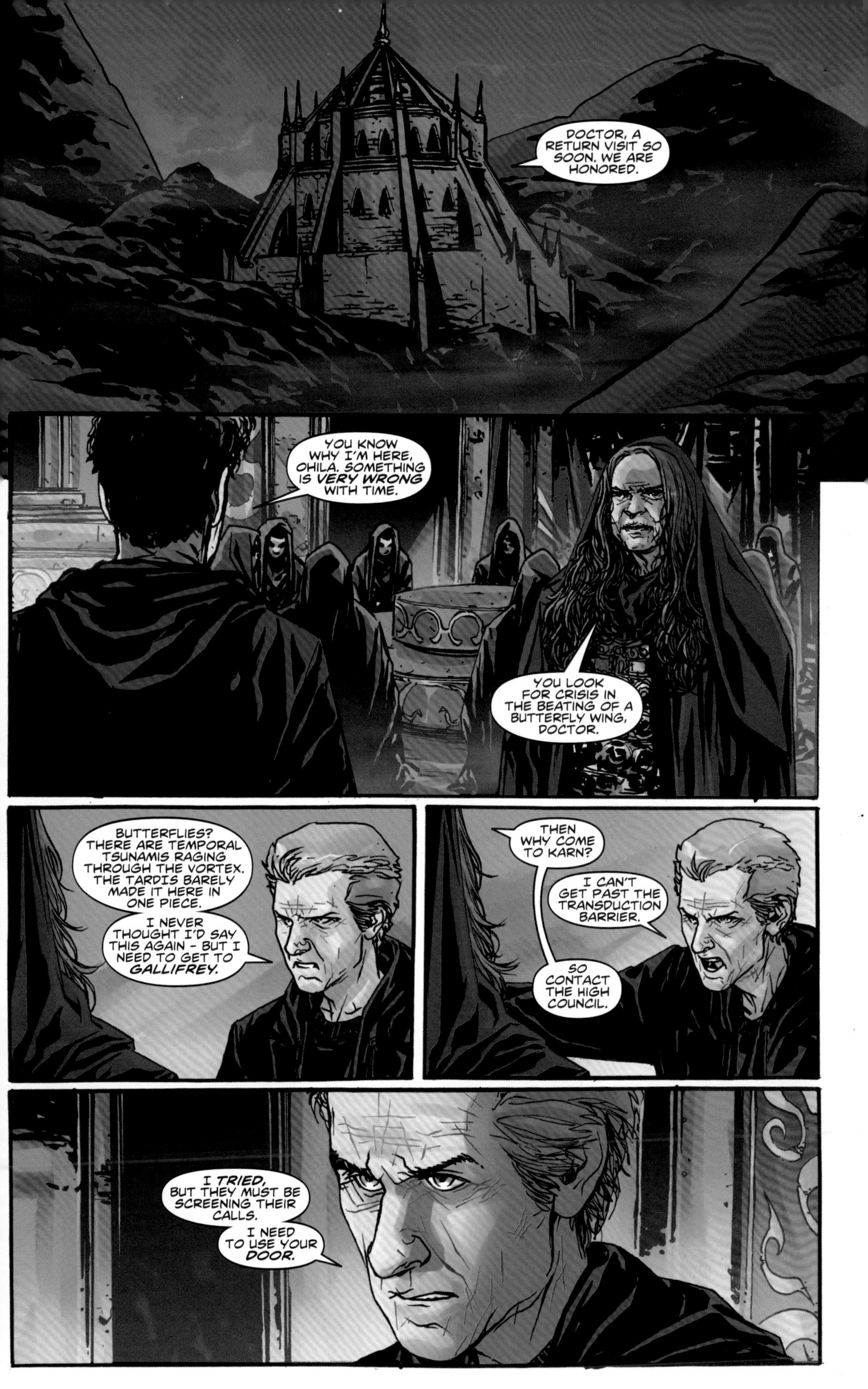
DOCTOR, A RETURN VISIT SO SOON. WE ARE HONORED.
YOU KNOW WHY I'M HERE, OHILA. SOMETHING IS VERY WRONG WITH TIME.
YOU LOOK FOR CRISIS IN THE BEATING OF A BUTTERFLY WING, DOCTOR.
BUTTERFLIES? THERE ARE TEMPORAL TSUNAMIS RAGING THROUGH THE VORTEX. THE TARDIS BARELY MADE IT HERE IN ONE PIECE.
I NEVER THOUGHT I'D SAY THIS AGAIN – BUT I NEED TO GET TO GALLIFREY.
THEN WHY COME TO KARN?
I CAN'T GET PAST THE TRANSDUCTION BARRIER.
SO CONTACT THE HIGH COUNCIL.
I TRIED, BUT THEY MUST BE SCREENING THEIR CALLS.
I NEED TO USE YOUR DOOR.

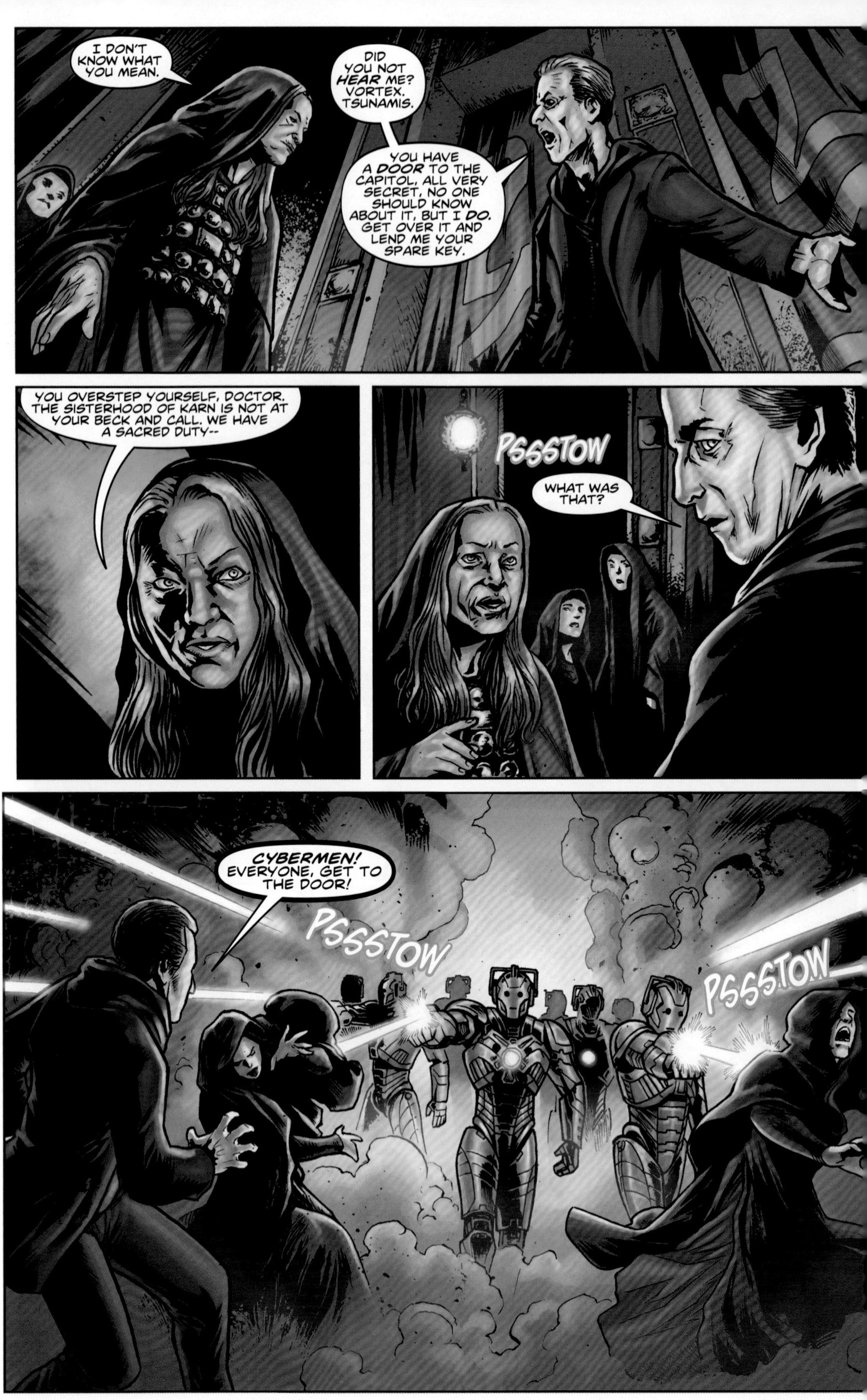
I DON'T KNOW WHAT YOU MEAN.
DID YOU NOT HEAR ME? VORTEX. TSUNAMIS.
YOU HAVE A DOOR TO THE CAPITOL, ALL VERY SECRET, NO ONE SHOULD KNOW ABOUT IT, BUT I DO. GET OVER IT AND LEND ME YOUR SPARE KEY.
YOU OVERSTEP YOURSELF, DOCTOR. THE SISTERHOOD OF KARN IS NOT AT YOUR BECK AND CALL. WE HAVE A SACRED DUTY--
PSSSTOW
WHAT WAS THAT?
CYBERMEN! EVERYONE, GET TO THE DOOR!
PSSSTOW
PSSSTOW

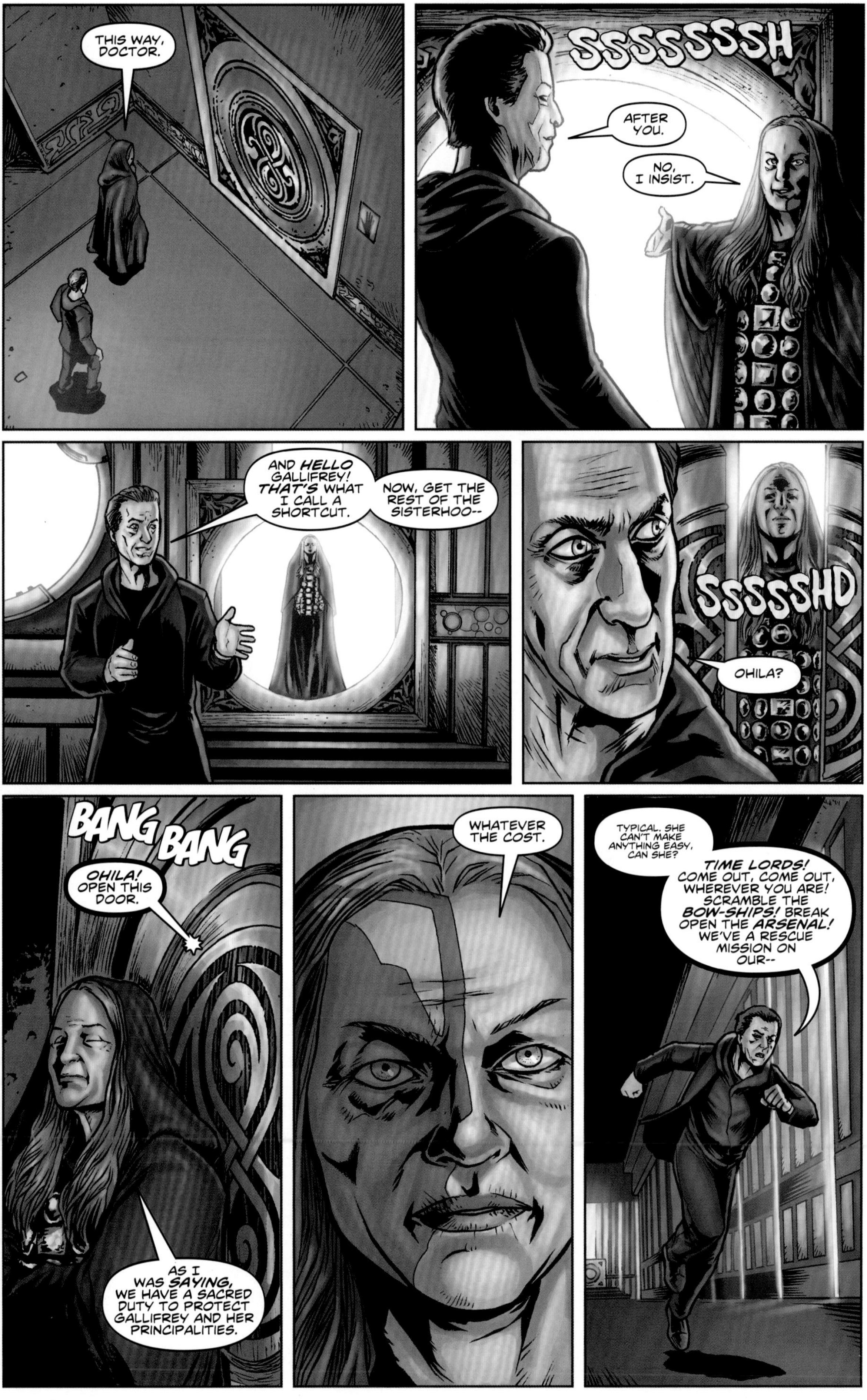
THIS WAY, DOCTOR.
SSSSSSSH
AFTER YOU.
NO, I INSIST.
AND HELLO GALLIFREY! THAT'S WHAT I CALL A SHORTCUT.
NOW, GET THE REST OF THE SISTERHOO--
SSSSSHD
OHILA?
BANG BANG
OHILA! OPEN THIS DOOR.
AS I WAS SAYING, WE HAVE A SACRED DUTY TO PROTECT GALLIFREY AND HER PRINCIPALITIES.
WHATEVER THE COST.
TYPICAL. SHE CAN'T MAKE ANYTHING EASY, CAN SHE?
TIME LORDS! COME OUT, COME OUT, WHEREVER YOU ARE! SCRAMBLE THE BOW-SHIPS! BREAK OPEN THE ARSENAL! WE'VE A RESCUE MISSION ON OUR--

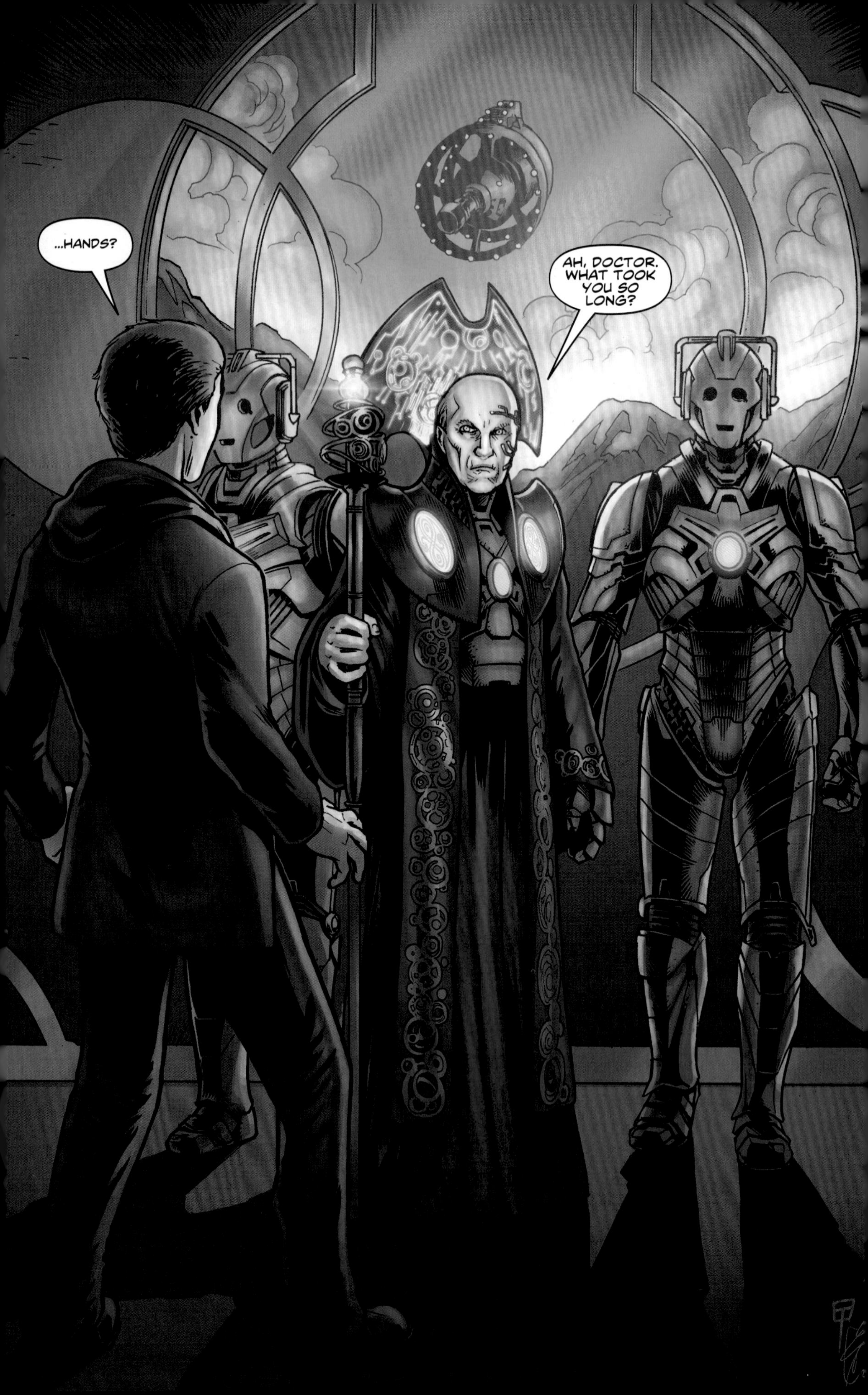
...HANDS?
AH, DOCTOR. WHAT TOOK YOU SO LONG?

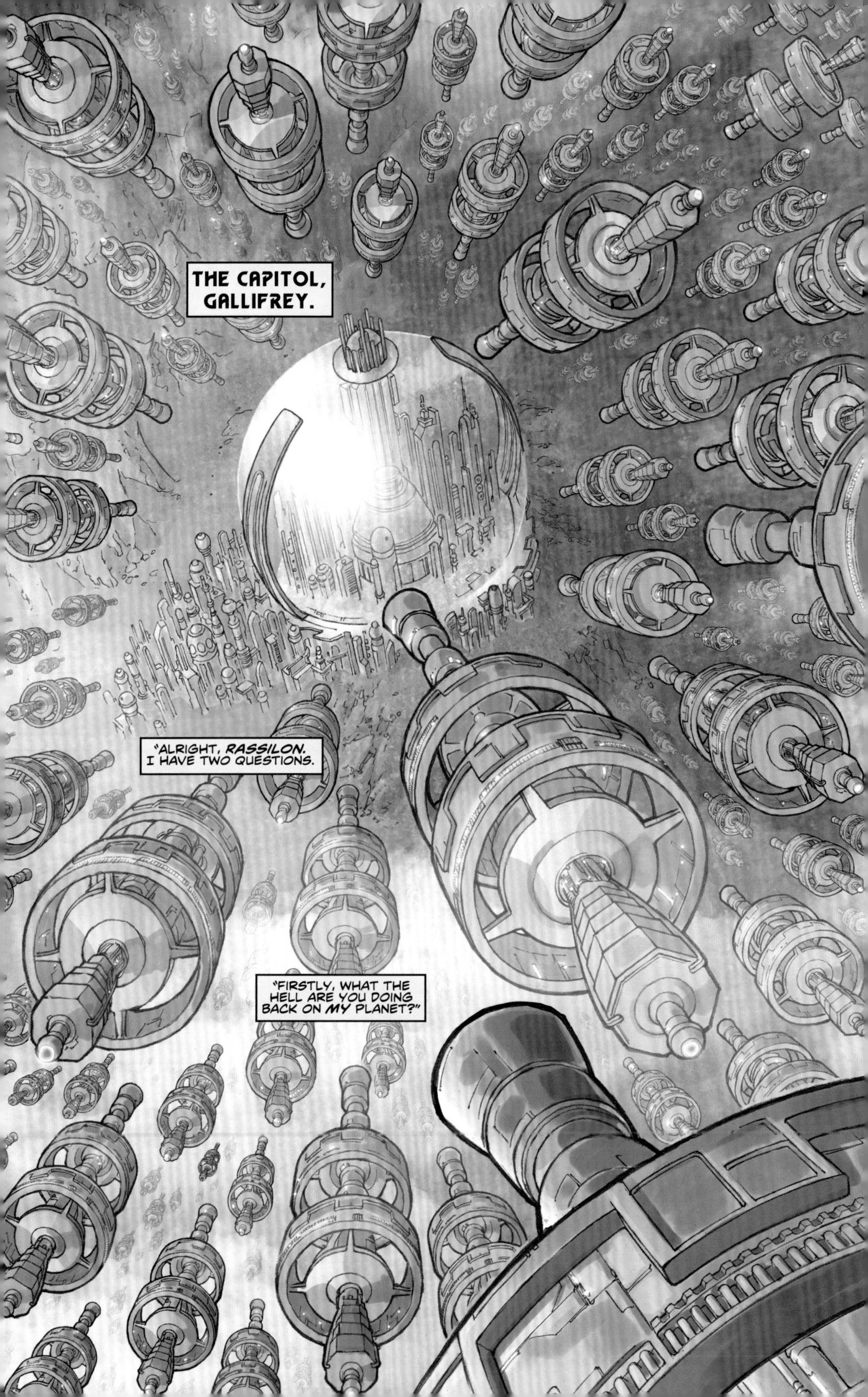
THE CAPITOL, GALLIFREY.
"ALRIGHT, RASSILON. I HAVE TWO QUESTIONS.
"FIRSTLY, WHAT THE HELL ARE YOU DOING BACK ON MY PLANET?"

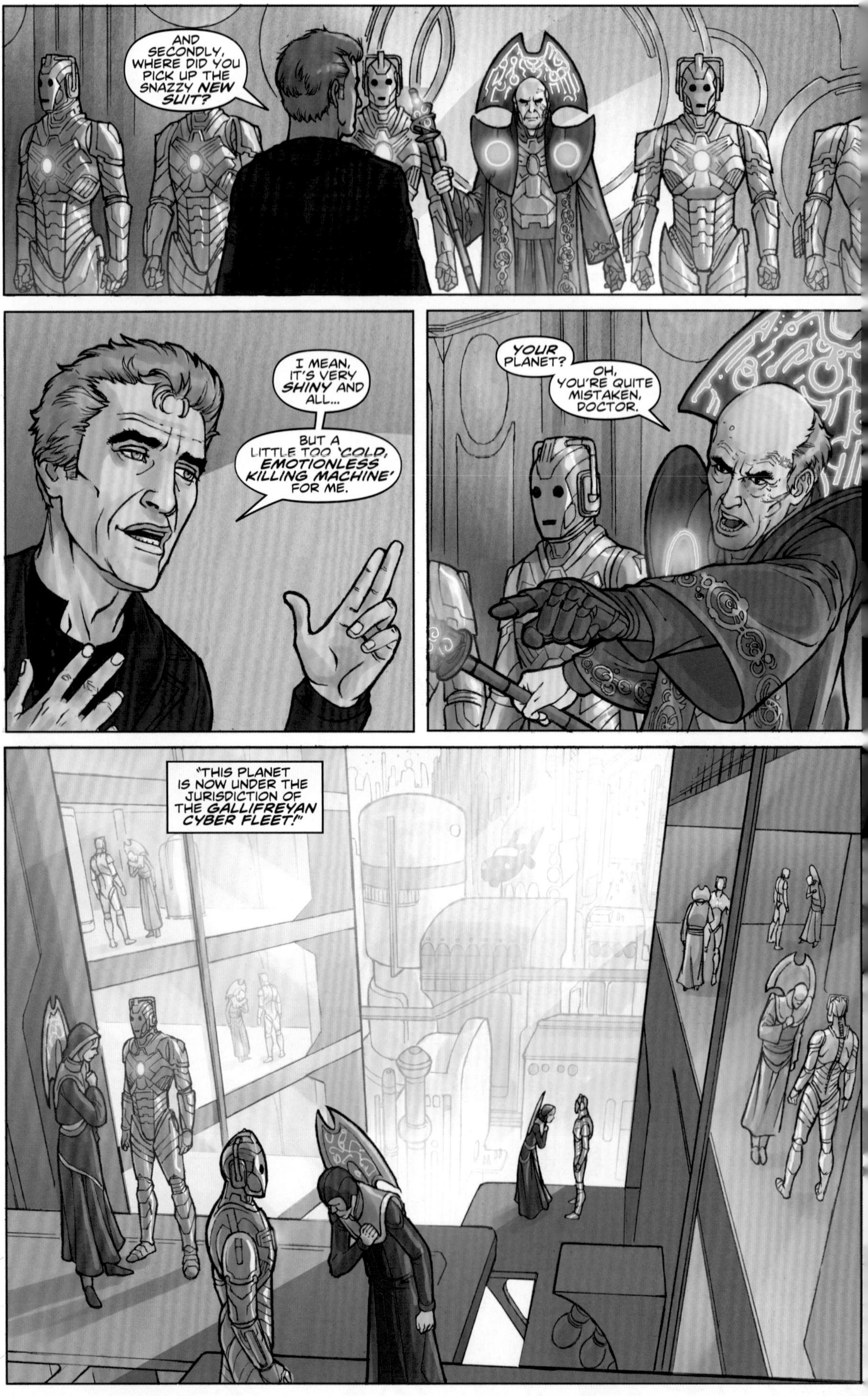
AND SECONDLY, WHERE DID YOU PICK UP THE SNAZZY NEW SUIT?
I MEAN, IT'S VERY SHINY AND ALL...
BUT A LITTLE TOO 'COLD, EMOTIONLESS KILLING MACHINE' FOR ME.
YOUR PLANET?
OH, YOU'RE QUITE MISTAKEN, DOCTOR.
"THIS PLANET IS NOW UNDER THE JURISDICTION OF THE GALLIFREYAN CYBER FLEET!"

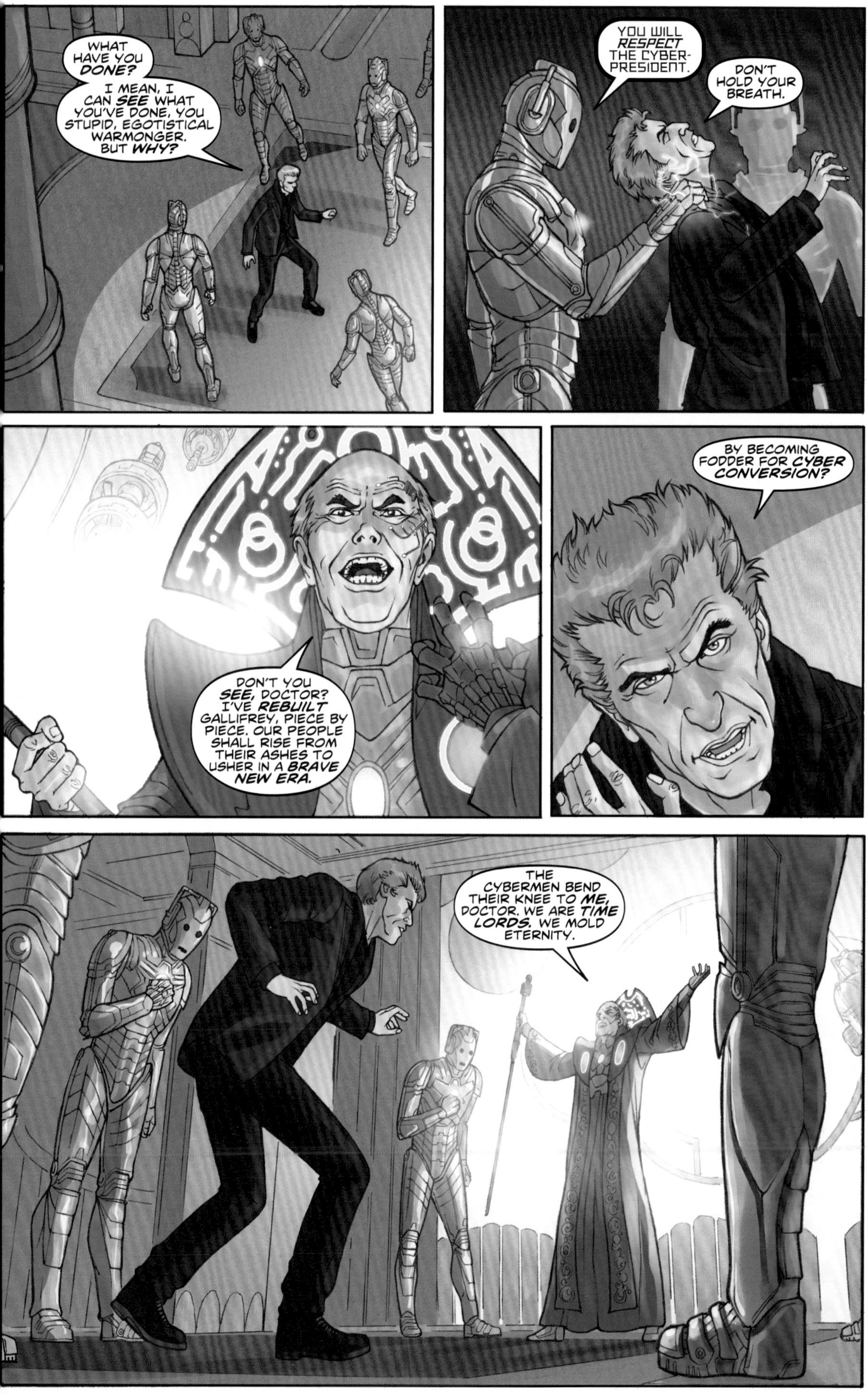
WHAT HAVE YOU DONE?
I MEAN, I CAN SEE WHAT YOU'VE DONE, YOU STUPID, EGOTISTICAL WARMONGER. BUT WHY?
YOU WILL RESPECT THE CYBER-PRESIDENT.
DON'T HOLD YOUR BREATH.
DON'T YOU SEE, DOCTOR? I'VE REBUILT GALLIFREY, PIECE BY PIECE. OUR PEOPLE SHALL RISE FROM THEIR ASHES TO USHER IN A BRAVE NEW ERA.
BY BECOMING FODDER FOR CYBER CONVERSION?
THE CYBERMEN BEND THEIR KNEE TO ME, DOCTOR. WE ARE TIME LORDS. WE MOLD ETERNITY.

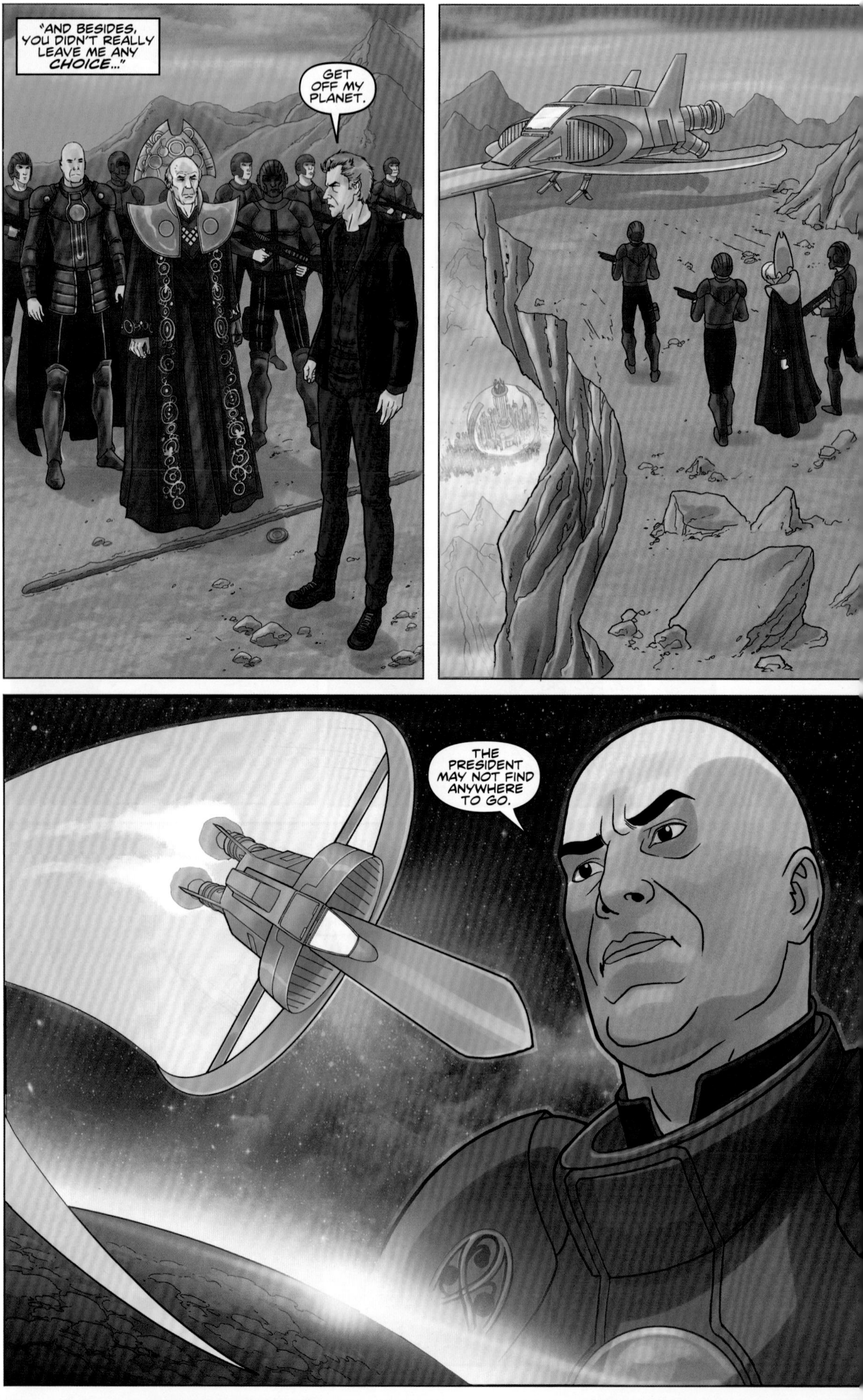
"AND BESIDES, YOU DIDN'T REALLY LEAVE ME ANY CHOICE..."
GET OFF MY PLANET.
THE PRESIDENT MAY NOT FIND ANYWHERE TO GO.

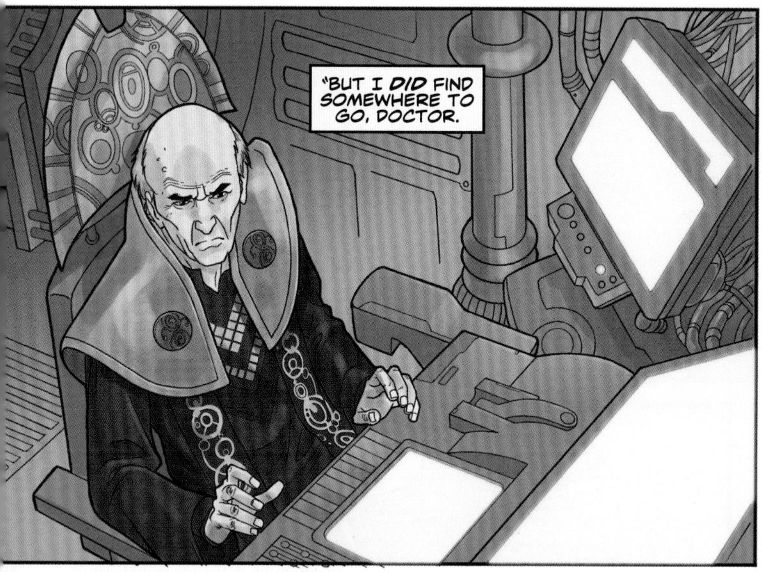
"BUT I *DID* FIND SOMEWHERE TO GO, DOCTOR.
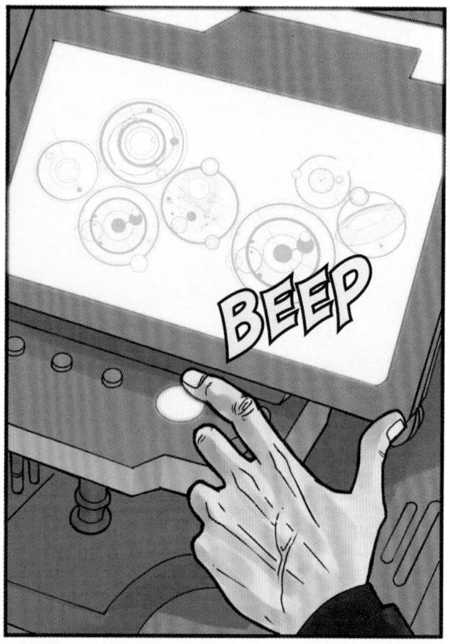
BEEP
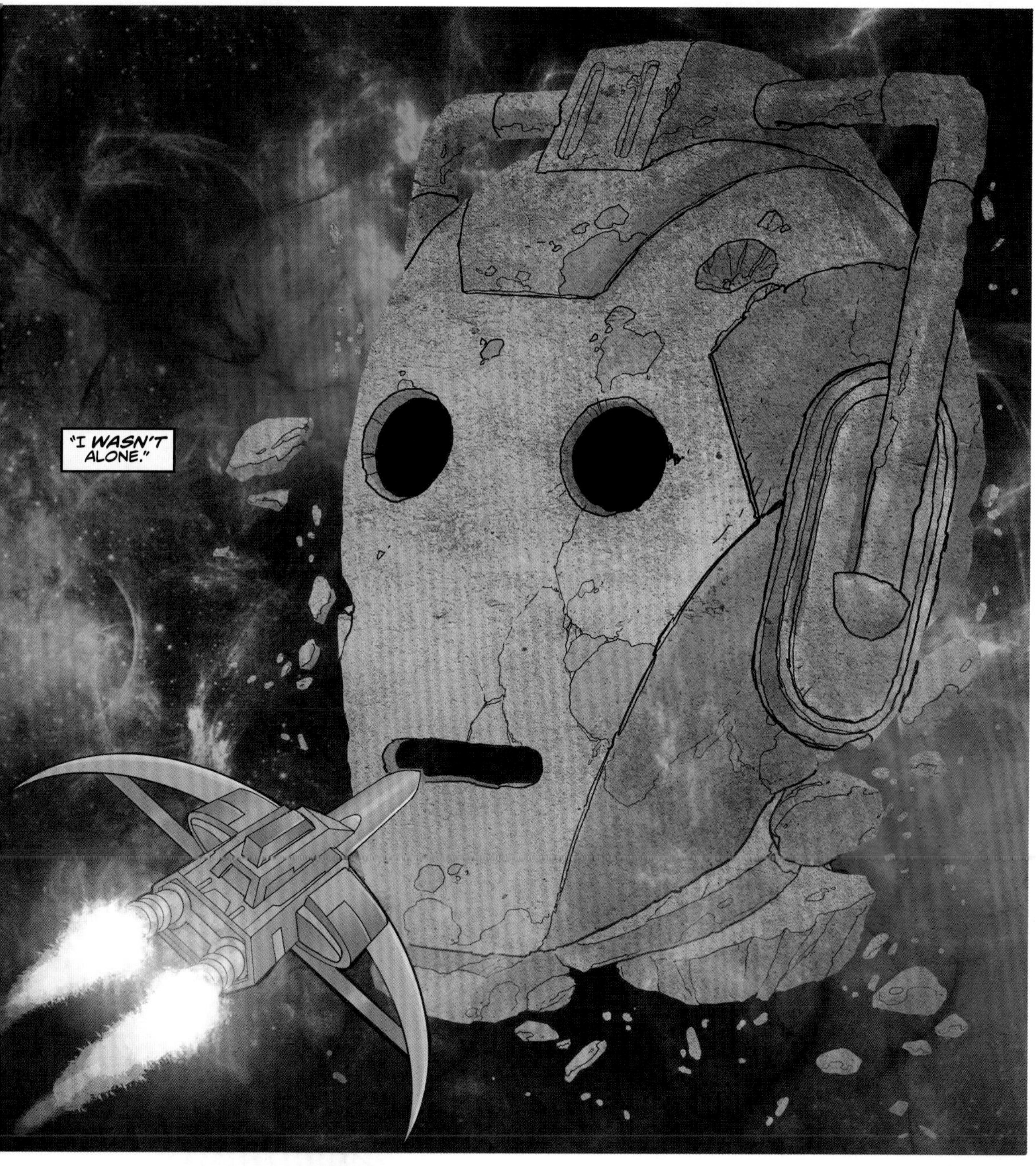
"I *WASN'T* ALONE."

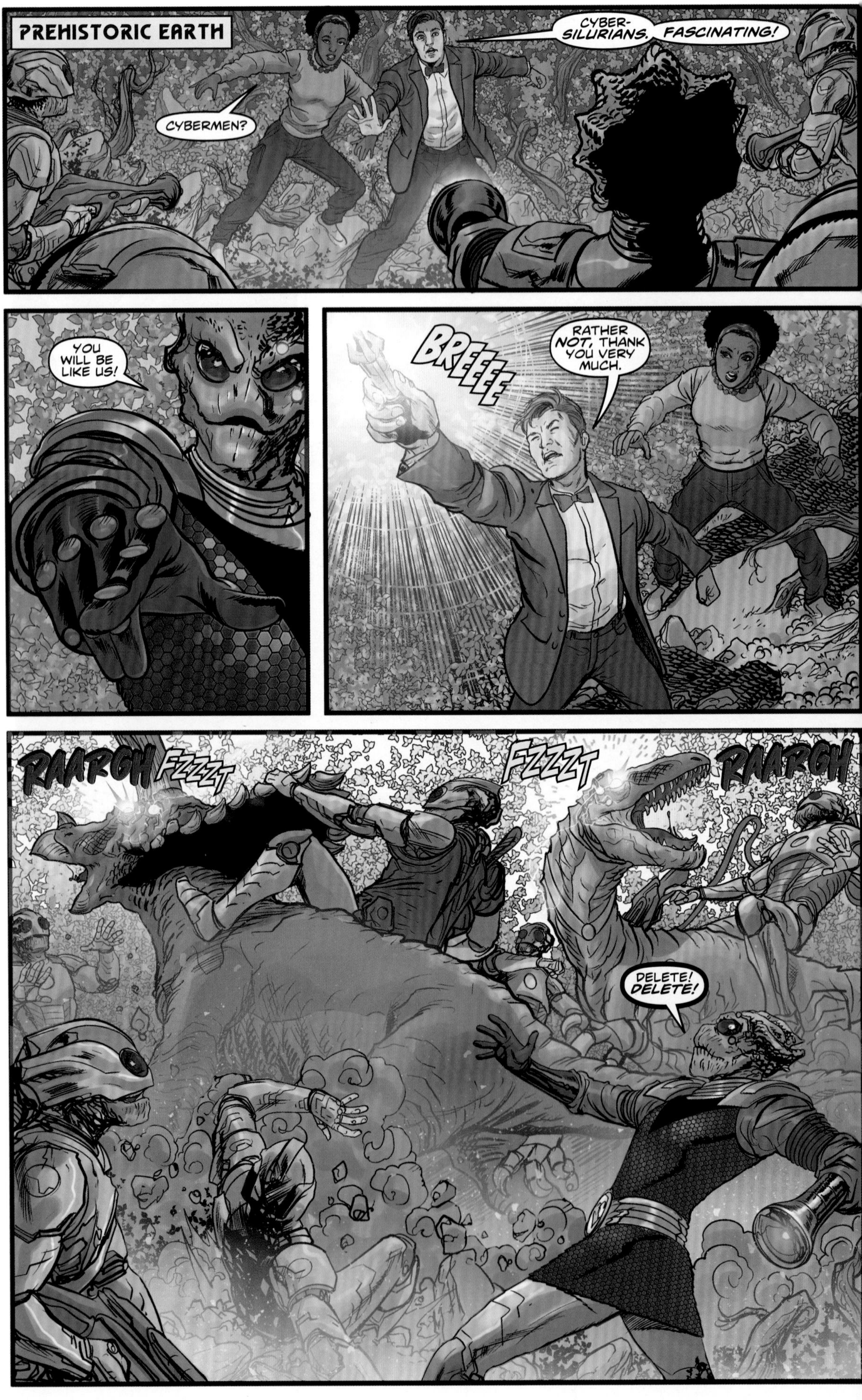
PREHISTORIC EARTH
CYBER-SILURIANS. FASCINATING!
CYBERMEN?
YOU WILL BE LIKE US!
BREEEE
RATHER NOT, THANK YOU VERY MUCH.
RAARGH FZZZT
FZZZT RAARGH
DELETE! DELETE!

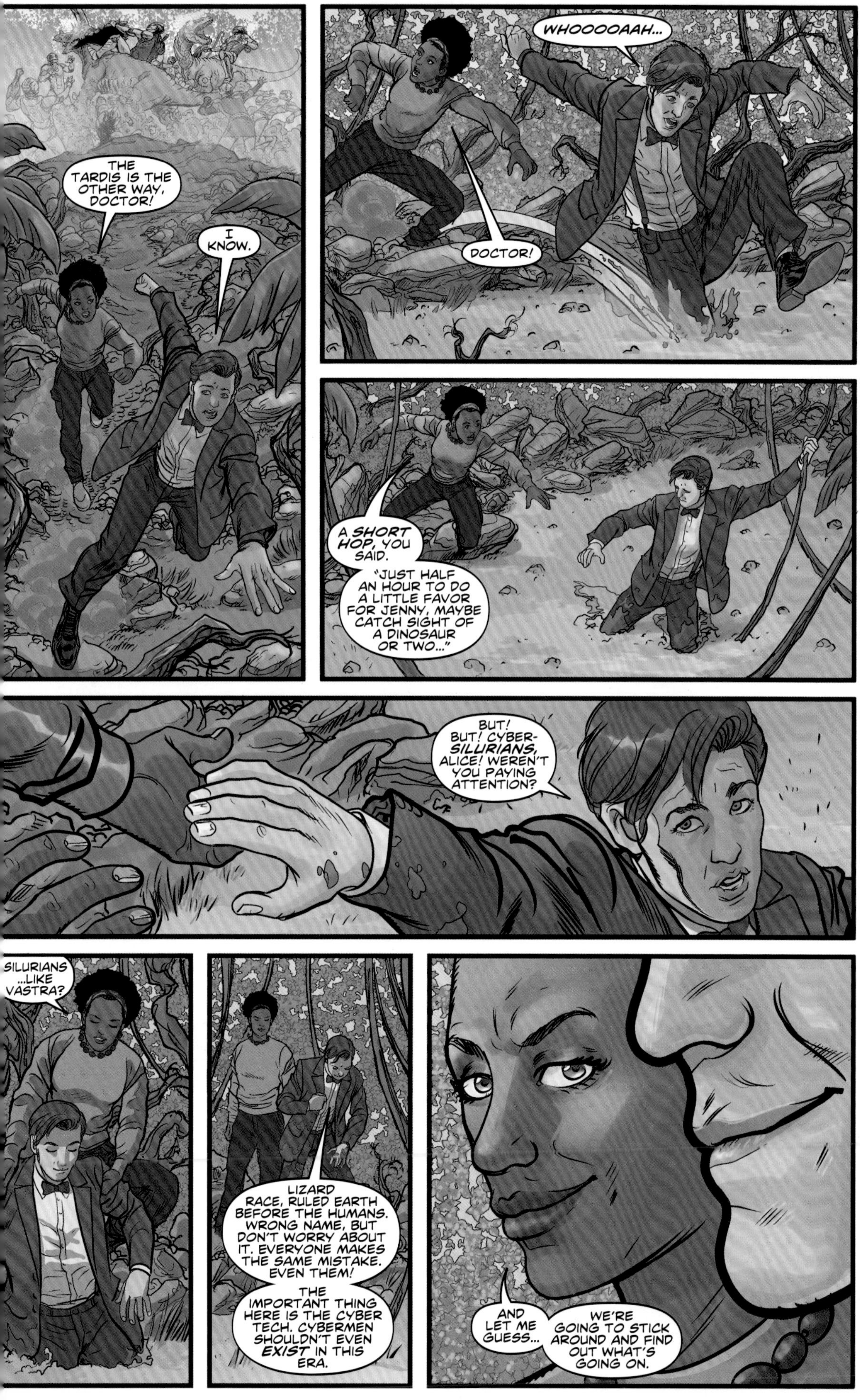
THE TARDIS IS THE OTHER WAY, DOCTOR!
I KNOW.
WHOOOOAAH...
DOCTOR!
A SHORT HOP, YOU SAID.
"JUST HALF AN HOUR TO DO A LITTLE FAVOR FOR JENNY, MAYBE CATCH SIGHT OF A DINOSAUR OR TWO..."
BUT! BUT! CYBER-SILURIANS, ALICE! WEREN'T YOU PAYING ATTENTION?
SILURIANS ...LIKE VASTRA?
LIZARD RACE, RULED EARTH BEFORE THE HUMANS. WRONG NAME, BUT DON'T WORRY ABOUT IT. EVERYONE MAKES THE SAME MISTAKE. EVEN THEM!
THE IMPORTANT THING HERE IS THE CYBER TECH. CYBERMEN SHOULDN'T EVEN EXIST IN THIS ERA.
AND LET ME GUESS...
WE'RE GOING TO STICK AROUND AND FIND OUT WHAT'S GOING ON.

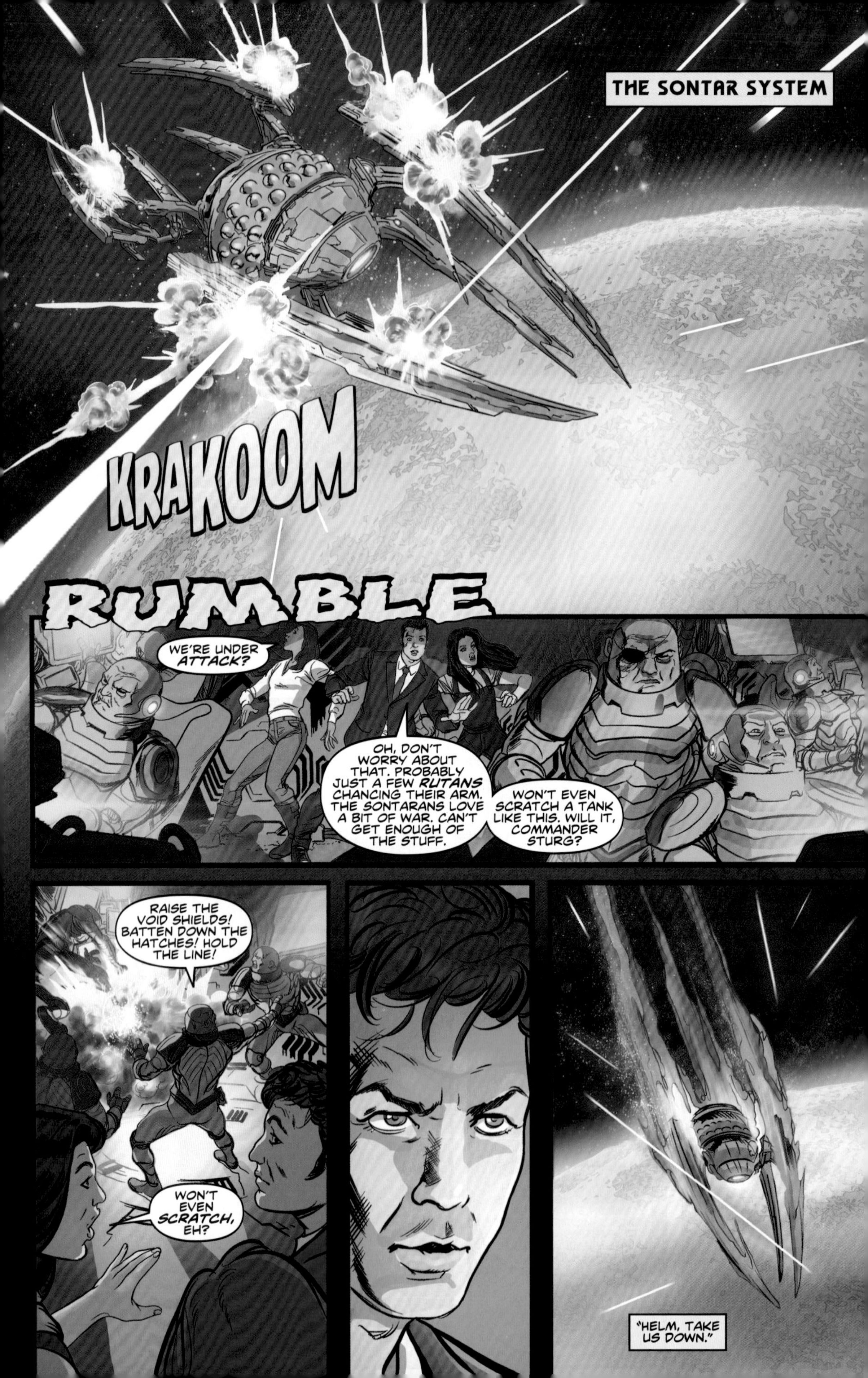
THE SONTAR SYSTEM
KRAKOOM
RUMBLE
WE'RE UNDER ATTACK?
OH, DON'T WORRY ABOUT THAT. PROBABLY JUST A FEW RUTANS CHANCING THEIR ARM. THE SONTARANS LOVE A BIT OF WAR. CAN'T GET ENOUGH OF THE STUFF.
WON'T EVEN SCRATCH A TANK LIKE THIS. WILL IT, COMMANDER STURG?
RAISE THE VOID SHIELDS! BATTEN DOWN THE HATCHES! HOLD THE LINE!
WON'T EVEN SCRATCH, EH?
"HELM, TAKE US DOWN."

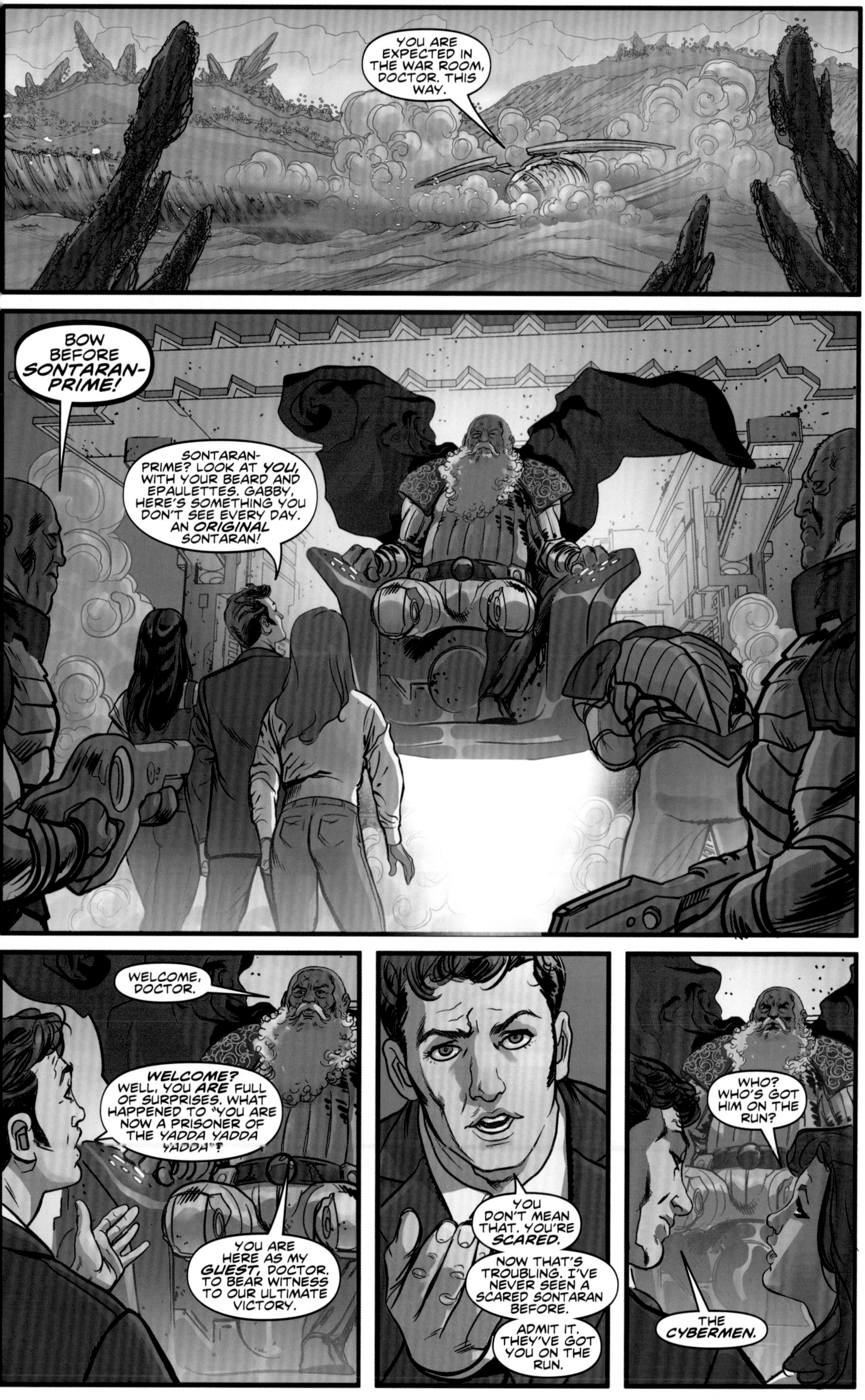
YOU ARE EXPECTED IN THE WAR ROOM, DOCTOR. THIS WAY.
BOW BEFORE SONTARAN-PRIME!
SONTARAN-PRIME? LOOK AT YOU, WITH YOUR BEARD AND EPAULETTES. GABBY, HERE'S SOMETHING YOU DON'T SEE EVERY DAY. AN ORIGINAL SONTARAN!
WELCOME, DOCTOR.
WELCOME? WELL, YOU ARE FULL OF SURPRISES. WHAT HAPPENED TO "YOU ARE NOW A PRISONER OF THE YADDA YADDA YADDA"?
YOU ARE HERE AS MY GUEST, DOCTOR. TO BEAR WITNESS TO OUR ULTIMATE VICTORY.
YOU DON'T MEAN THAT. YOU'RE SCARED.
NOW THAT'S TROUBLING. I'VE NEVER SEEN A SCARED SONTARAN BEFORE.
ADMIT IT. THEY'VE GOT YOU ON THE RUN.
WHO? WHO'S GOT HIM ON THE RUN?
THE CYBERMEN.

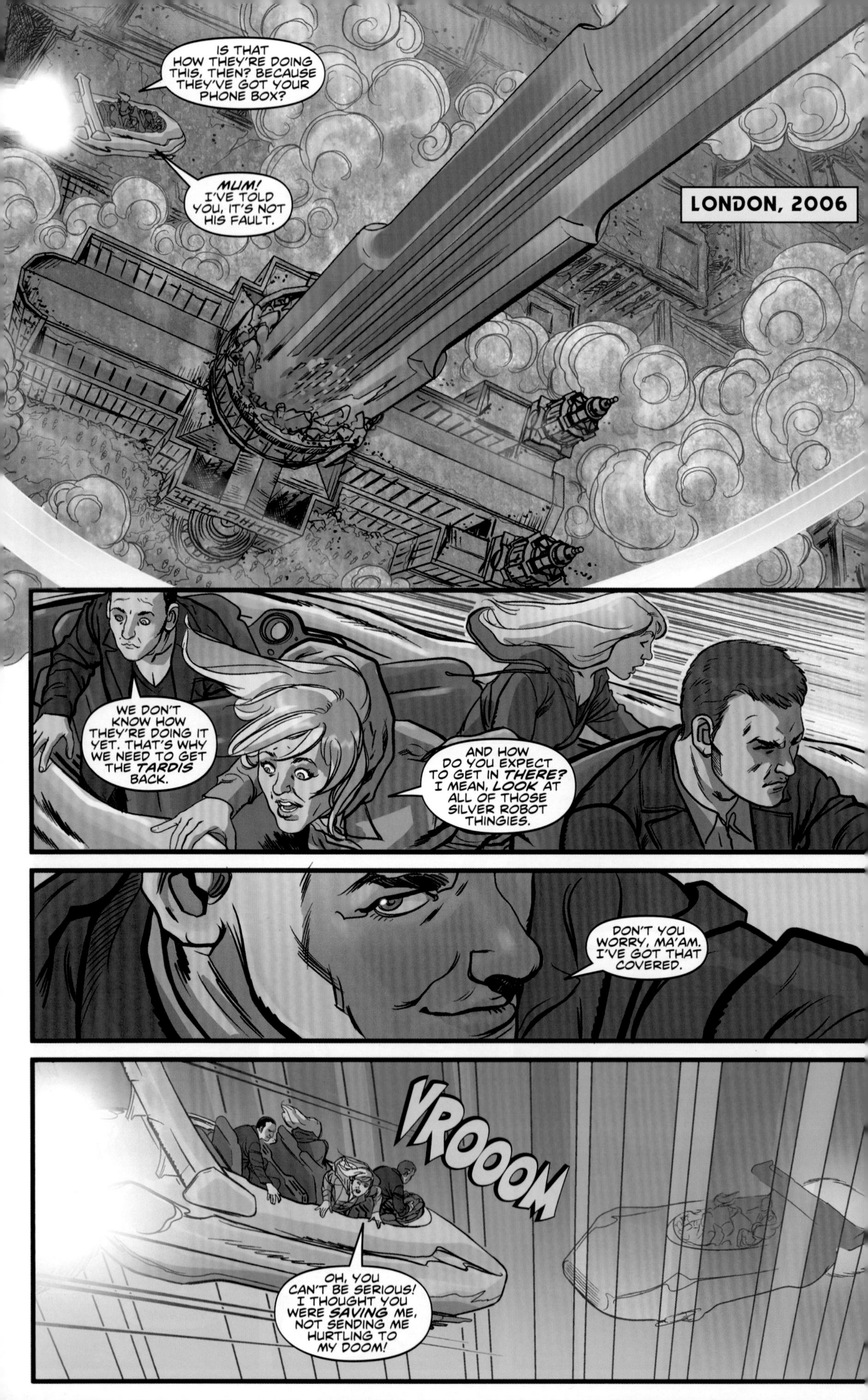
IS THAT HOW THEY'RE DOING THIS, THEN? BECAUSE THEY'VE GOT YOUR PHONE BOX?
MUM! I'VE TOLD YOU, IT'S NOT HIS FAULT.
LONDON, 2006
WE DON'T KNOW HOW THEY'RE DOING IT YET. THAT'S WHY WE NEED TO GET THE TARDIS BACK.
AND HOW DO YOU EXPECT TO GET IN THERE? I MEAN, LOOK AT ALL OF THOSE SILVER ROBOT THINGIES.
DON'T YOU WORRY, MA'AM. I'VE GOT THAT COVERED.
VROOOM
OH, YOU CAN'T BE SERIOUS! I THOUGHT YOU WERE SAVING ME, NOT SENDING ME HURTLING TO MY DOOM!

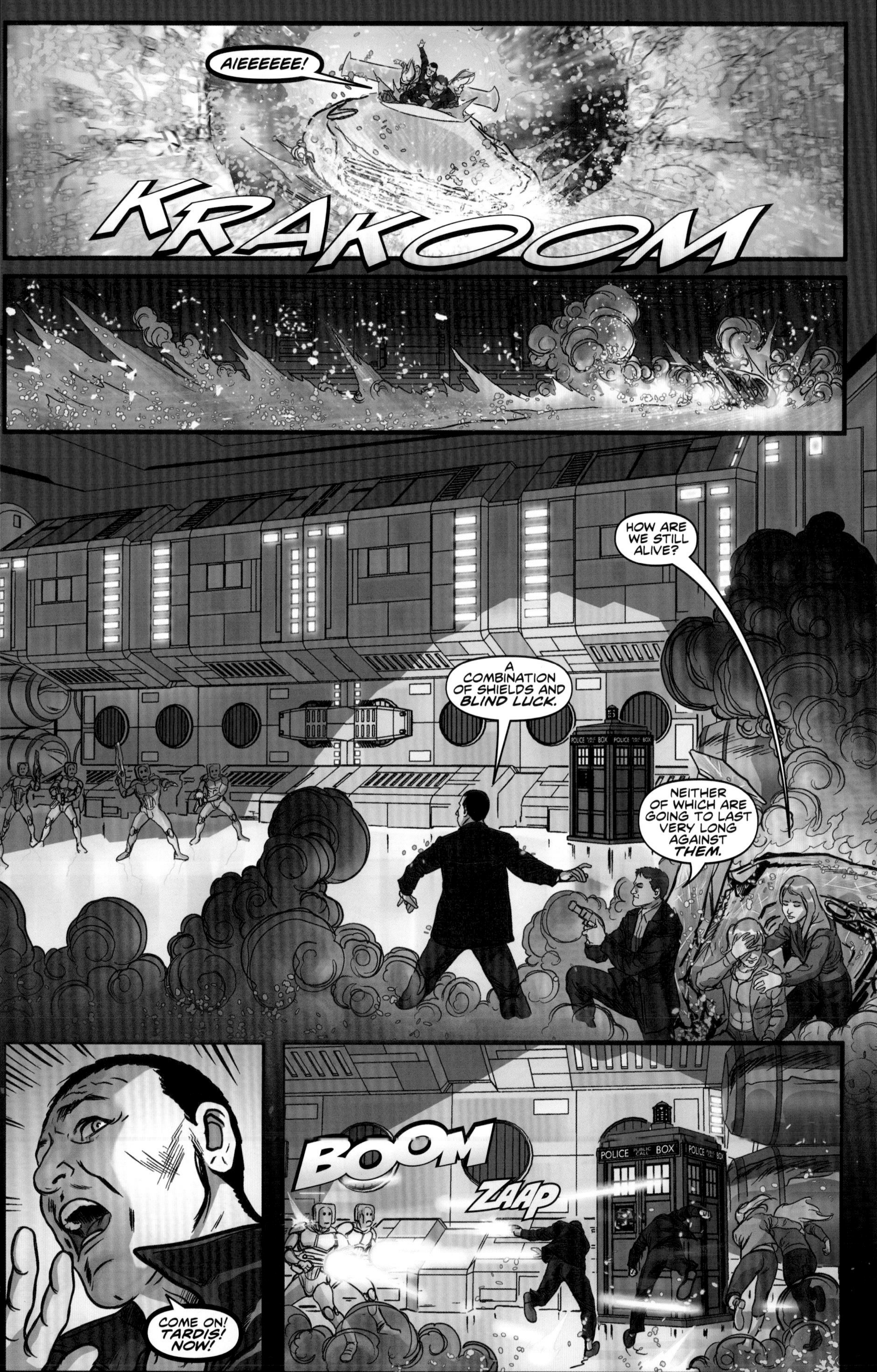
AIEEEEEE!
KRAKOOM
HOW ARE WE STILL ALIVE?
A COMBINATION OF SHIELDS AND BLIND LUCK.
NEITHER OF WHICH ARE GOING TO LAST VERY LONG AGAINST THEM.
POLICE PUBLIC CALL BOX
COME ON! TARDIS! NOW!
BOOM
ZAAP
POLICE PUBLIC CALL BOX

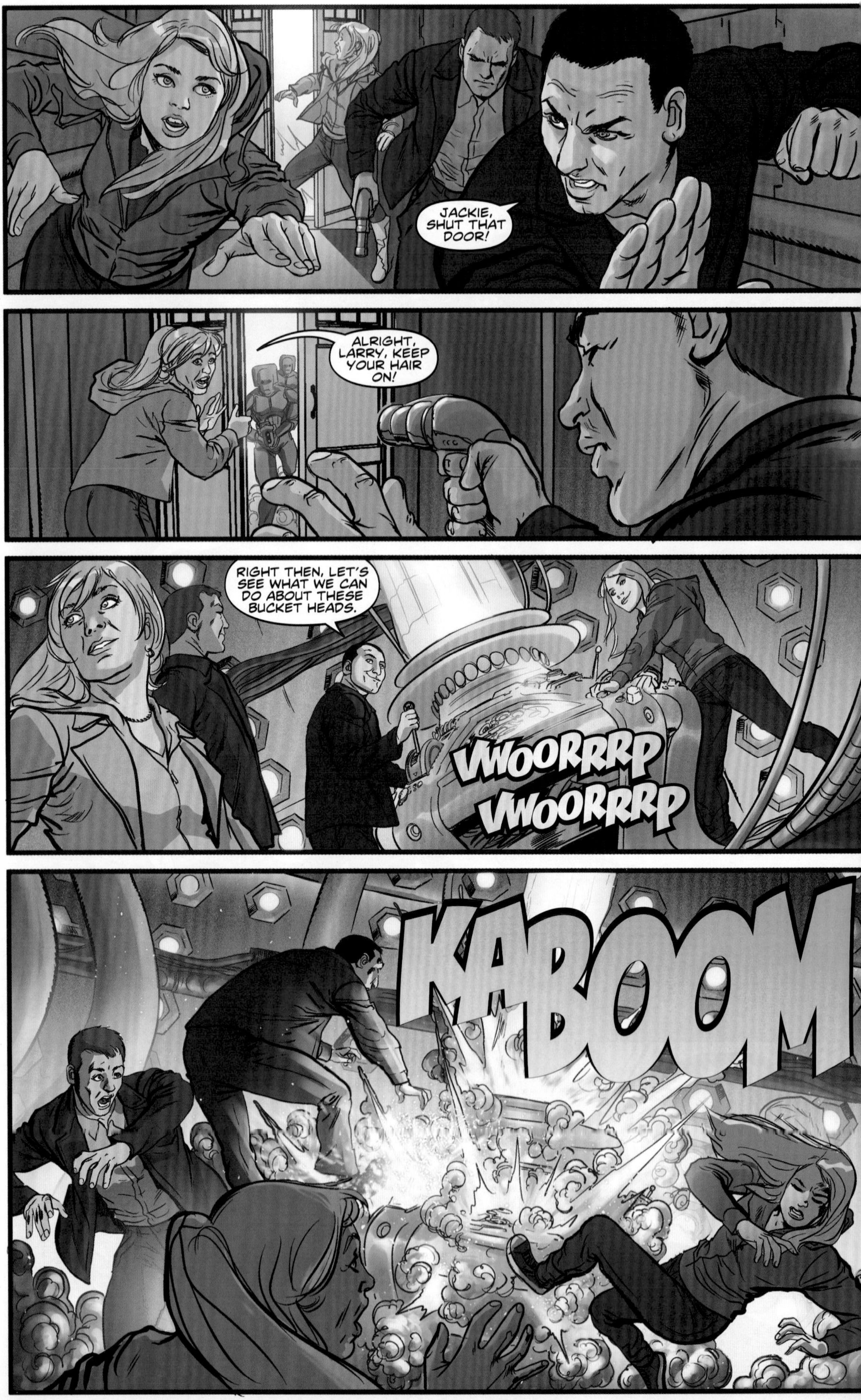
JACKIE, SHUT THAT DOOR!
ALRIGHT, LARRY, KEEP YOUR HAIR ON!
RIGHT THEN, LET'S SEE WHAT WE CAN DO ABOUT THESE BUCKET HEADS.
VWOORRRP
VWOORRRP
KABOOM

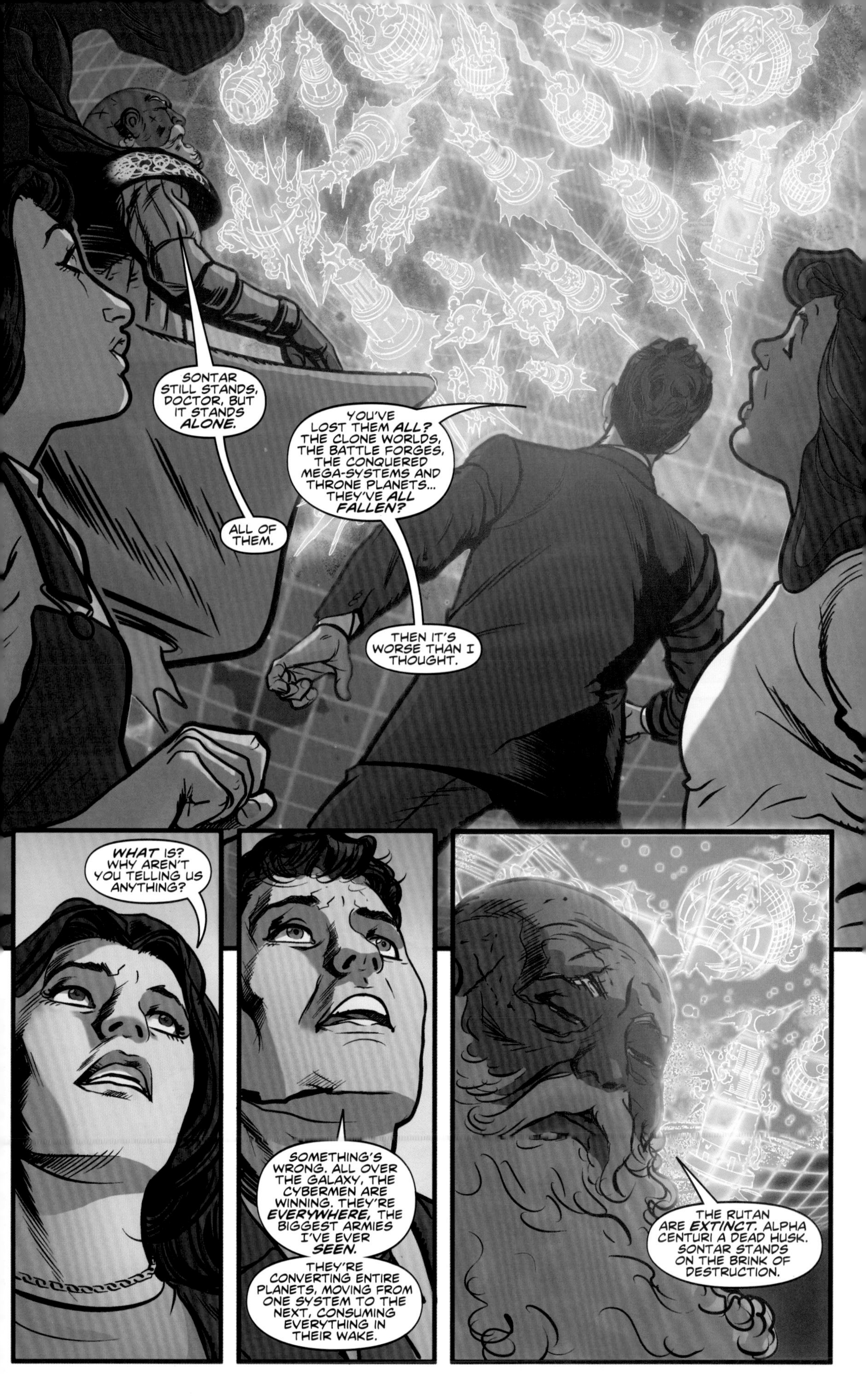
SONTAR STILL STANDS, DOCTOR, BUT IT STANDS ALONE.
YOU'VE LOST THEM ALL? THE CLONE WORLDS, THE BATTLE FORGES, THE CONQUERED MEGA-SYSTEMS AND THRONE PLANETS... THEY'VE ALL FALLEN?
ALL OF THEM.
THEN IT'S WORSE THAN I THOUGHT.
WHAT IS? WHY AREN'T YOU TELLING US ANYTHING?
SOMETHING'S WRONG. ALL OVER THE GALAXY, THE CYBERMEN ARE WINNING. THEY'RE EVERYWHERE, THE BIGGEST ARMIES I'VE EVER SEEN.
THEY'RE CONVERTING ENTIRE PLANETS, MOVING FROM ONE SYSTEM TO THE NEXT, CONSUMING EVERYTHING IN THEIR WAKE.
THE RUTAN ARE EXTINCT. ALPHA CENTURI A DEAD HUSK. SONTAR STANDS ON THE BRINK OF DESTRUCTION.

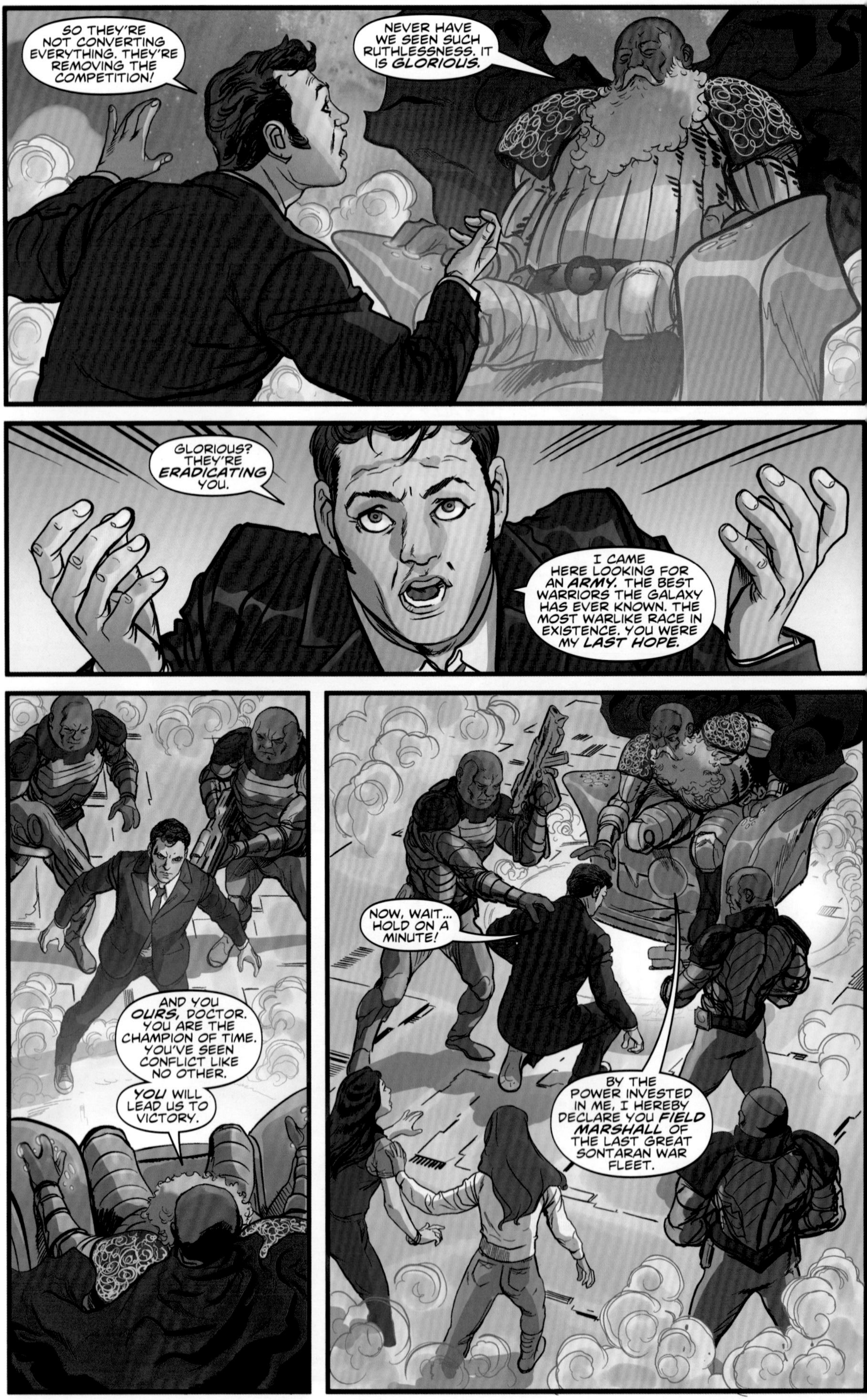
SO THEY'RE NOT CONVERTING EVERYTHING. THEY'RE REMOVING THE COMPETITION!
NEVER HAVE WE SEEN SUCH RUTHLESSNESS. IT IS GLORIOUS.
GLORIOUS? THEY'RE ERADICATING YOU.
I CAME HERE LOOKING FOR AN ARMY. THE BEST WARRIORS THE GALAXY HAS EVER KNOWN. THE MOST WARLIKE RACE IN EXISTENCE. YOU WERE MY LAST HOPE.
AND YOU OURS, DOCTOR. YOU ARE THE CHAMPION OF TIME. YOU'VE SEEN CONFLICT LIKE NO OTHER.
YOU WILL LEAD US TO VICTORY.
NOW, WAIT... HOLD ON A MINUTE!
BY THE POWER INVESTED IN ME, I HEREBY DECLARE YOU FIELD MARSHALL OF THE LAST GREAT SONTARAN WAR FLEET.

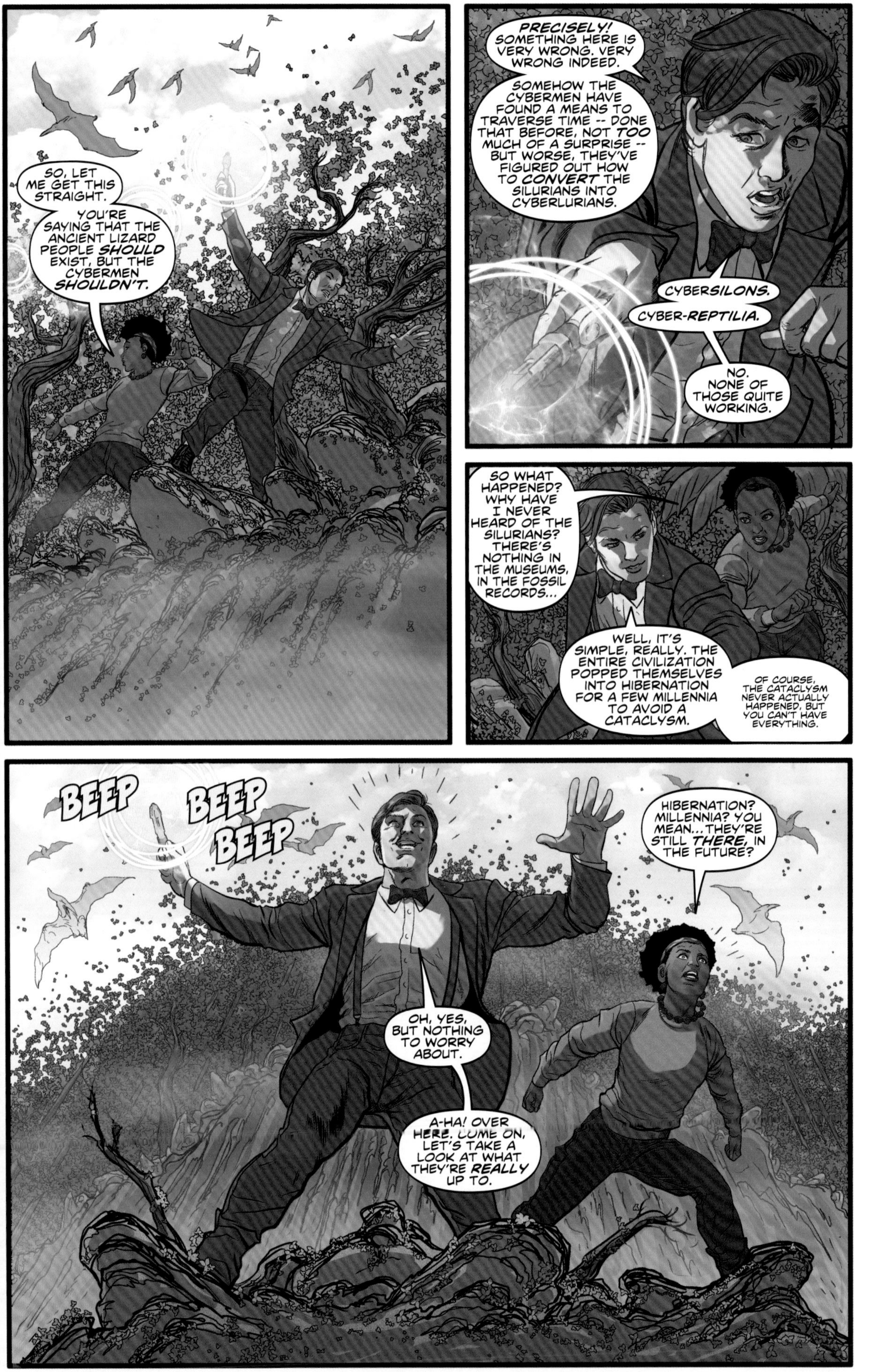
SO, LET ME GET THIS STRAIGHT.
YOU'RE SAYING THAT THE ANCIENT LIZARD PEOPLE *SHOULD* EXIST, BUT THE CYBERMEN *SHOULDN'T*.
PRECISELY! SOMETHING HERE IS VERY WRONG. VERY WRONG INDEED.
SOMEHOW THE CYBERMEN HAVE FOUND A MEANS TO TRAVERSE TIME -- DONE THAT BEFORE, NOT *TOO* MUCH OF A SURPRISE -- BUT WORSE, THEY'VE FIGURED OUT HOW TO *CONVERT* THE SILURIANS INTO CYBERLURIANS.
CYBER*SILONS*.
CYBER-*REPTILIA*.
NO. NONE OF THOSE QUITE WORKING.
SO WHAT HAPPENED? WHY HAVE I NEVER HEARD OF THE SILURIANS? THERE'S NOTHING IN THE MUSEUMS, IN THE FOSSIL RECORDS...
WELL, IT'S SIMPLE, REALLY. THE ENTIRE CIVILIZATION POPPED THEMSELVES INTO HIBERNATION FOR A FEW MILLENNIA TO AVOID A CATACLYSM.
OF COURSE, THE CATACLYSM NEVER ACTUALLY HAPPENED, BUT YOU CAN'T HAVE EVERYTHING.
BEEP
BEEP
BEEP
HIBERNATION? MILLENNIA? YOU MEAN...THEY'RE STILL *THERE*, IN THE FUTURE?
OH, YES, BUT NOTHING TO WORRY ABOUT.
A-HA! OVER HERE. COME ON, LET'S TAKE A LOOK AT WHAT THEY'RE *REALLY* UP TO.

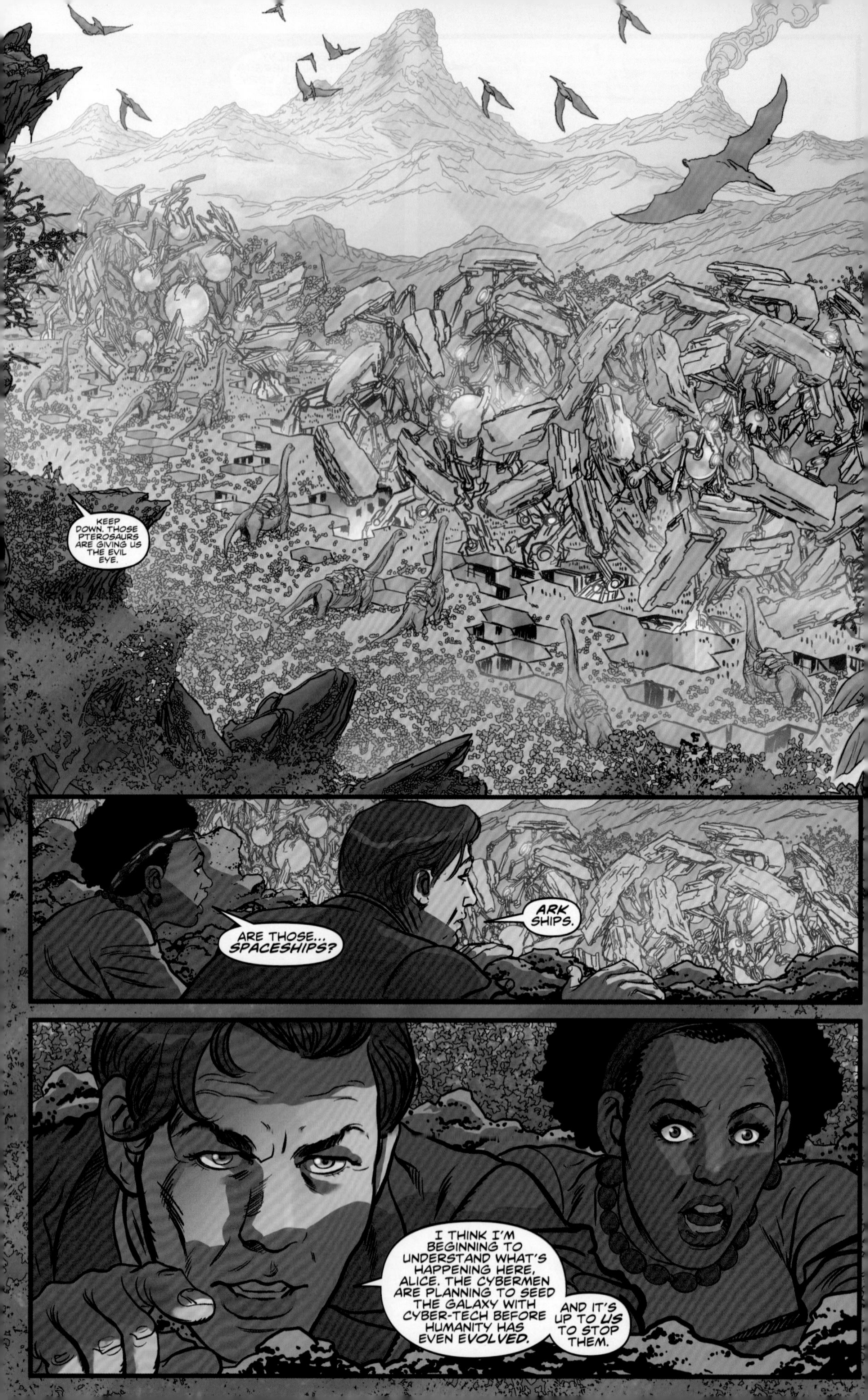
KEEP DOWN. THOSE PTEROSAURS ARE GIVING US THE EVIL EYE.
ARE THOSE... SPACESHIPS?
ARK SHIPS.
I THINK I'M BEGINNING TO UNDERSTAND WHAT'S HAPPENING HERE, ALICE. THE CYBERMEN ARE PLANNING TO SEED THE GALAXY WITH CYBER-TECH BEFORE HUMANITY HAS EVEN EVOLVED.
AND IT'S UP TO US TO STOP THEM.

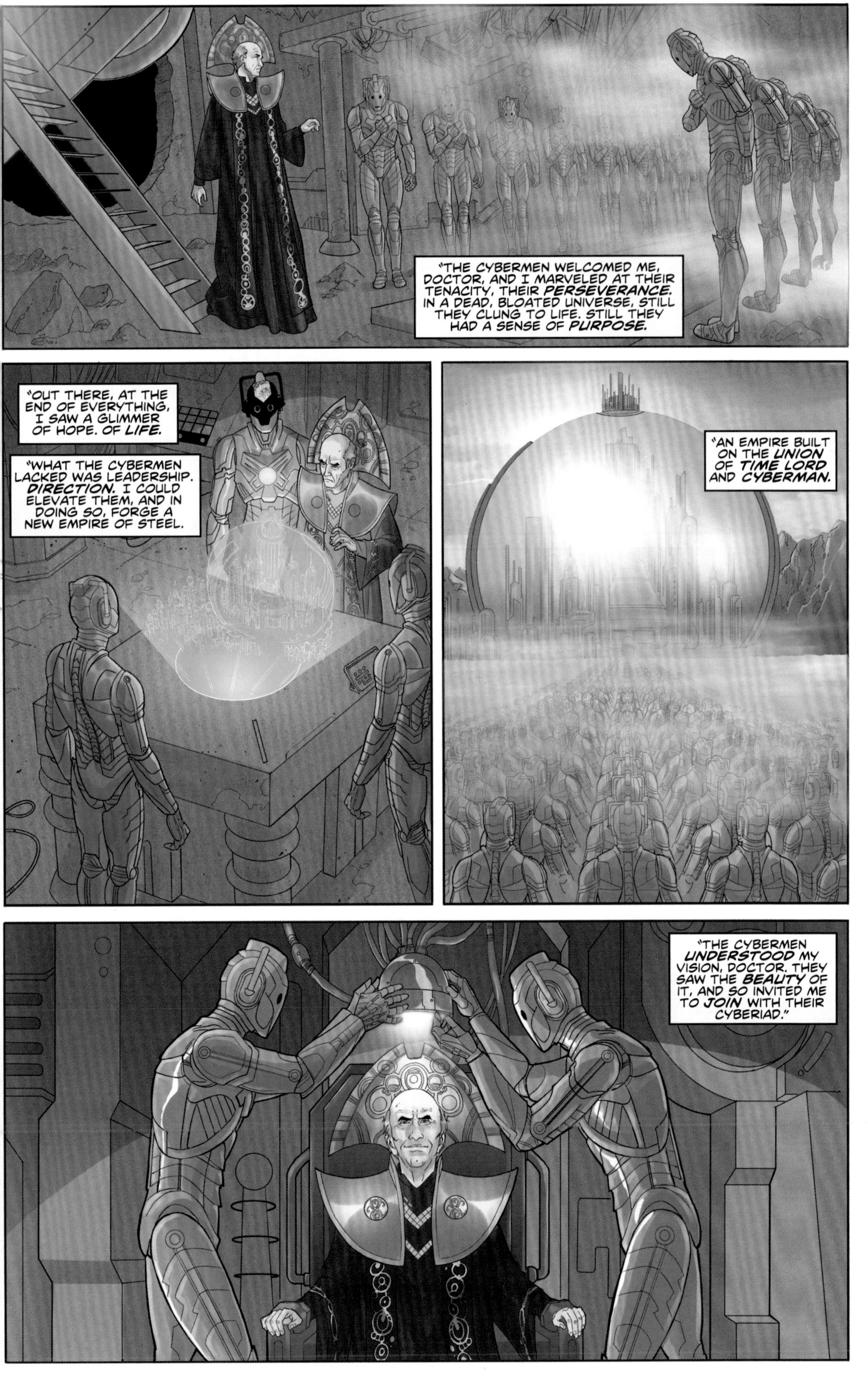
"THE CYBERMEN WELCOMED ME, DOCTOR, AND I MARVELED AT THEIR TENACITY, THEIR PERSEVERANCE. IN A DEAD, BLOATED UNIVERSE, STILL THEY CLUNG TO LIFE. STILL THEY HAD A SENSE OF PURPOSE.
"OUT THERE, AT THE END OF EVERYTHING, I SAW A GLIMMER OF HOPE. OF LIFE.
"WHAT THE CYBERMEN LACKED WAS LEADERSHIP. DIRECTION. I COULD ELEVATE THEM, AND IN DOING SO, FORGE A NEW EMPIRE OF STEEL.
"AN EMPIRE BUILT ON THE UNION OF TIME LORD AND CYBERMAN.
"THE CYBERMEN UNDERSTOOD MY VISION, DOCTOR. THEY SAW THE BEAUTY OF IT, AND SO INVITED ME TO JOIN WITH THEIR CYBERIAD."

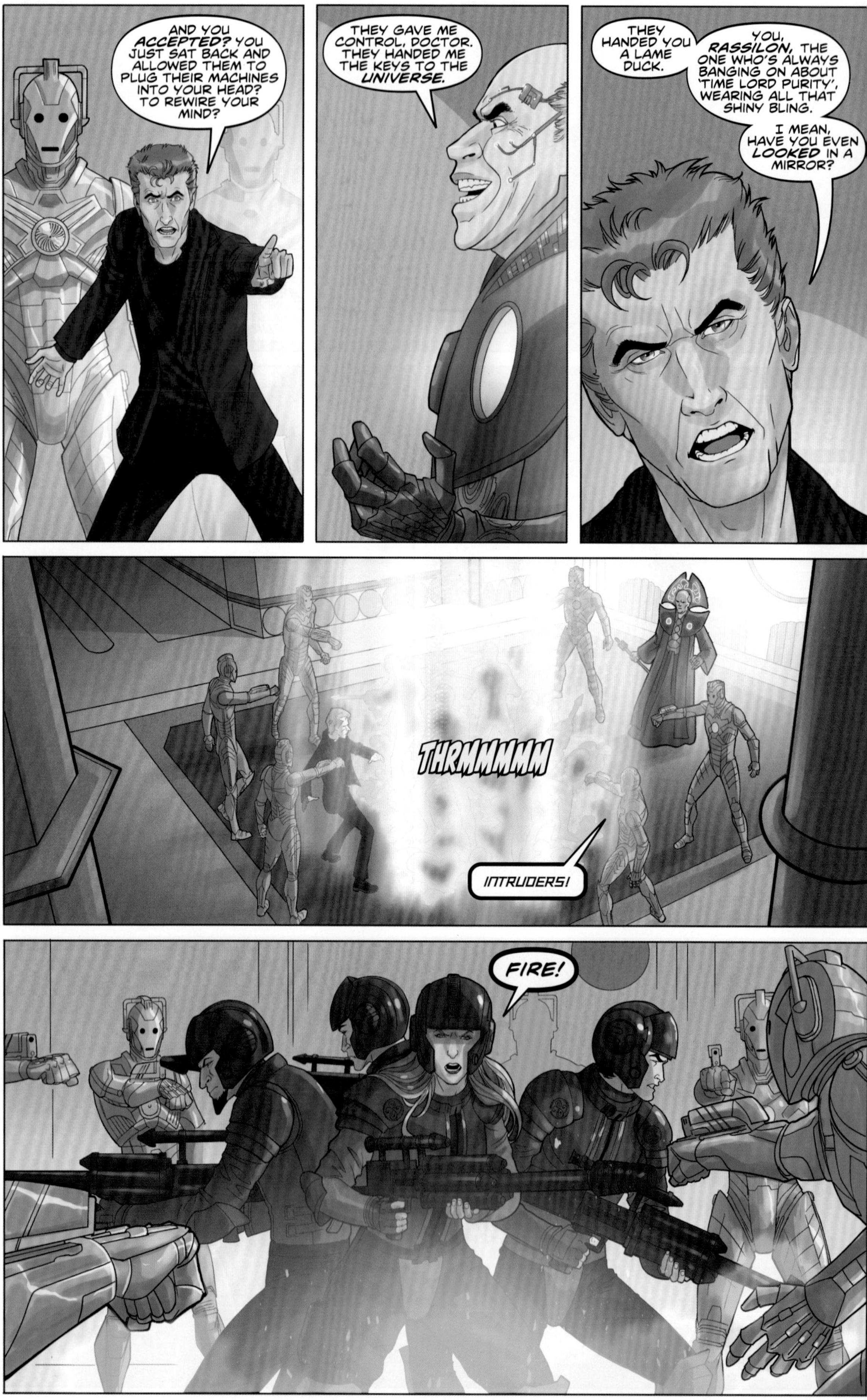
AND YOU ACCEPTED? YOU JUST SAT BACK AND ALLOWED THEM TO PLUG THEIR MACHINES INTO YOUR HEAD? TO REWIRE YOUR MIND?
THEY GAVE ME CONTROL, DOCTOR. THEY HANDED ME THE KEYS TO THE UNIVERSE.
THEY HANDED YOU A LAME DUCK.
YOU, RASSILON, THE ONE WHO'S ALWAYS BANGING ON ABOUT 'TIME LORD PURITY', WEARING ALL THAT SHINY BLING.
I MEAN, HAVE YOU EVEN LOOKED IN A MIRROR?
THRMMMMM
INTRUDERS!
FIRE!

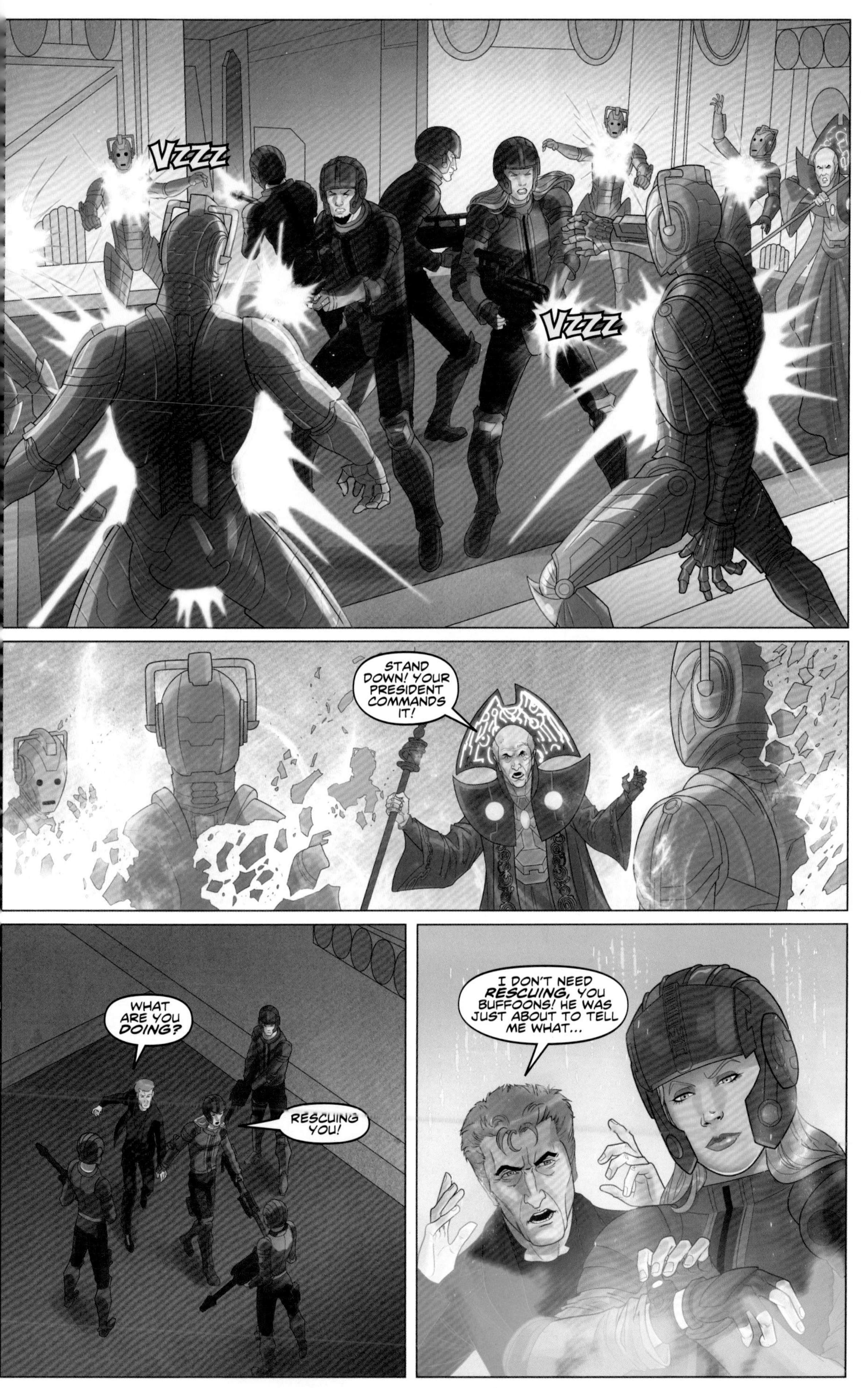
VZZZ
VZZZ
STAND DOWN! YOUR PRESIDENT COMMANDS IT!
WHAT ARE YOU DOING?
RESCUING YOU!
I DON'T NEED RESCUING, YOU BUFFOONS! HE WAS JUST ABOUT TO TELL ME WHAT...

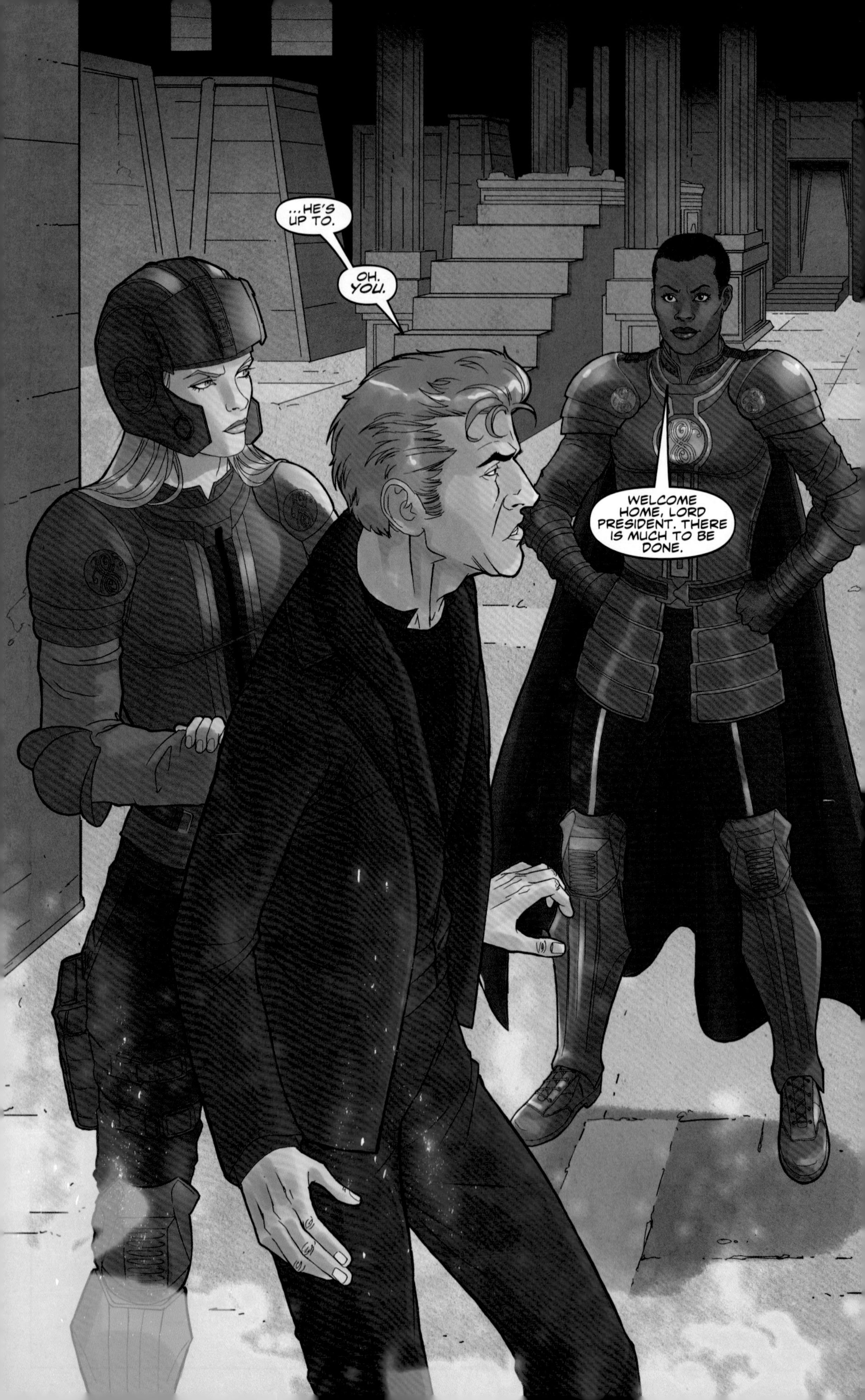
...HE'S UP TO.
OH. YOU.
WELCOME HOME, LORD PRESIDENT. THERE IS MUCH TO BE DONE.

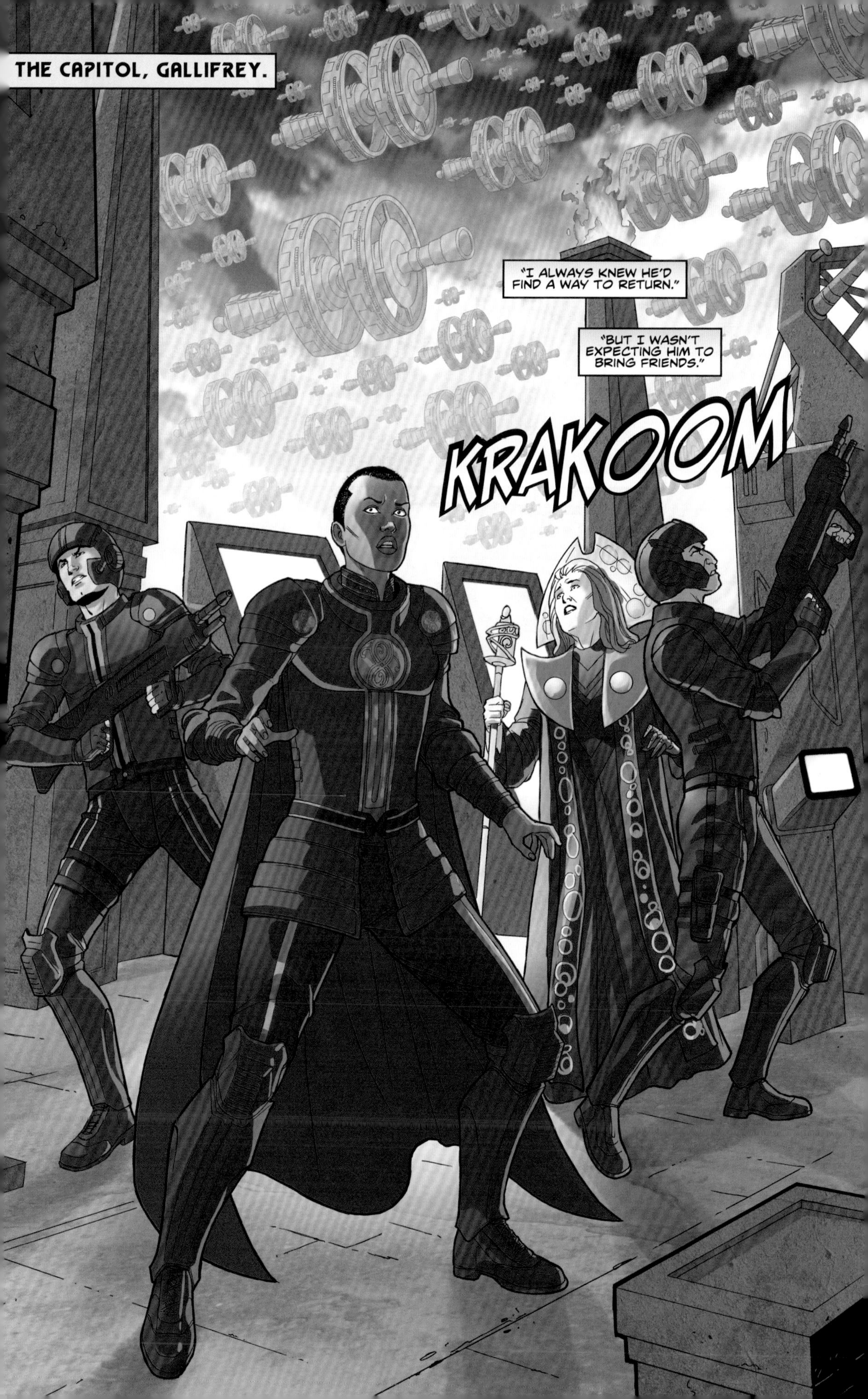
THE CAPITOL, GALLIFREY.
"I ALWAYS KNEW HE'D FIND A WAY TO RETURN."
"BUT I WASN'T EXPECTING HIM TO BRING FRIENDS."
KRAKOOM

THRMMMMM

VZZZZZ

ARRGH!

ARRGH!

THOOM

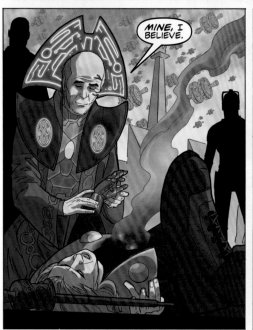

MINE, I BELIEVE.

ROUND UP THE REST OF THE TIME LORDS.

TELL THEM THEIR *PRESIDENT* HAS RETURNED.

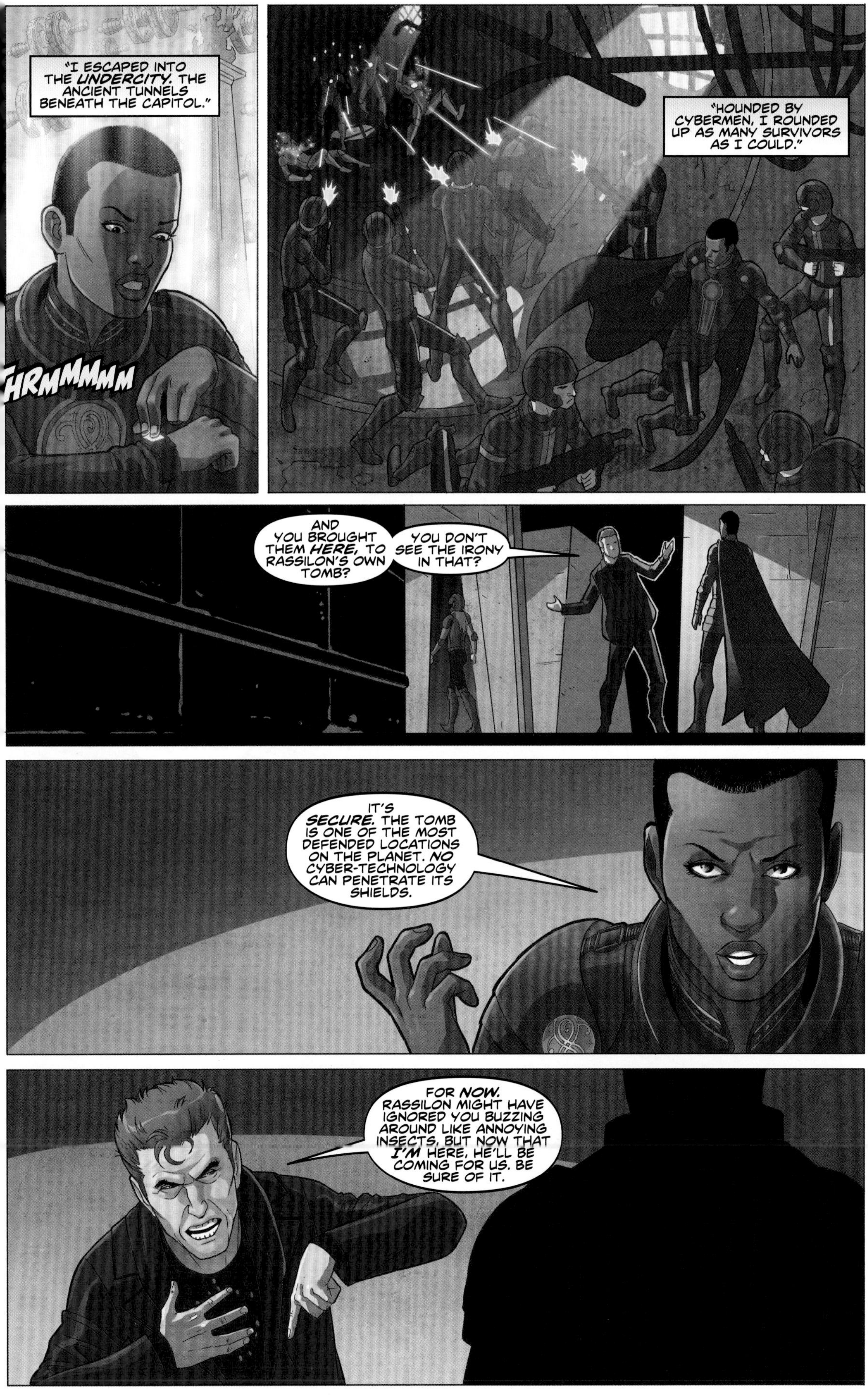
"I ESCAPED INTO THE UNDERCITY. THE ANCIENT TUNNELS BENEATH THE CAPITOL."
THRMMMMM
"HOUNDED BY CYBERMEN, I ROUNDED UP AS MANY SURVIVORS AS I COULD."
AND YOU BROUGHT THEM HERE, TO RASSILON'S OWN TOMB?
YOU DON'T SEE THE IRONY IN THAT?
IT'S SECURE. THE TOMB IS ONE OF THE MOST DEFENDED LOCATIONS ON THE PLANET. NO CYBER-TECHNOLOGY CAN PENETRATE ITS SHIELDS.
FOR NOW. RASSILON MIGHT HAVE IGNORED YOU BUZZING AROUND LIKE ANNOYING INSECTS, BUT NOW THAT I'M HERE, HE'LL BE COMING FOR US. BE SURE OF IT.

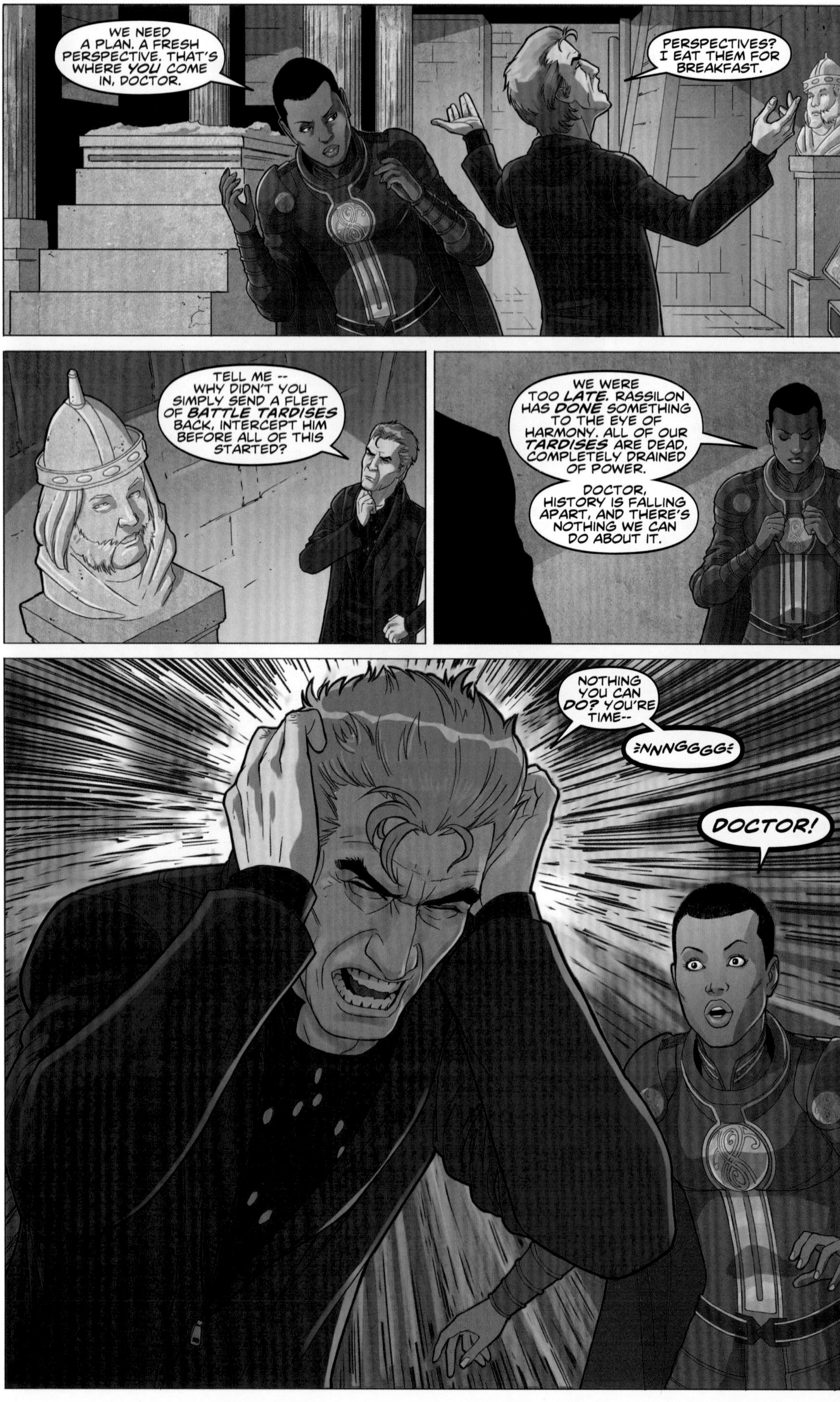
WE NEED A PLAN. A FRESH PERSPECTIVE. THAT'S WHERE YOU COME IN, DOCTOR.
PERSPECTIVES? I EAT THEM FOR BREAKFAST.
TELL ME -- WHY DIDN'T YOU SIMPLY SEND A FLEET OF BATTLE TARDISES BACK, INTERCEPT HIM BEFORE ALL OF THIS STARTED?
WE WERE TOO LATE. RASSILON HAS DONE SOMETHING TO THE EYE OF HARMONY. ALL OF OUR TARDISES ARE DEAD, COMPLETELY DRAINED OF POWER.
DOCTOR, HISTORY IS FALLING APART, AND THERE'S NOTHING WE CAN DO ABOUT IT.
NOTHING YOU CAN DO? YOU'RE TIME--
NNNGGGG
DOCTOR!

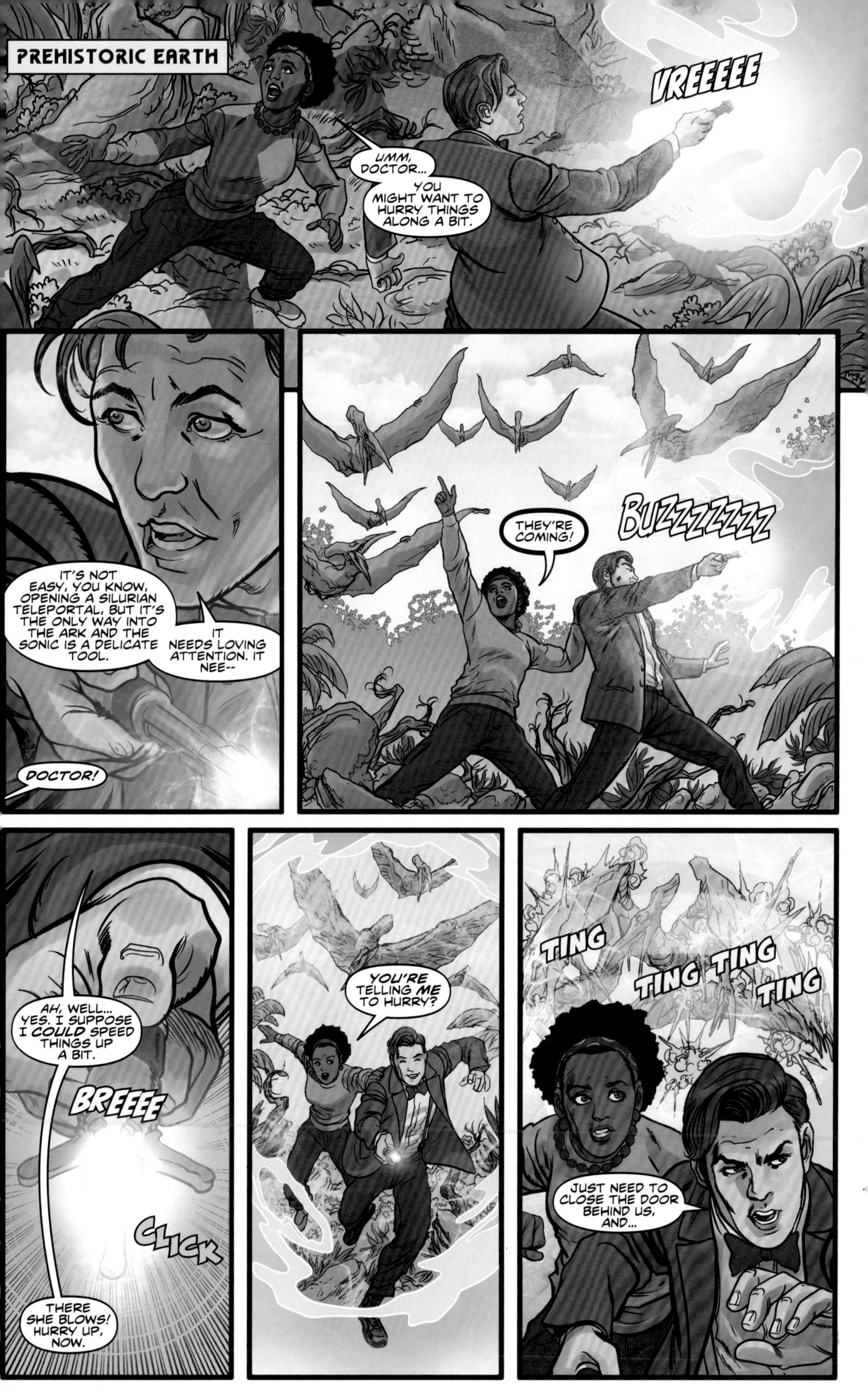

PREHISTORIC EARTH
VREEEEE
UMM, DOCTOR...
YOU MIGHT WANT TO HURRY THINGS ALONG A BIT.
IT'S NOT EASY, YOU KNOW, OPENING A SILURIAN TELEPORTAL, BUT IT'S THE ONLY WAY INTO THE ARK AND THE SONIC IS A DELICATE TOOL.
IT NEEDS LOVING ATTENTION. IT NEE--
DOCTOR!
THEY'RE COMING!
BUZZZZZZZ
AH, WELL... YES. I SUPPOSE I COULD SPEED THINGS UP A BIT.
BREEEE
CLICK
THERE SHE BLOWS! HURRY UP, NOW.
YOU'RE TELLING ME TO HURRY?
TING
TING TING
TING
JUST NEED TO CLOSE THE DOOR BEHIND US, AND...

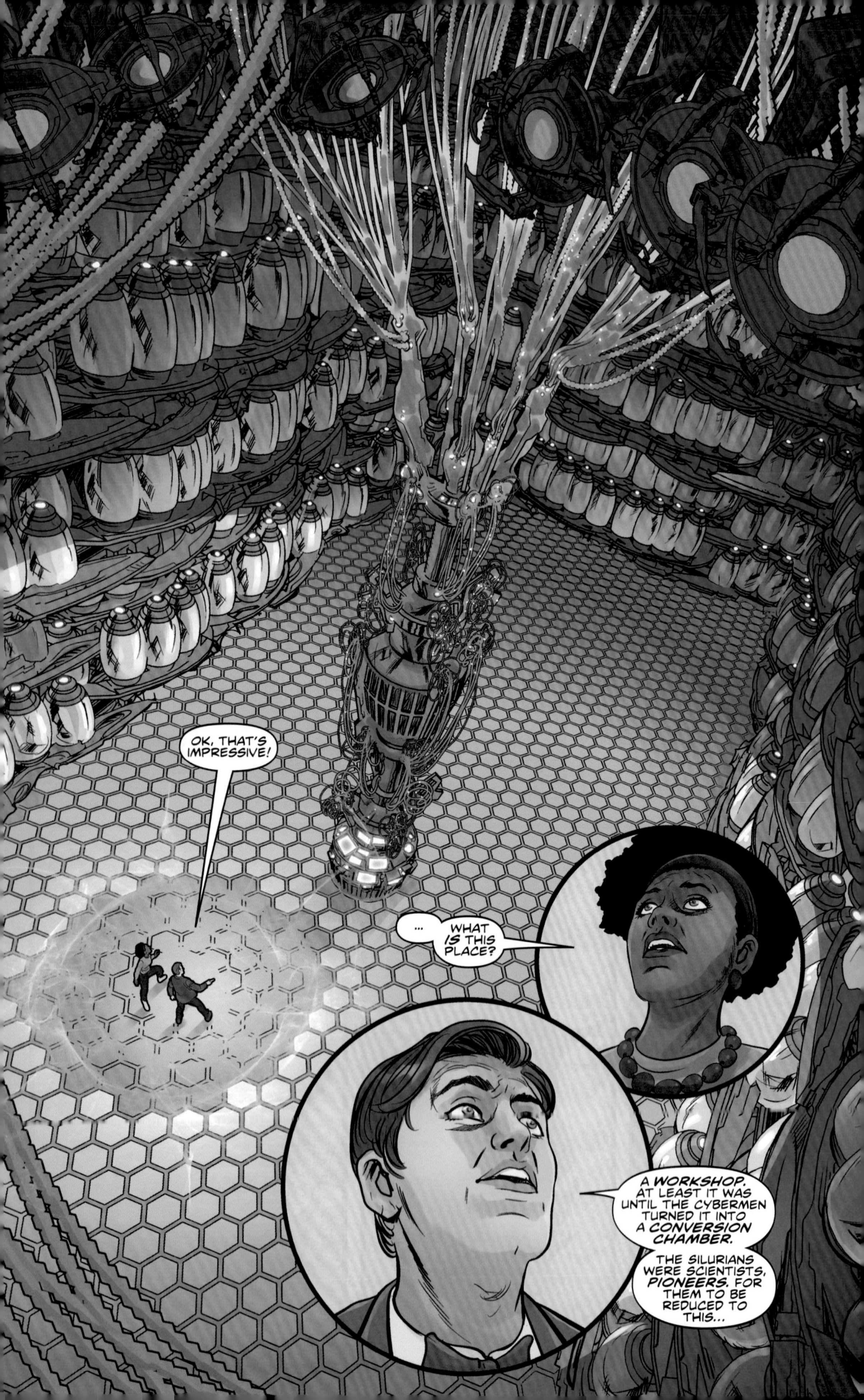

OK, THAT'S IMPRESSIVE!
... WHAT IS THIS PLACE?
A WORKSHOP. AT LEAST IT WAS UNTIL THE CYBERMEN TURNED IT INTO A CONVERSION CHAMBER.
THE SILURIANS WERE SCIENTISTS, PIONEERS. FOR THEM TO BE REDUCED TO THIS...

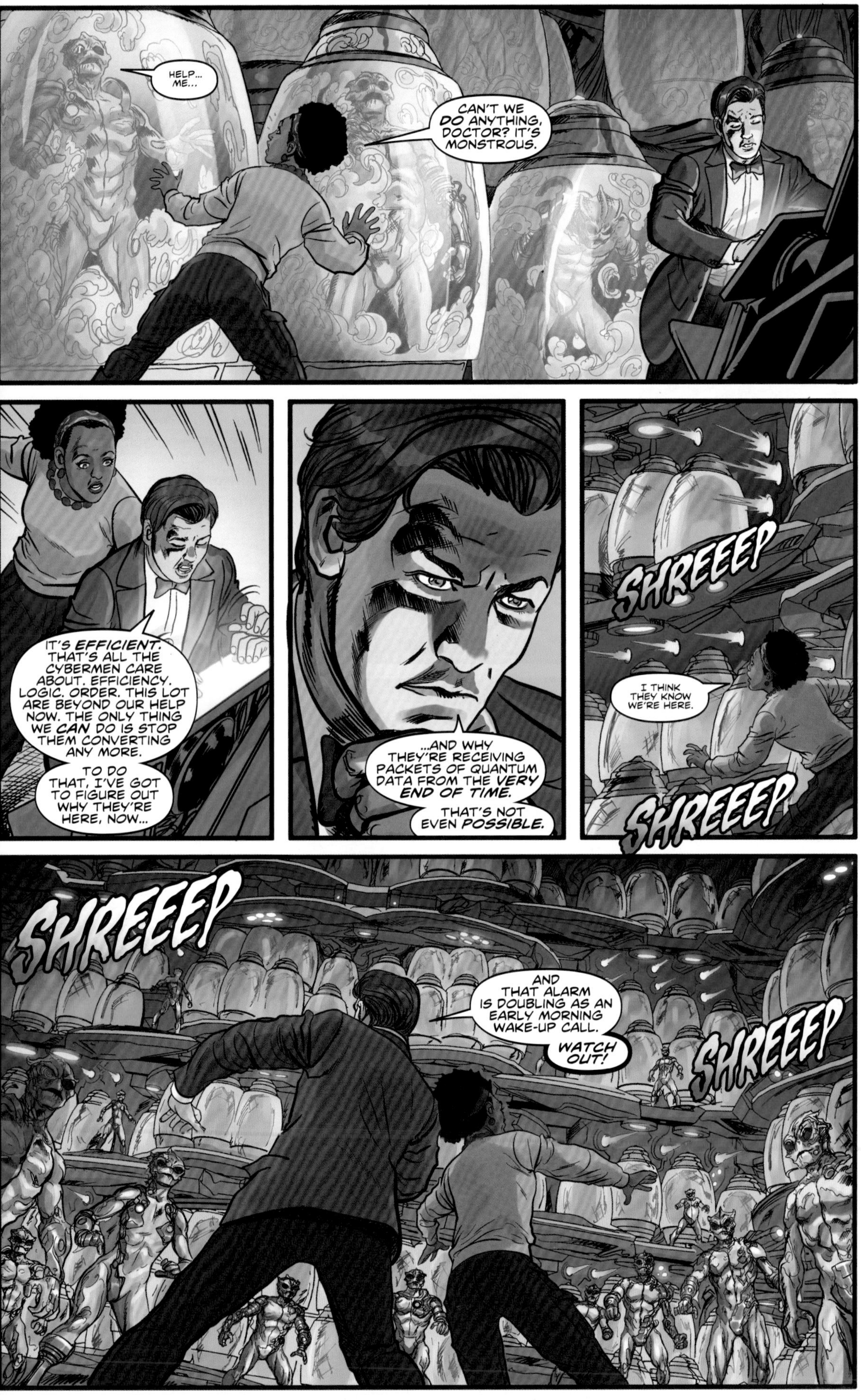
HELP... ME...
CAN'T WE DO ANYTHING, DOCTOR? IT'S MONSTROUS.
IT'S EFFICIENT. THAT'S ALL THE CYBERMEN CARE ABOUT. EFFICIENCY. LOGIC. ORDER. THIS LOT ARE BEYOND OUR HELP NOW. THE ONLY THING WE CAN DO IS STOP THEM CONVERTING ANY MORE.
TO DO THAT, I'VE GOT TO FIGURE OUT WHY THEY'RE HERE, NOW...
...AND WHY THEY'RE RECEIVING PACKETS OF QUANTUM DATA FROM THE VERY END OF TIME.
THAT'S NOT EVEN POSSIBLE.
SHREEEP
I THINK THEY KNOW WE'RE HERE.
SHREEEP
SHREEEP
AND THAT ALARM IS DOUBLING AS AN EARLY MORNING WAKE-UP CALL.
WATCH OUT!
SHREEEP

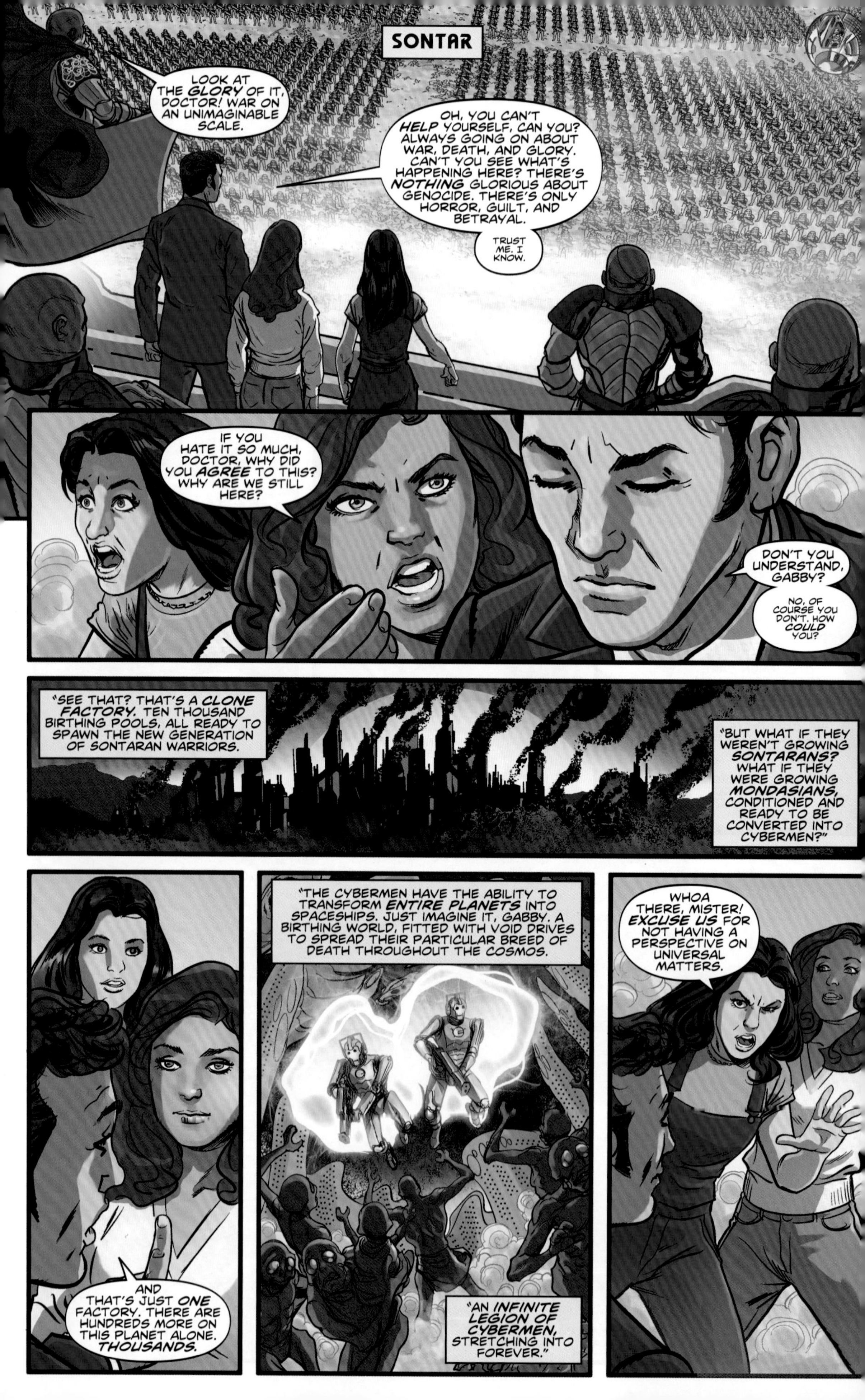
SONTAR
LOOK AT THE GLORY OF IT, DOCTOR! WAR ON AN UNIMAGINABLE SCALE.
OH, YOU CAN'T HELP YOURSELF, CAN YOU? ALWAYS GOING ON ABOUT WAR, DEATH, AND GLORY. CAN'T YOU SEE WHAT'S HAPPENING HERE? THERE'S NOTHING GLORIOUS ABOUT GENOCIDE. THERE'S ONLY HORROR, GUILT, AND BETRAYAL.
TRUST ME. I KNOW.
IF YOU HATE IT SO MUCH, DOCTOR, WHY DID YOU AGREE TO THIS? WHY ARE WE STILL HERE?
DON'T YOU UNDERSTAND, GABBY?
NO, OF COURSE YOU DON'T. HOW COULD YOU?
"SEE THAT? THAT'S A CLONE FACTORY. TEN THOUSAND BIRTHING POOLS, ALL READY TO SPAWN THE NEW GENERATION OF SONTARAN WARRIORS.
"BUT WHAT IF THEY WEREN'T GROWING SONTARANS? WHAT IF THEY WERE GROWING MONDASIANS, CONDITIONED AND READY TO BE CONVERTED INTO CYBERMEN?"
AND THAT'S JUST ONE FACTORY. THERE ARE HUNDREDS MORE ON THIS PLANET ALONE. THOUSANDS.
"THE CYBERMEN HAVE THE ABILITY TO TRANSFORM ENTIRE PLANETS INTO SPACESHIPS. JUST IMAGINE IT, GABBY. A BIRTHING WORLD, FITTED WITH VOID DRIVES TO SPREAD THEIR PARTICULAR BREED OF DEATH THROUGHOUT THE COSMOS.
"AN INFINITE LEGION OF CYBERMEN, STRETCHING INTO FOREVER."
WHOA THERE, MISTER! EXCUSE US FOR NOT HAVING A PERSPECTIVE ON UNIVERSAL MATTERS.

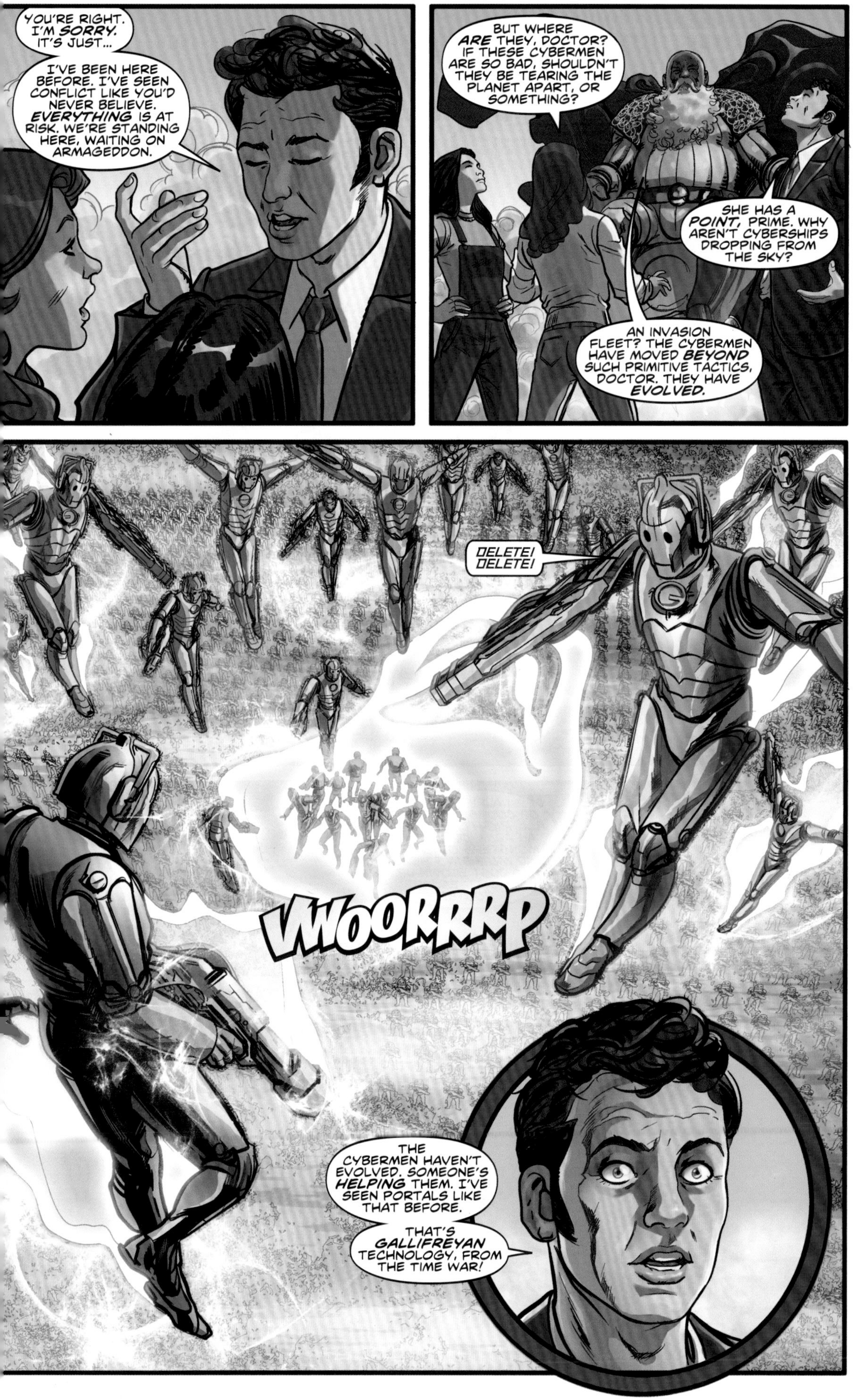
YOU'RE RIGHT. I'M SORRY. IT'S JUST...
I'VE BEEN HERE BEFORE. I'VE SEEN CONFLICT LIKE YOU'D NEVER BELIEVE. EVERYTHING IS AT RISK. WE'RE STANDING HERE, WAITING ON ARMAGEDDON.
BUT WHERE ARE THEY, DOCTOR? IF THESE CYBERMEN ARE SO BAD, SHOULDN'T THEY BE TEARING THE PLANET APART, OR SOMETHING?
SHE HAS A POINT, PRIME. WHY AREN'T CYBERSHIPS DROPPING FROM THE SKY?
AN INVASION FLEET? THE CYBERMEN HAVE MOVED BEYOND SUCH PRIMITIVE TACTICS, DOCTOR. THEY HAVE EVOLVED.
DELETE! DELETE!
VWOORRRP
THE CYBERMEN HAVEN'T EVOLVED. SOMEONE'S HELPING THEM. I'VE SEEN PORTALS LIKE THAT BEFORE.
THAT'S GALLIFREYAN TECHNOLOGY, FROM THE TIME WAR!

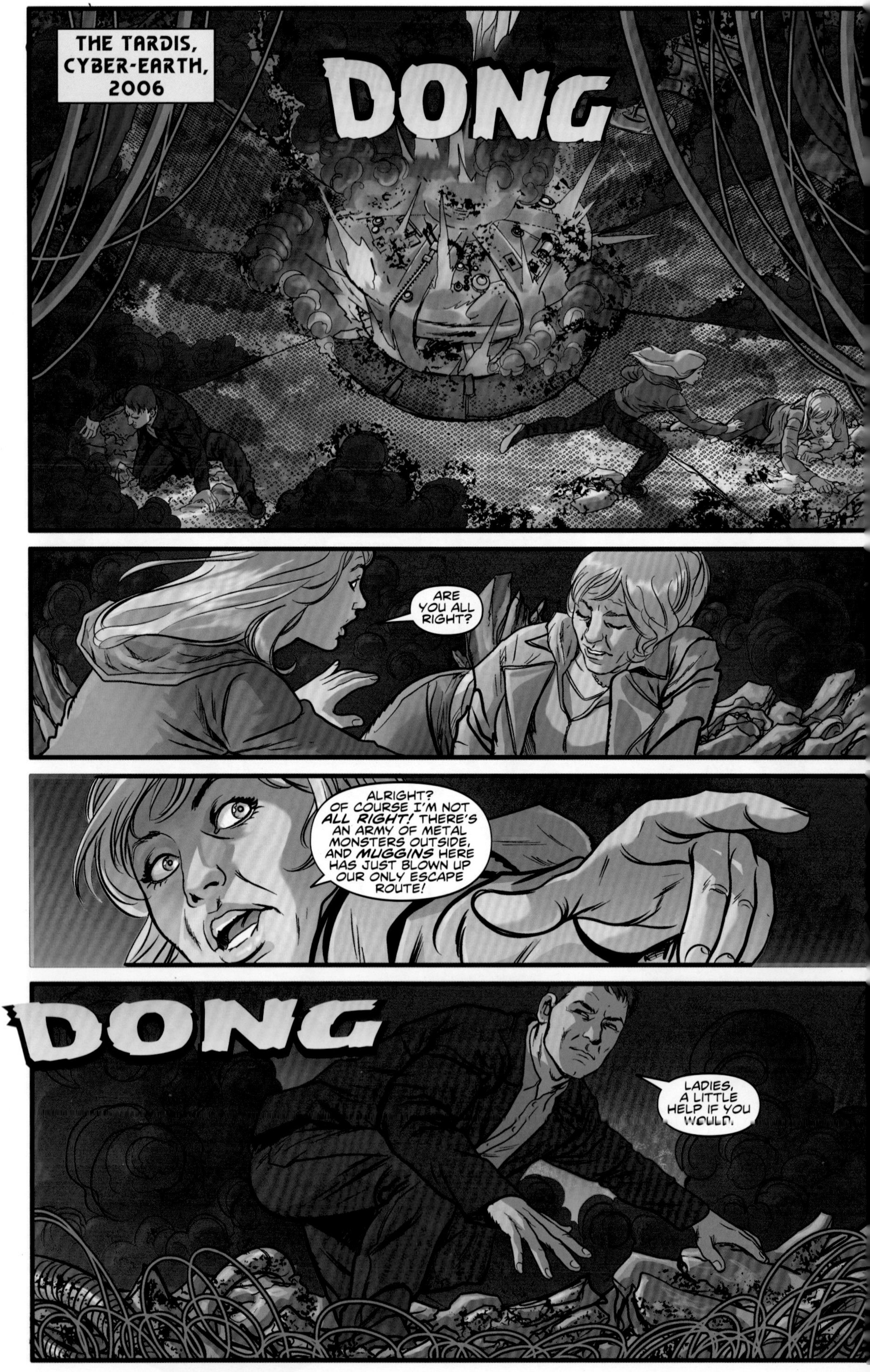
THE TARDIS, CYBER-EARTH, 2006
DONG
ARE YOU ALL RIGHT?
ALRIGHT? OF COURSE I'M NOT ALL RIGHT! THERE'S AN ARMY OF METAL MONSTERS OUTSIDE, AND MUGGINS HERE HAS JUST BLOWN UP OUR ONLY ESCAPE ROUTE!
DONG
LADIES, A LITTLE HELP IF YOU WOULD.

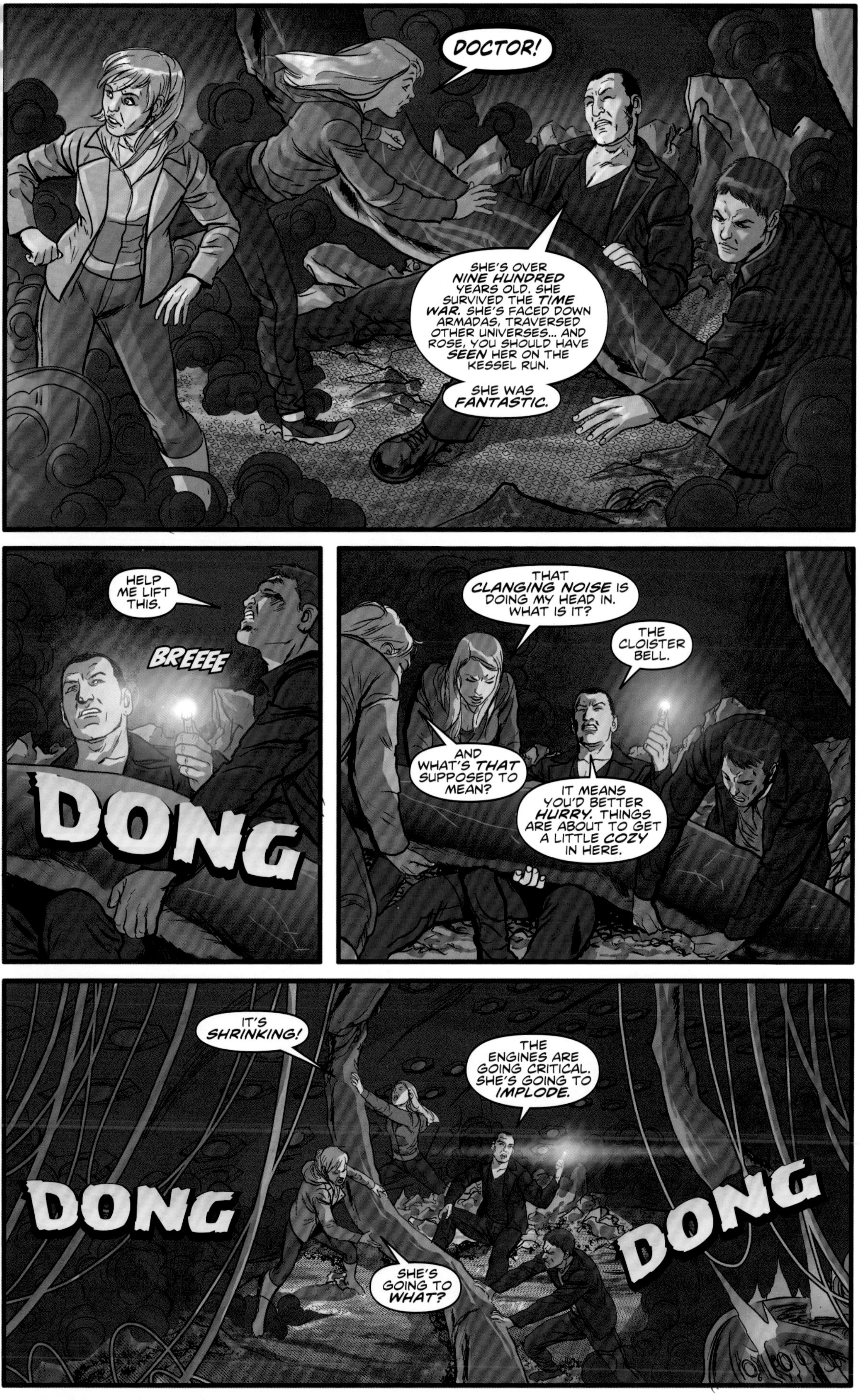
DOCTOR!
SHE'S OVER NINE HUNDRED YEARS OLD. SHE SURVIVED THE TIME WAR. SHE'S FACED DOWN ARMADAS, TRAVERSED OTHER UNIVERSES... AND ROSE, YOU SHOULD HAVE SEEN HER ON THE KESSEL RUN.
SHE WAS FANTASTIC.
HELP ME LIFT THIS.
BREEEE
DONG
THAT CLANGING NOISE IS DOING MY HEAD IN. WHAT IS IT?
THE CLOISTER BELL.
AND WHAT'S THAT SUPPOSED TO MEAN?
IT MEANS YOU'D BETTER HURRY. THINGS ARE ABOUT TO GET A LITTLE COZY IN HERE.
IT'S SHRINKING!
THE ENGINES ARE GOING CRITICAL. SHE'S GOING TO IMPLODE.
DONG
SHE'S GOING TO WHAT?
DONG

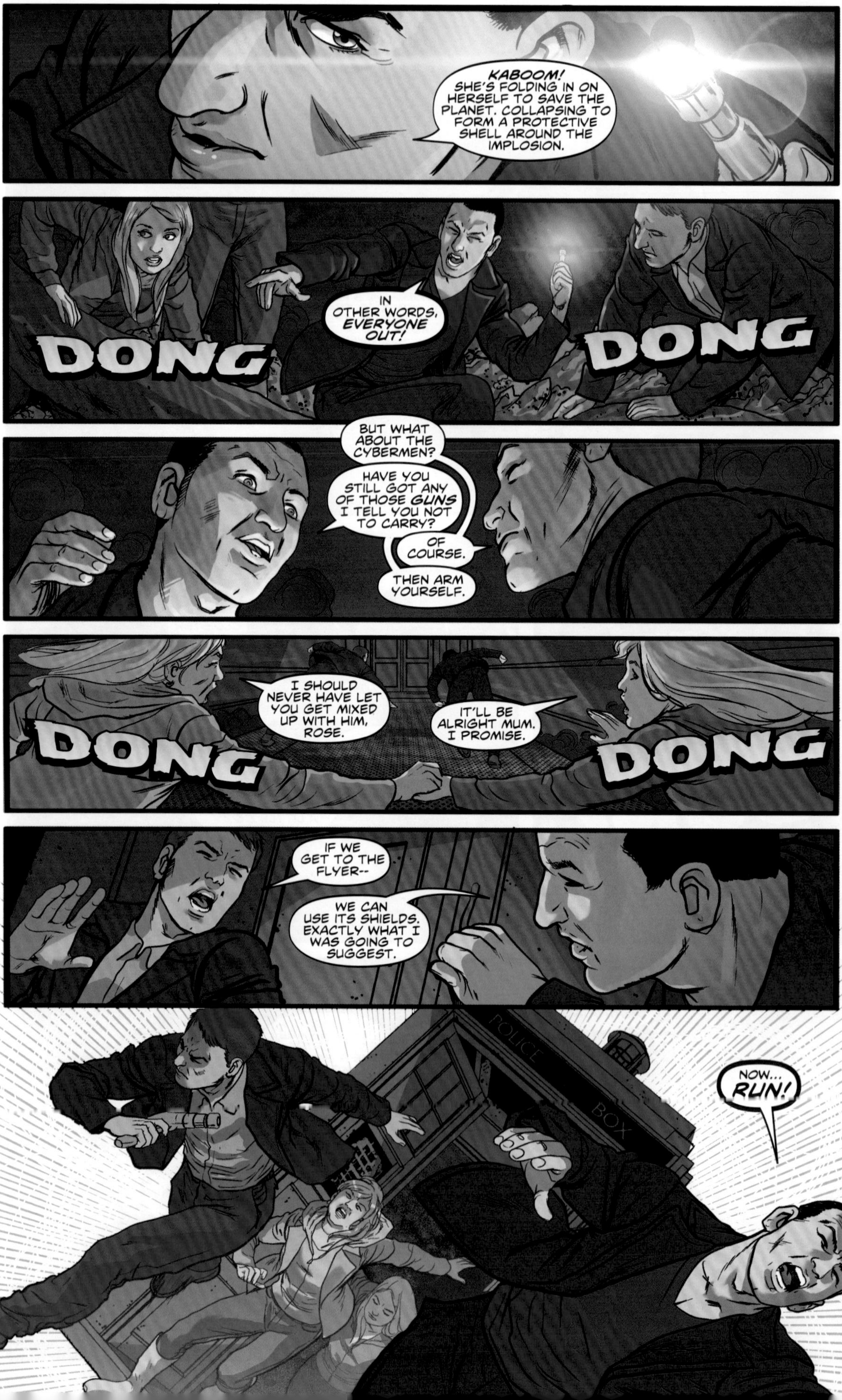
KABOOM! SHE'S FOLDING IN ON HERSELF TO SAVE THE PLANET. COLLAPSING TO FORM A PROTECTIVE SHELL AROUND THE IMPLOSION.
DONG
IN OTHER WORDS, EVERYONE OUT!
DONG
BUT WHAT ABOUT THE CYBERMEN?
HAVE YOU STILL GOT ANY OF THOSE GUNS I TELL YOU NOT TO CARRY?
OF COURSE.
THEN ARM YOURSELF.
DONG
I SHOULD NEVER HAVE LET YOU GET MIXED UP WITH HIM, ROSE.
IT'LL BE ALRIGHT MUM. I PROMISE.
DONG
IF WE GET TO THE FLYER--
WE CAN USE ITS SHIELDS. EXACTLY WHAT I WAS GOING TO SUGGEST.
POLICE
BOX
NOW... RUN!

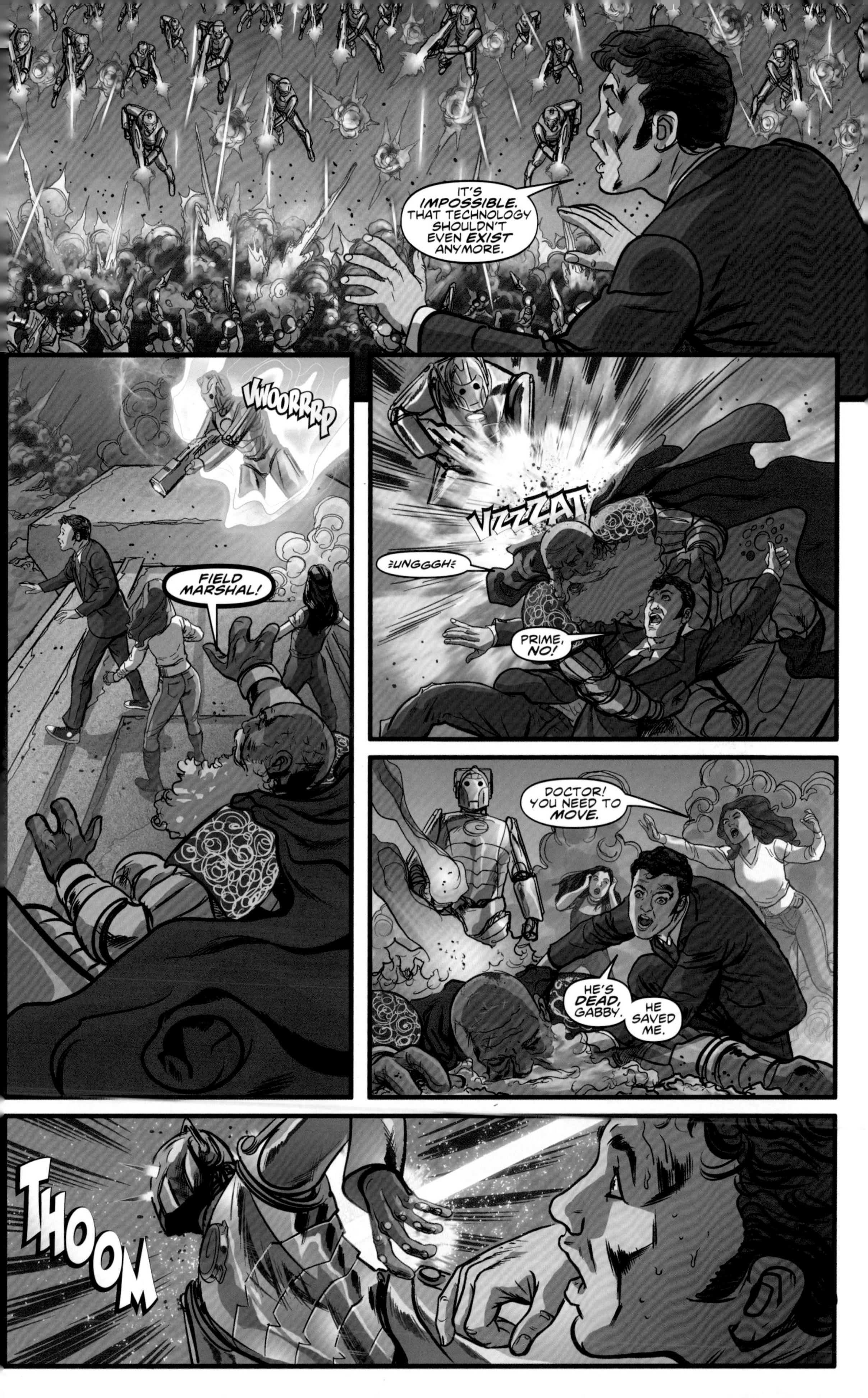
IT'S IMPOSSIBLE. THAT TECHNOLOGY SHOULDN'T EVEN EXIST ANYMORE.
VWOORRRP
FIELD MARSHAL!
VIZZZAT
UNGGGH
PRIME, NO!
DOCTOR! YOU NEED TO MOVE.
HE'S DEAD, GABBY.
HE SAVED ME.
THOOM

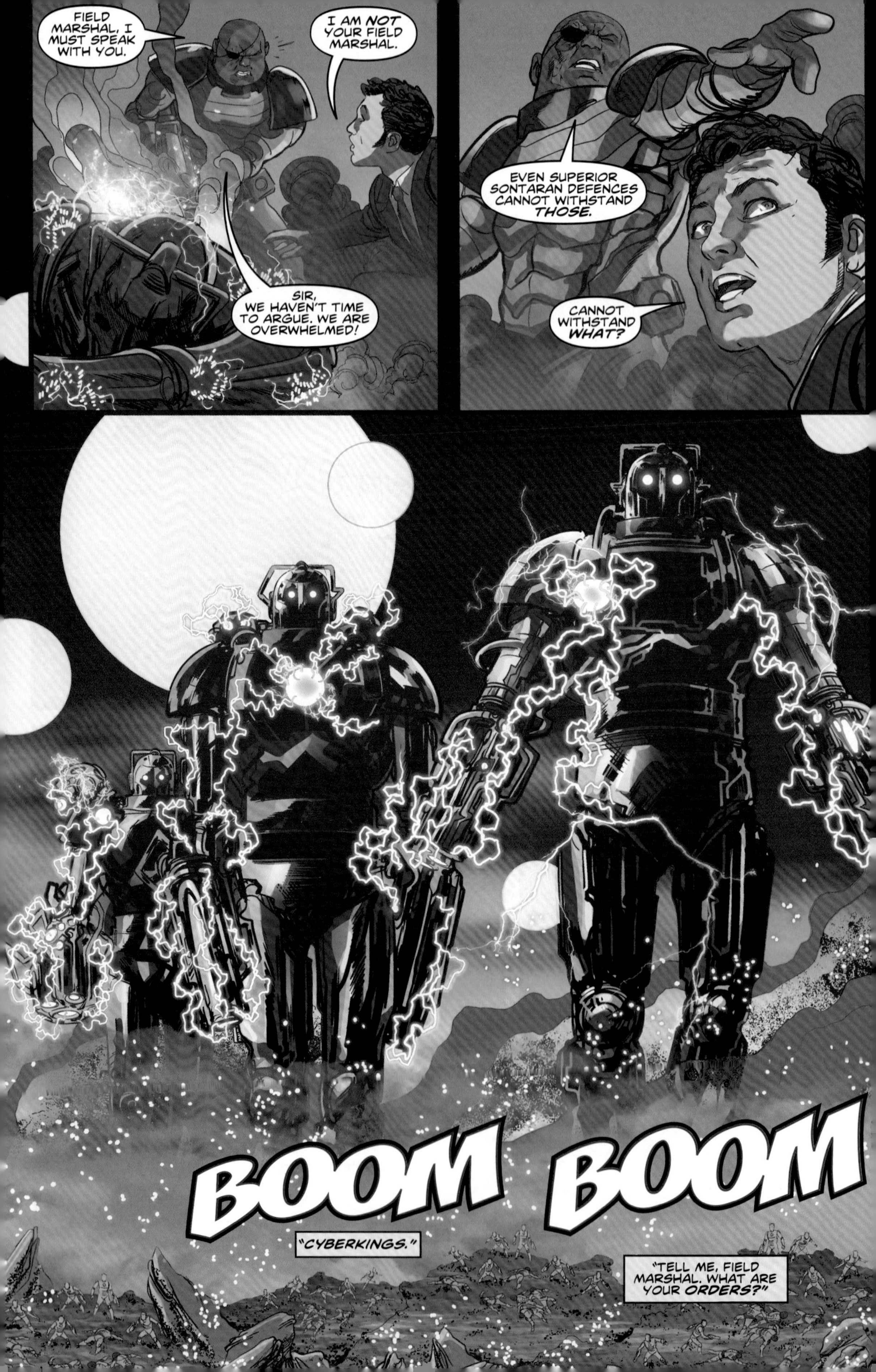
FIELD MARSHAL, I MUST SPEAK WITH YOU.
I AM NOT YOUR FIELD MARSHAL.
SIR, WE HAVEN'T TIME TO ARGUE. WE ARE OVERWHELMED!
EVEN SUPERIOR SONTARAN DEFENCES CANNOT WITHSTAND THOSE.
CANNOT WITHSTAND WHAT?
BOOM BOOM
"CYBERKINGS."
"TELL ME, FIELD MARSHAL. WHAT ARE YOUR ORDERS?"

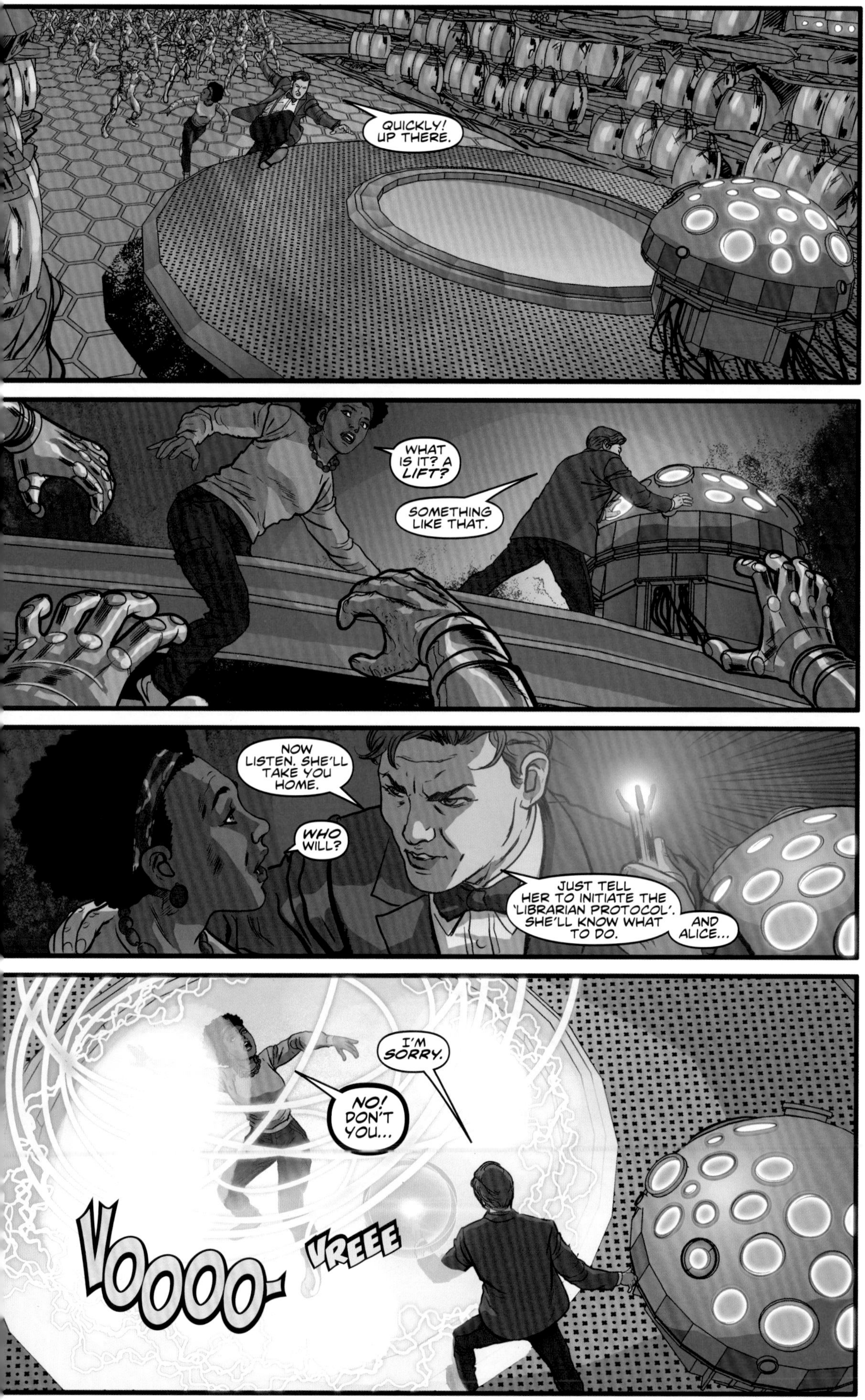
QUICKLY! UP THERE.
WHAT IS IT? A LIFT?
SOMETHING LIKE THAT.
NOW LISTEN. SHE'LL TAKE YOU HOME.
WHO WILL?
JUST TELL HER TO INITIATE THE 'LIBRARIAN PROTOCOL'. SHE'LL KNOW WHAT TO DO.
AND ALICE...
I'M SORRY.
NO! DON'T YOU...
VOOOO-
VREEE

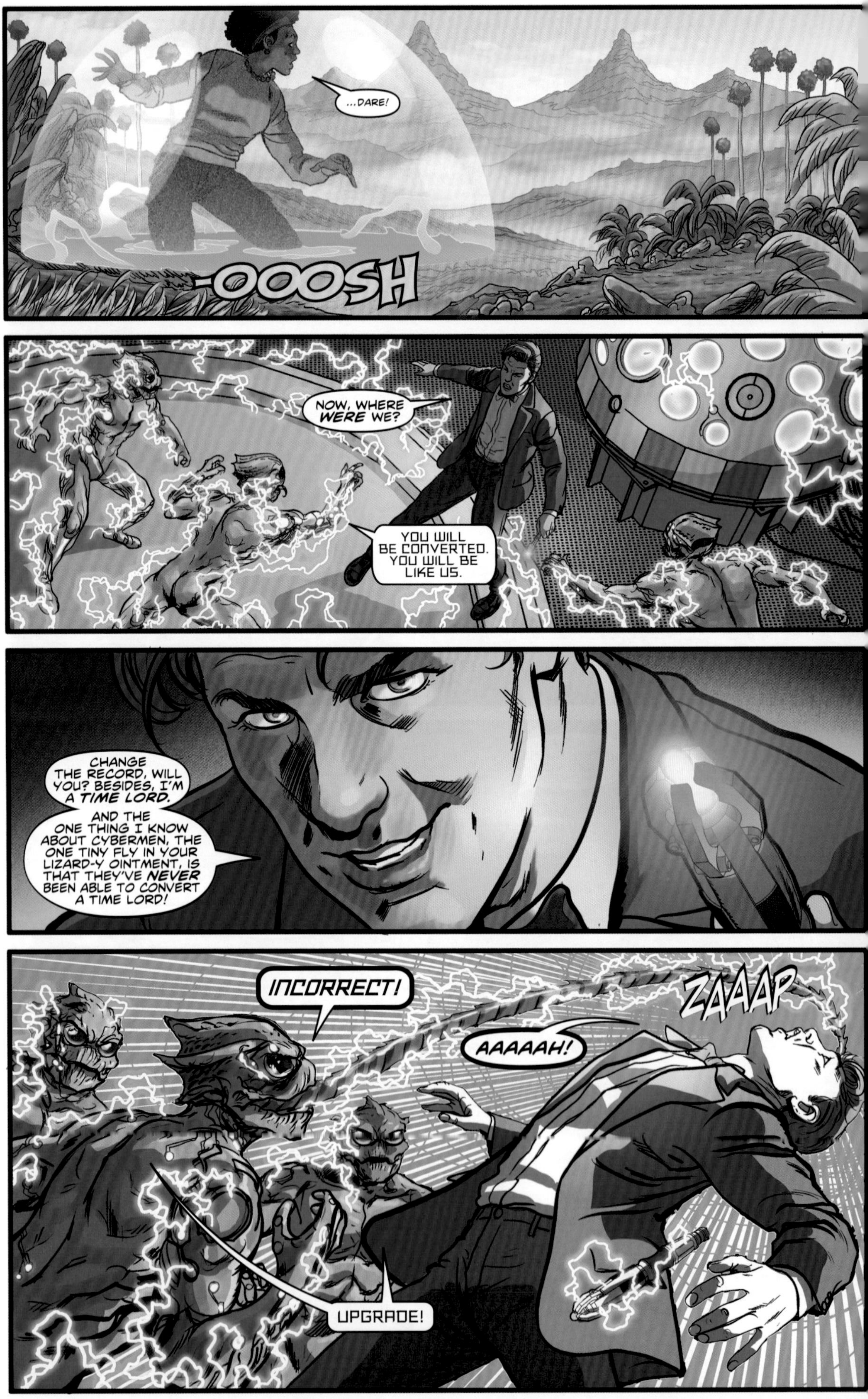
...DARE!
-OOOSH
NOW, WHERE WERE WE?
YOU WILL BE CONVERTED. YOU WILL BE LIKE US.
CHANGE THE RECORD, WILL YOU? BESIDES, I'M A TIME LORD.
AND THE ONE THING I KNOW ABOUT CYBERMEN, THE ONE TINY FLY IN YOUR LIZARD-Y OINTMENT, IS THAT THEY'VE NEVER BEEN ABLE TO CONVERT A TIME LORD!
INCORRECT!
ZAAAP
AAAAAH!
UPGRADE!

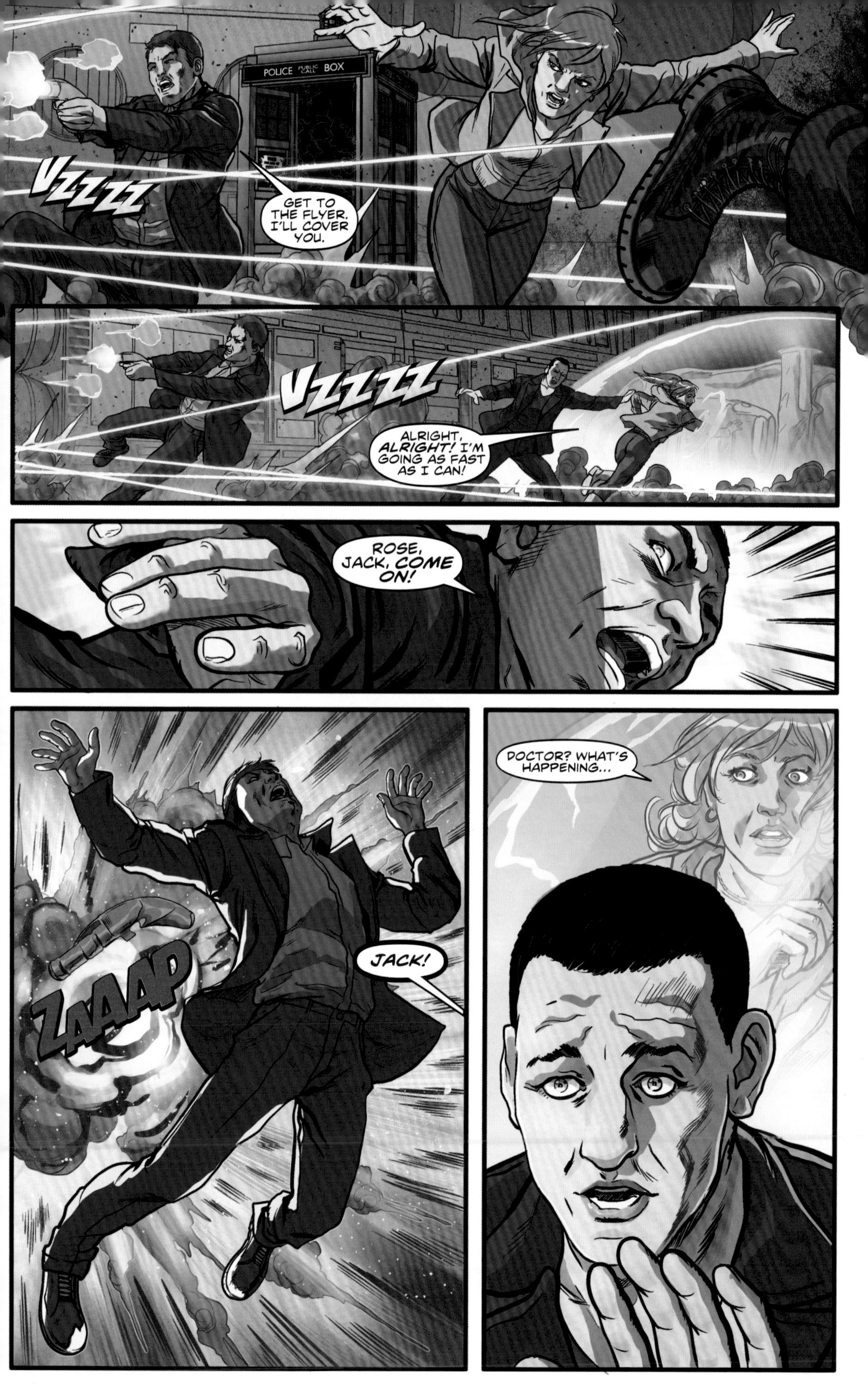
POLICE PUBLIC CALL BOX
VZZZZ
GET TO THE FLYER. I'LL COVER YOU.
VZZZZ
ALRIGHT, ALRIGHT! I'M GOING AS FAST AS I CAN!
ROSE, JACK, COME ON!
ZAAAP
JACK!
DOCTOR? WHAT'S HAPPENING...

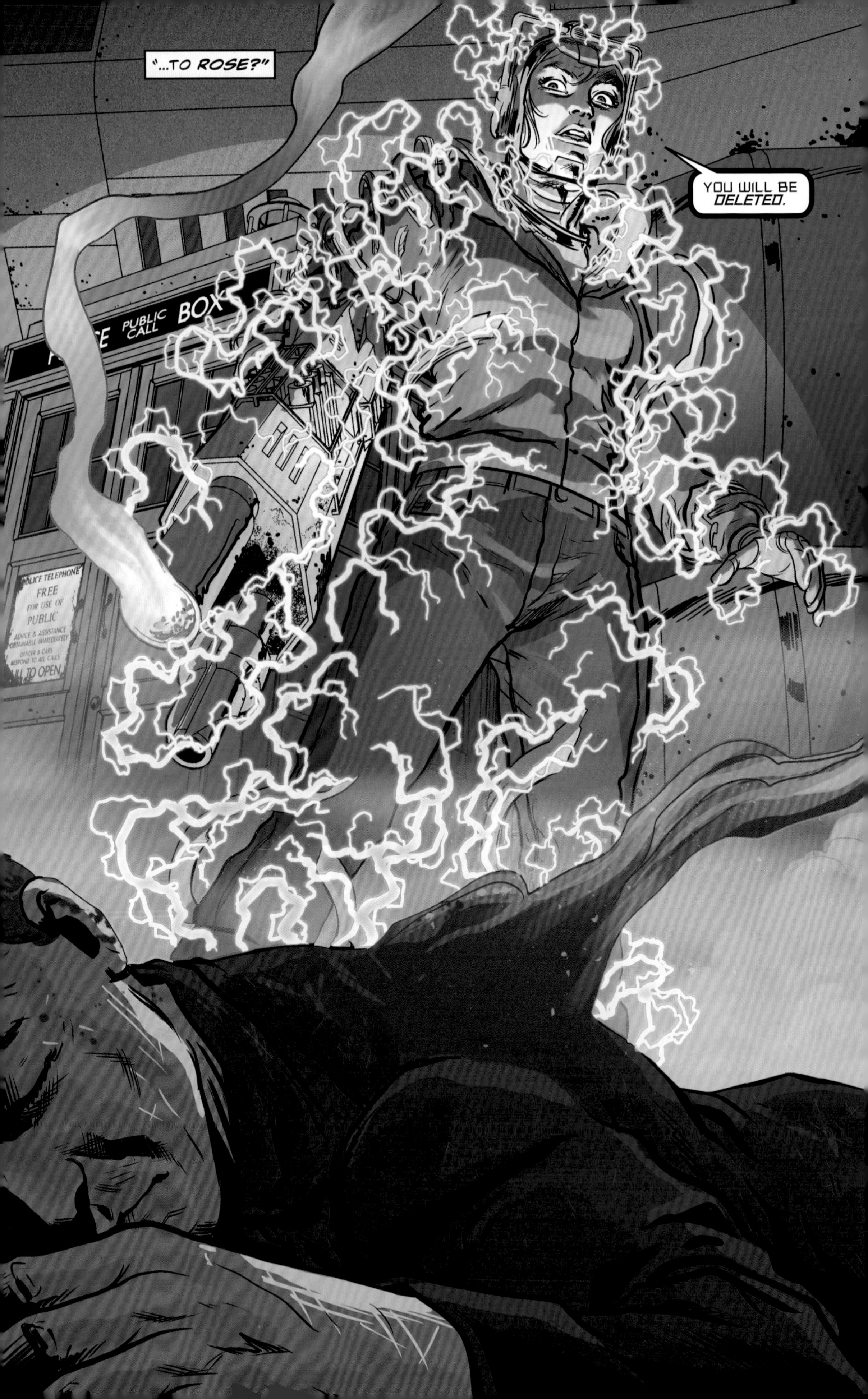
"...TO ROSE?"
YOU WILL BE DELETED.
POLICE PUBLIC CALL BOX
POLICE TELEPHONE
FREE
FOR USE OF
PUBLIC
ADVICE & ASSISTANCE
OBTAINABLE IMMEDIATELY
OFFICER & CARS
RESPOND TO ALL CALLS
PULL TO OPEN

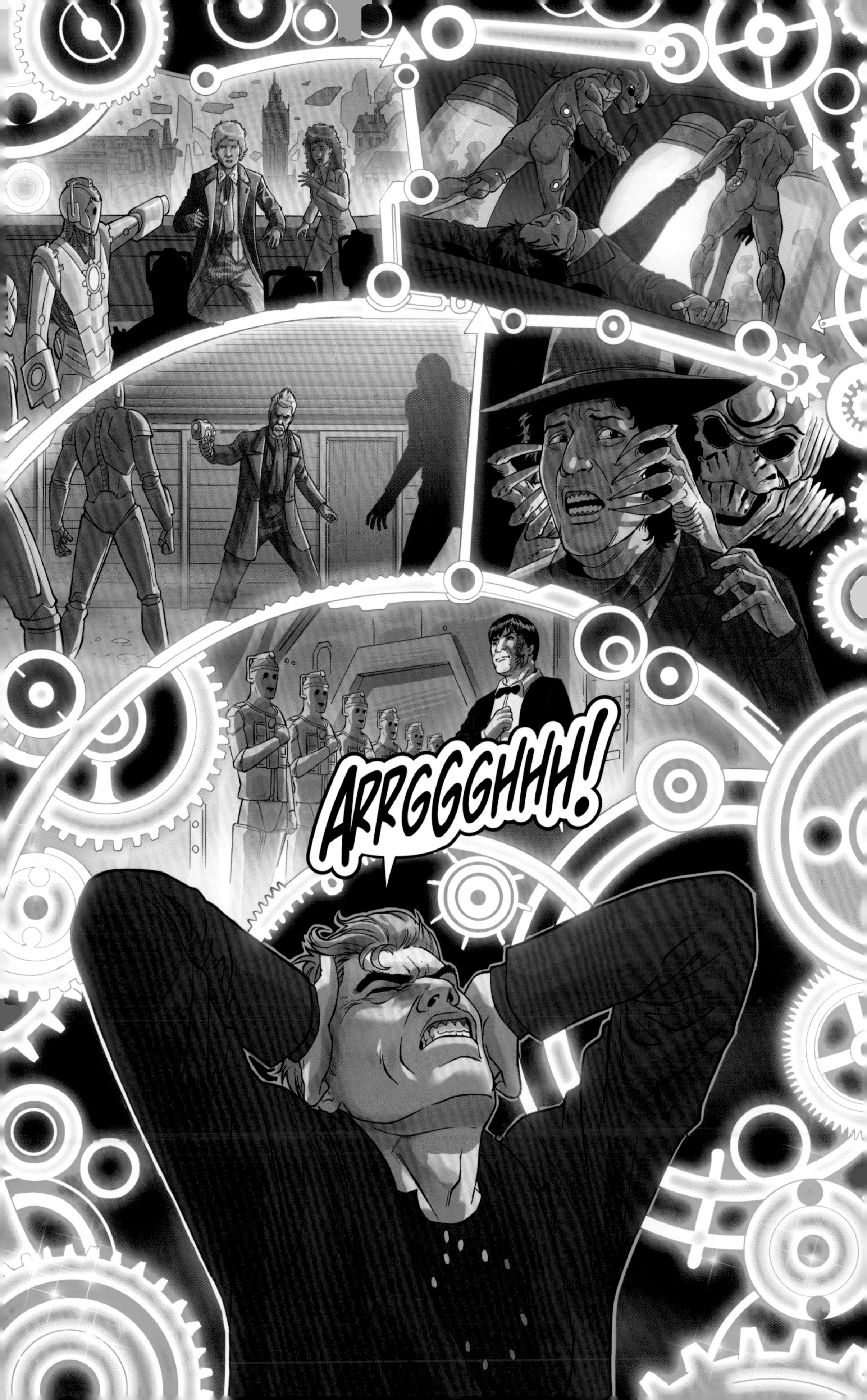
ARRGGGHHH!

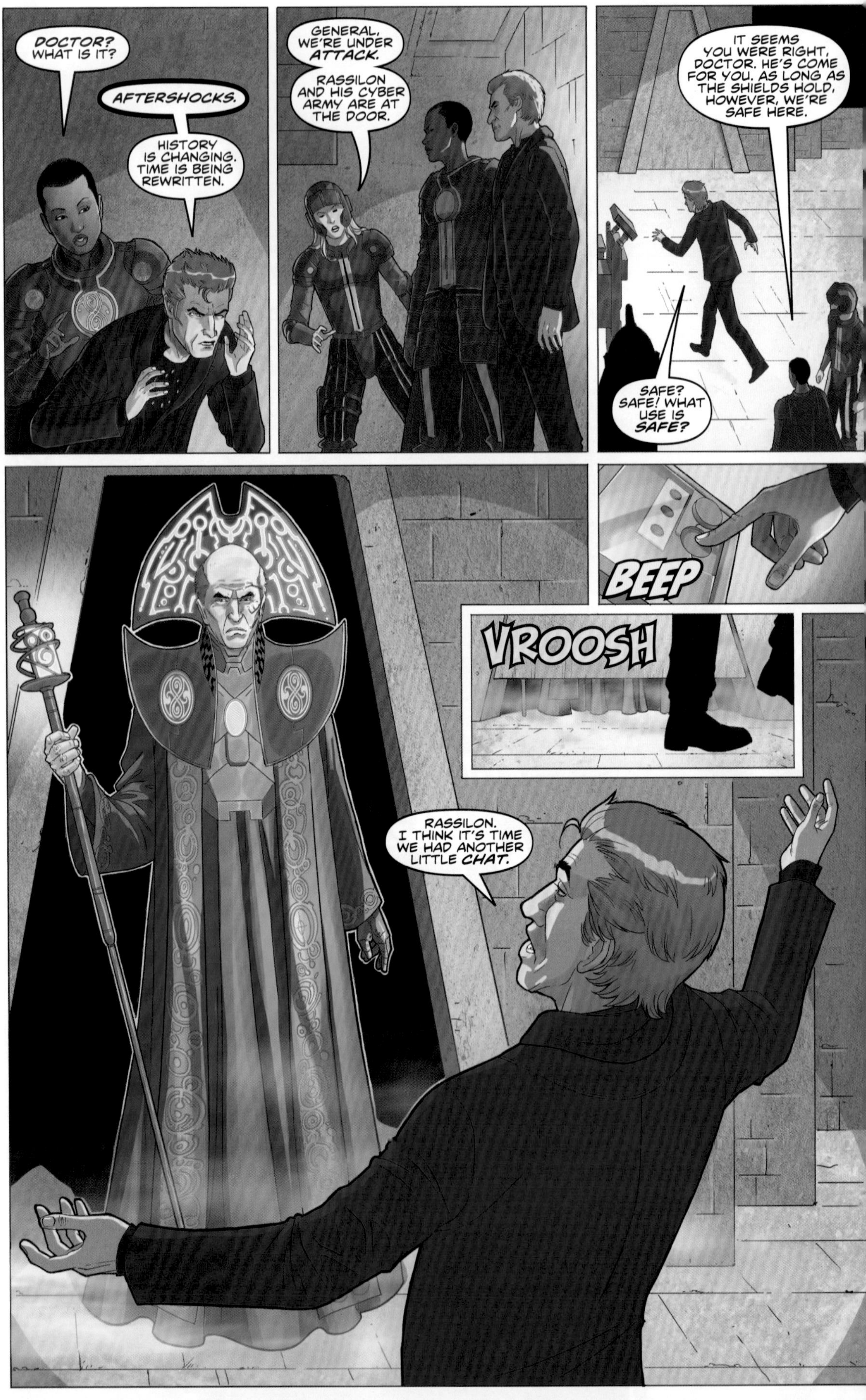
DOCTOR? WHAT IS IT?
AFTERSHOCKS.
HISTORY IS CHANGING. TIME IS BEING REWRITTEN.
GENERAL, WE'RE UNDER ATTACK.
RASSILON AND HIS CYBER ARMY ARE AT THE DOOR.
IT SEEMS YOU WERE RIGHT, DOCTOR. HE'S COME FOR YOU. AS LONG AS THE SHIELDS HOLD, HOWEVER, WE'RE SAFE HERE.
SAFE? SAFE! WHAT USE IS SAFE?
BEEP
VROOSH
RASSILON. I THINK IT'S TIME WE HAD ANOTHER LITTLE CHAT.

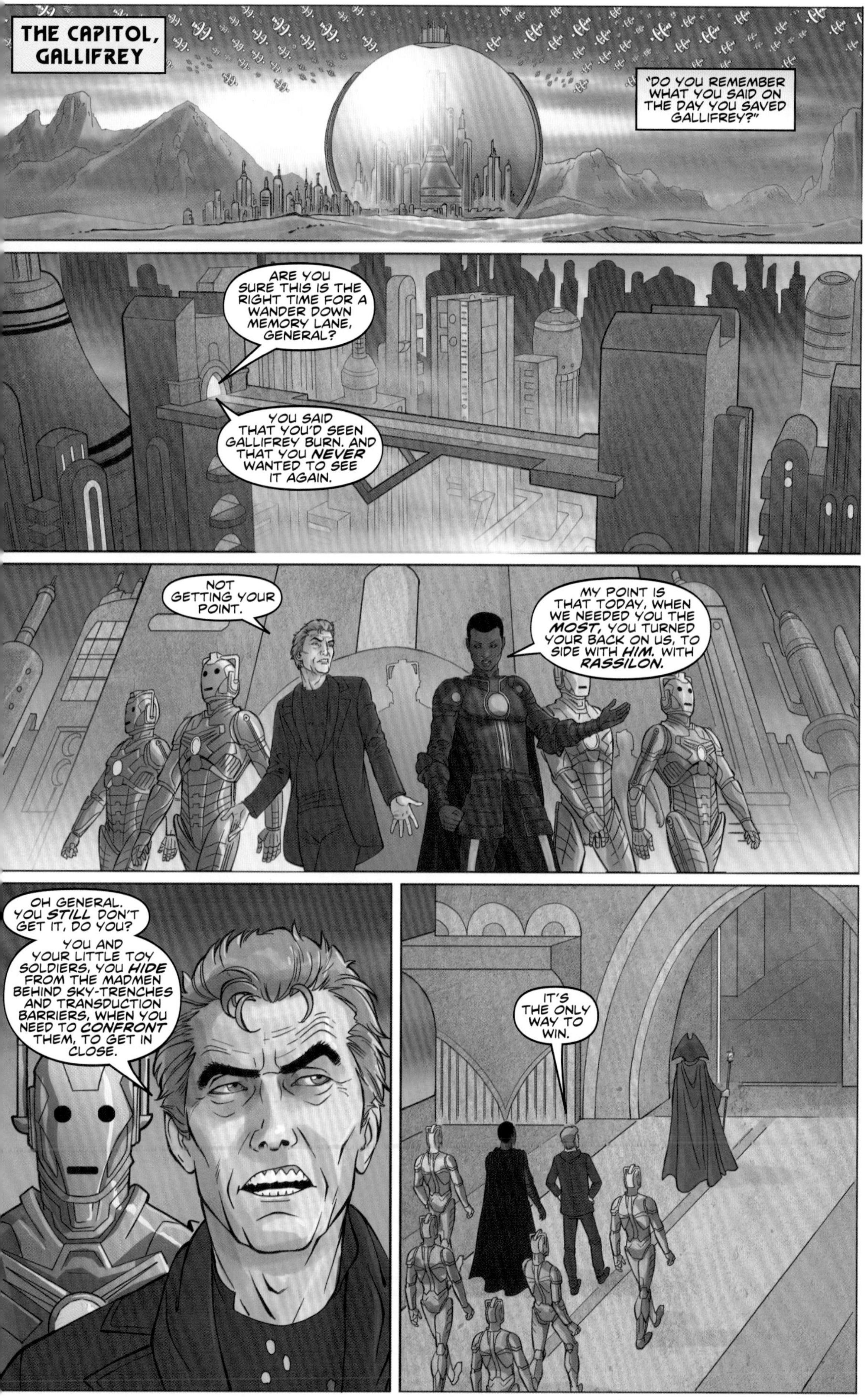
THE CAPITOL, GALLIFREY
"DO YOU REMEMBER WHAT YOU SAID ON THE DAY YOU SAVED GALLIFREY?"
ARE YOU SURE THIS IS THE RIGHT TIME FOR A WANDER DOWN MEMORY LANE, GENERAL?
YOU SAID THAT YOU'D SEEN GALLIFREY BURN. AND THAT YOU NEVER WANTED TO SEE IT AGAIN.
NOT GETTING YOUR POINT.
MY POINT IS THAT TODAY, WHEN WE NEEDED YOU THE MOST, YOU TURNED YOUR BACK ON US, TO SIDE WITH HIM. WITH RASSILON.
OH GENERAL. YOU STILL DON'T GET IT, DO YOU?
YOU AND YOUR LITTLE TOY SOLDIERS, YOU HIDE FROM THE MADMEN BEHIND SKY-TRENCHES AND TRANSDUCTION BARRIERS, WHEN YOU NEED TO CONFRONT THEM, TO GET IN CLOSE.
IT'S THE ONLY WAY TO WIN.

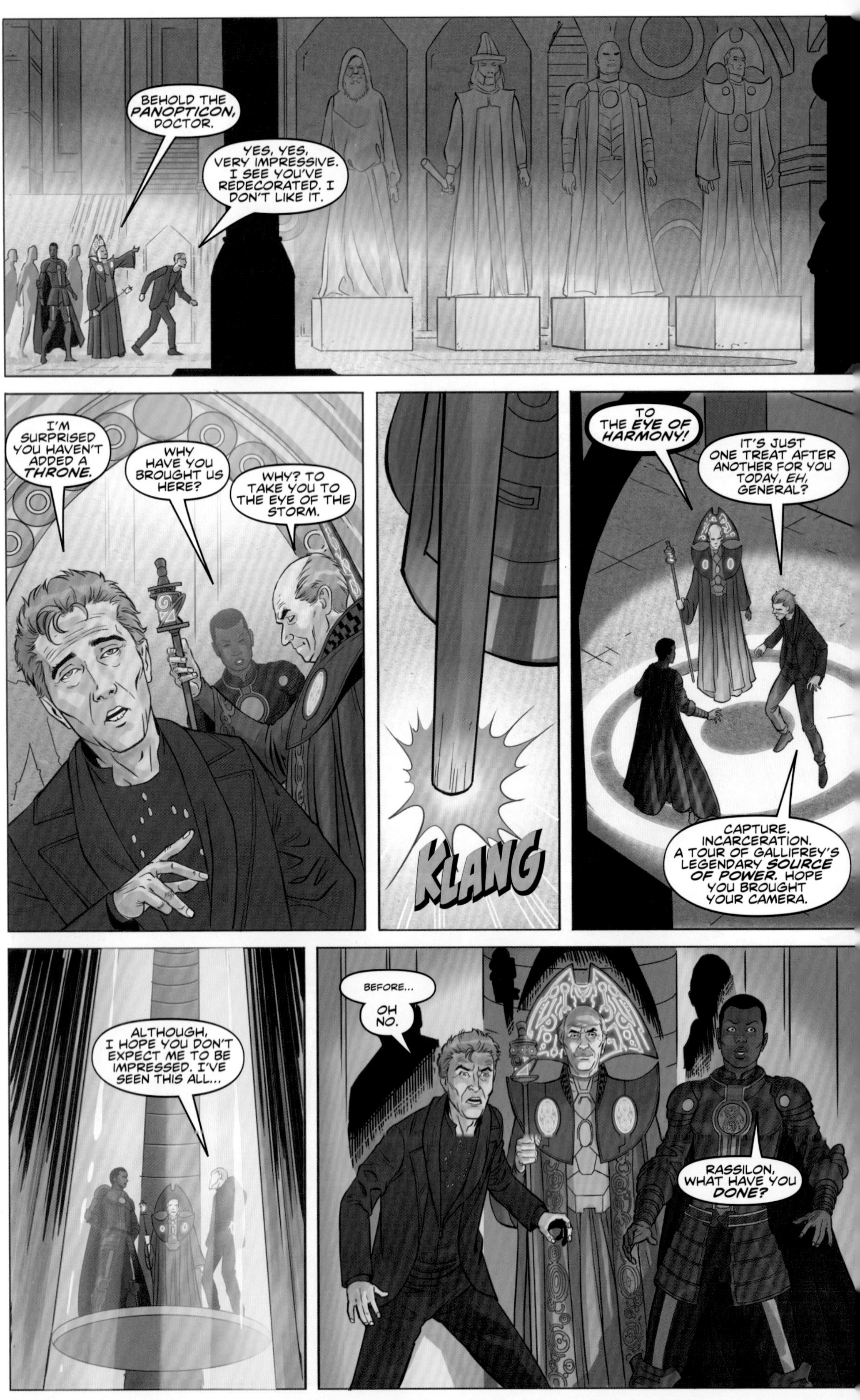
BEHOLD THE PANOPTICON, DOCTOR.
YES, YES, VERY IMPRESSIVE. I SEE YOU'VE REDECORATED. I DON'T LIKE IT.
I'M SURPRISED YOU HAVEN'T ADDED A THRONE.
WHY HAVE YOU BROUGHT US HERE?
WHY? TO TAKE YOU TO THE EYE OF THE STORM.
KLANG
TO THE EYE OF HARMONY!
IT'S JUST ONE TREAT AFTER ANOTHER FOR YOU TODAY, EH, GENERAL?
CAPTURE. INCARCERATION. A TOUR OF GALLIFREY'S LEGENDARY SOURCE OF POWER. HOPE YOU BROUGHT YOUR CAMERA.
ALTHOUGH, I HOPE YOU DON'T EXPECT ME TO BE IMPRESSED. I'VE SEEN THIS ALL...
BEFORE...
OH NO.
RASSILON, WHAT HAVE YOU DONE?

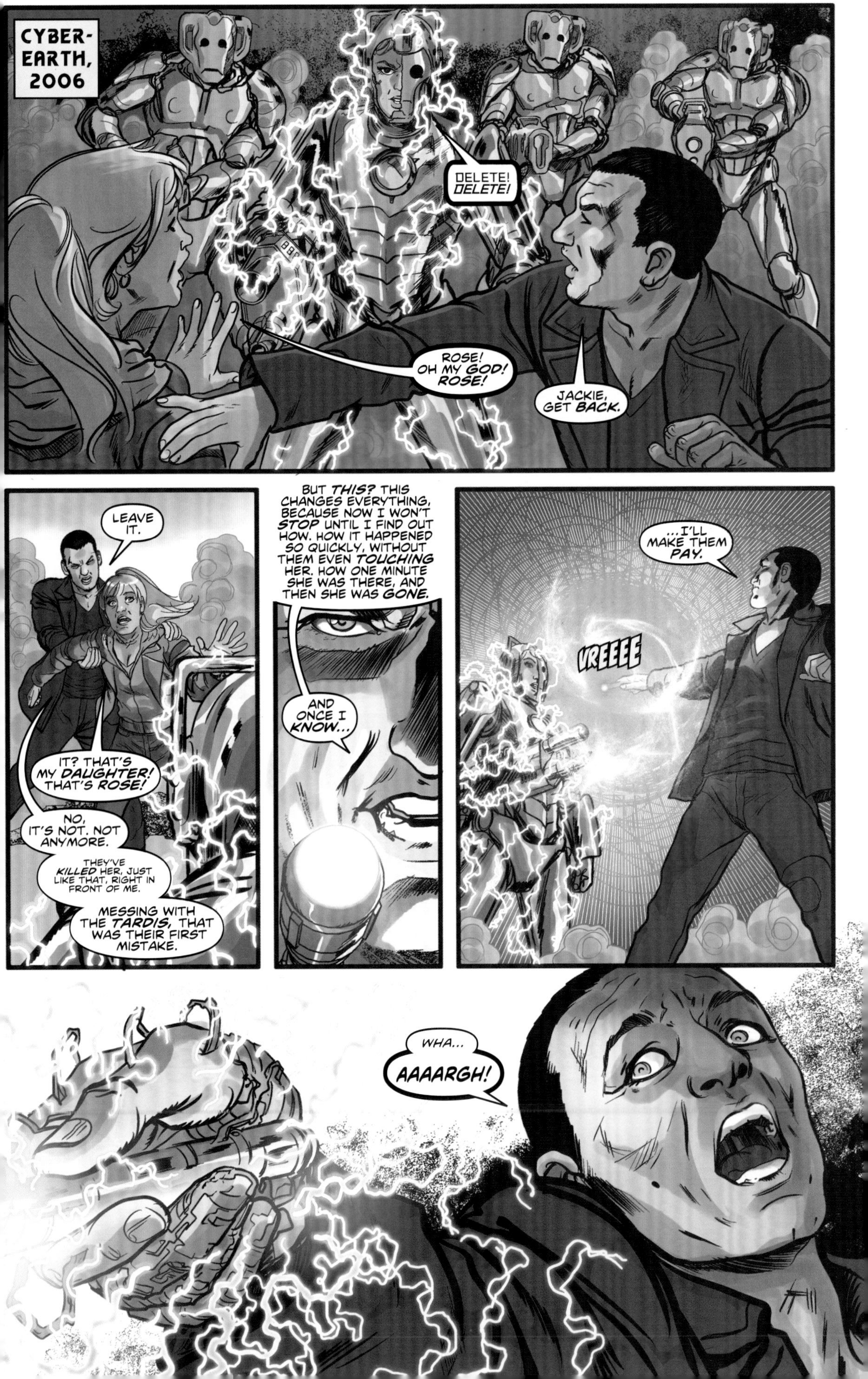
CYBER-EARTH, 2006
DELETE! DELETE!
ROSE! OH MY GOD! ROSE!
JACKIE, GET BACK.
LEAVE IT.
IT? THAT'S MY DAUGHTER! THAT'S ROSE!
NO, IT'S NOT. NOT ANYMORE.
THEY'VE KILLED HER, JUST LIKE THAT, RIGHT IN FRONT OF ME.
MESSING WITH THE TARDIS, THAT WAS THEIR FIRST MISTAKE.
BUT THIS? THIS CHANGES EVERYTHING, BECAUSE NOW I WON'T STOP UNTIL I FIND OUT HOW. HOW IT HAPPENED SO QUICKLY, WITHOUT THEM EVEN TOUCHING HER. HOW ONE MINUTE SHE WAS THERE, AND THEN SHE WAS GONE.
AND ONCE I KNOW...
...I'LL MAKE THEM PAY.
VREEEE
WHA...
AAAARGH!

YOU *BELONG* TO US! YOU SHALL *BE* LIKE US!

NOT ON YOUR LIFE.

DOCTOR! THIS WAY.

WHAT ARE YOU DOING?

SAVING YOU... BECAUSE YOU'RE THE ONLY ONE WHO CAN SAVE ROSE.

JACKIE, SHE CAN'T--

NO. I WON'T LISTEN TO THAT. SHE *BELIEVES* IN YOU. SHE *TRUSTS* YOU. YOU WON'T LET HER DOWN.

JUST TELL ME HOW TO *FLY* THIS THING.

IT'S NOT GOING ANYWHERE.

THEN WHAT ARE YOU DOING?

ALTERING THE PARTICULATE FILTER ON THE *SHIELDS*.

FIRST *ROSE*, THEN MY SONIC. IT'S IN THE *AIR* NOW, JACKIE. *CYBERNIZATION AS AIRBORNE VIRUS.* INVISIBLE. DEADLY. IT'S *FANTASTIC*.

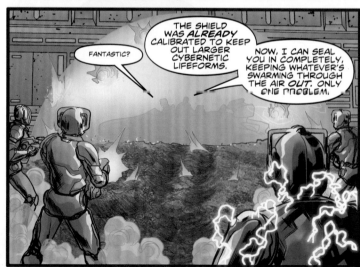

FANTASTIC?

THE SHIELD WAS *ALREADY* CALIBRATED TO KEEP OUT LARGER CYBERNETIC LIFEFORMS.

NOW, I CAN SEAL YOU IN COMPLETELY, KEEPING WHATEVER'S SWARMING THROUGH THE AIR *OUT*. ONLY ONE PROBLEM.

YOU'RE IN HERE WITH *ME*.

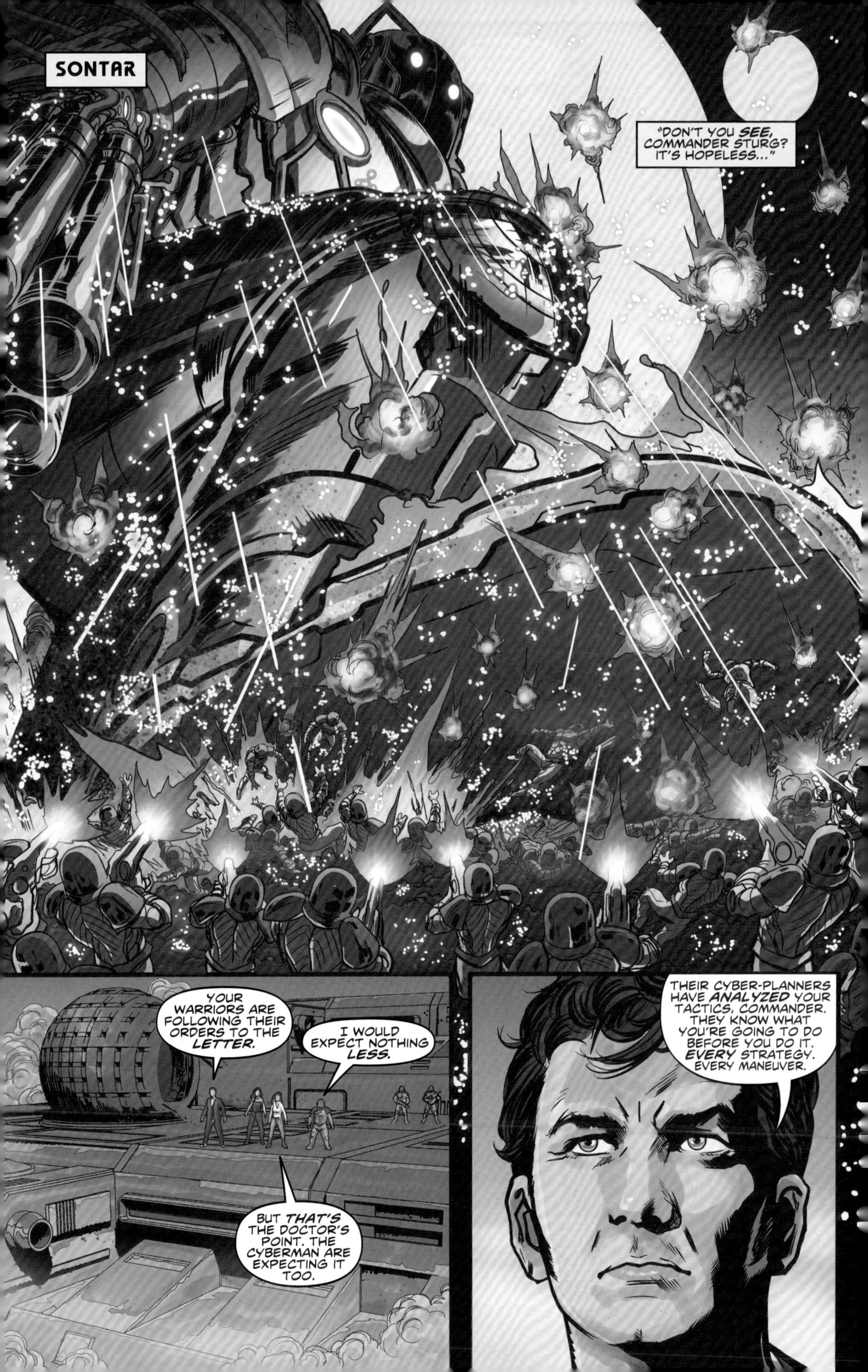
SONTAR
"DON'T YOU SEE, COMMANDER STURG? IT'S HOPELESS..."
YOUR WARRIORS ARE FOLLOWING THEIR ORDERS TO THE LETTER.
I WOULD EXPECT NOTHING LESS.
BUT THAT'S THE DOCTOR'S POINT. THE CYBERMAN ARE EXPECTING IT TOO.
THEIR CYBER-PLANNERS HAVE ANALYZED YOUR TACTICS, COMMANDER. THEY KNOW WHAT YOU'RE GOING TO DO BEFORE YOU DO IT. EVERY STRATEGY. EVERY MANEUVER.

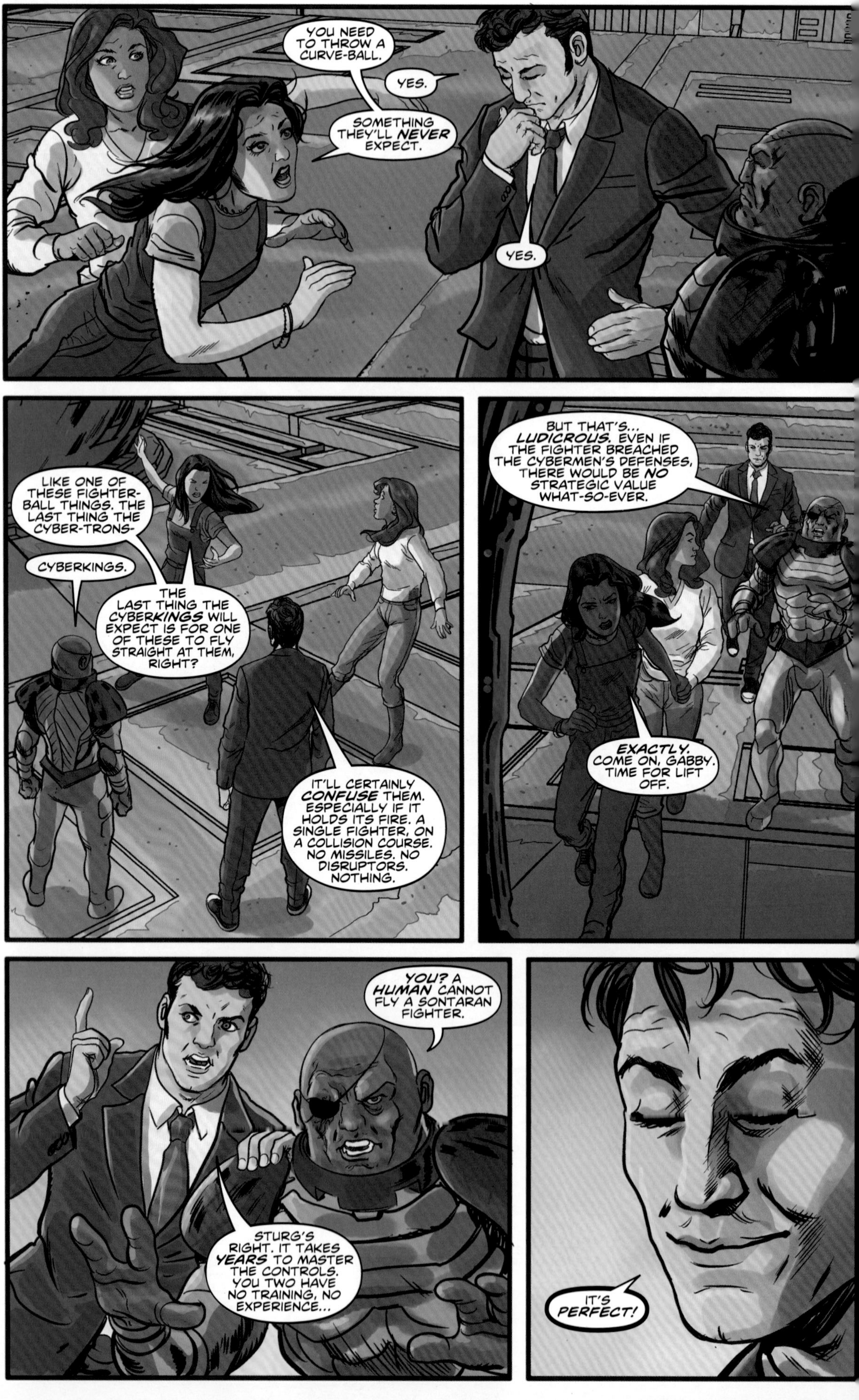
YOU NEED TO THROW A CURVE-BALL.
YES.
SOMETHING THEY'LL NEVER EXPECT.
YES.
LIKE ONE OF THESE FIGHTER-BALL THINGS. THE LAST THING THE CYBER-TRONS-
CYBERKINGS.
THE LAST THING THE CYBERKINGS WILL EXPECT IS FOR ONE OF THESE TO FLY STRAIGHT AT THEM, RIGHT?
IT'LL CERTAINLY CONFUSE THEM. ESPECIALLY IF IT HOLDS ITS FIRE. A SINGLE FIGHTER, ON A COLLISION COURSE. NO MISSILES. NO DISRUPTORS. NOTHING.
BUT THAT'S... LUDICROUS. EVEN IF THE FIGHTER BREACHED THE CYBERMEN'S DEFENSES, THERE WOULD BE NO STRATEGIC VALUE WHAT-SO-EVER.
EXACTLY. COME ON, GABBY. TIME FOR LIFT OFF.
YOU? A HUMAN CANNOT FLY A SONTARAN FIGHTER.
STURG'S RIGHT. IT TAKES YEARS TO MASTER THE CONTROLS. YOU TWO HAVE NO TRAINING, NO EXPERIENCE...
IT'S PERFECT!

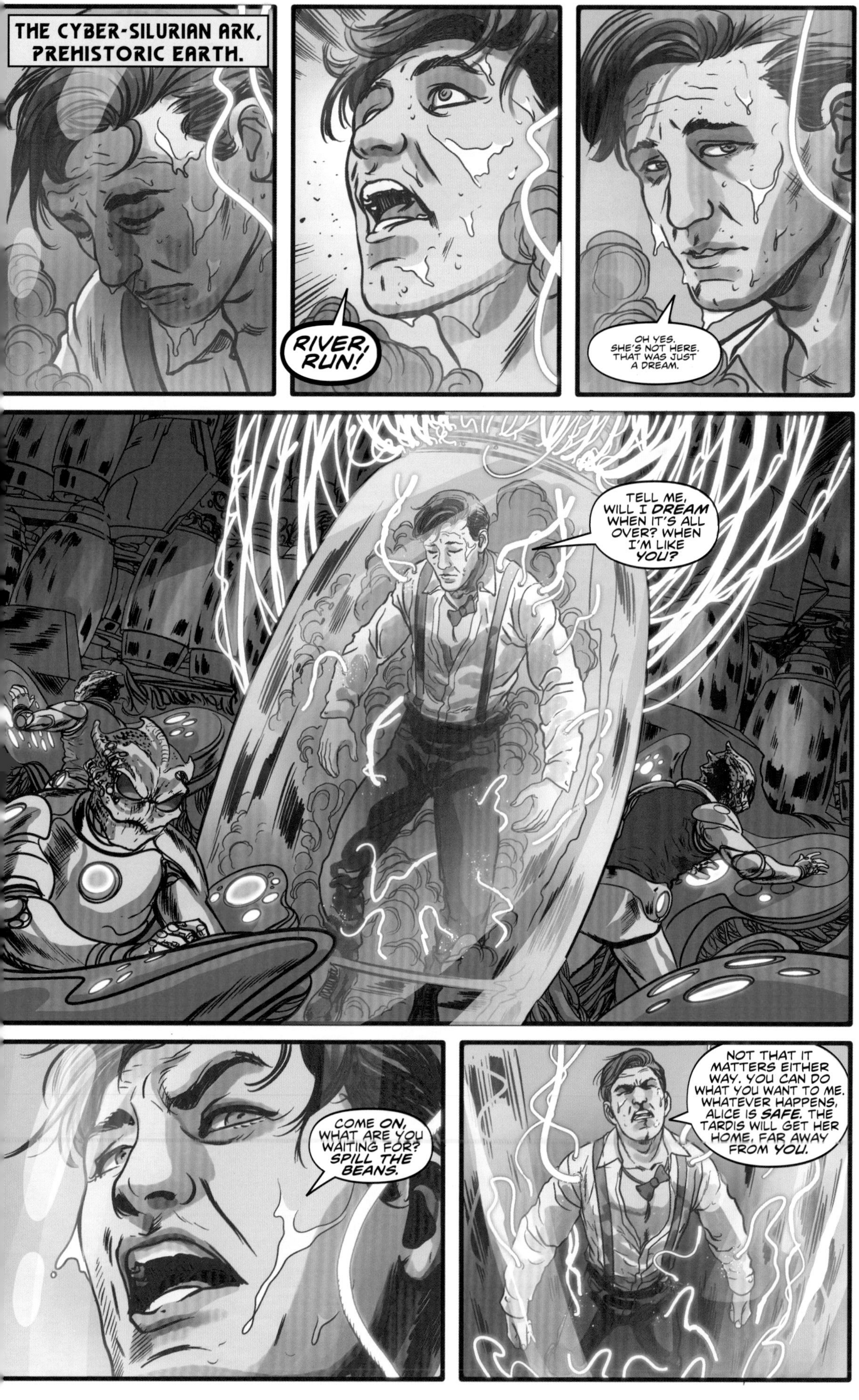
THE CYBER-SILURIAN ARK, PREHISTORIC EARTH.
RIVER, RUN!
OH YES. SHE'S NOT HERE. THAT WAS JUST A DREAM.
TELL ME, WILL I DREAM WHEN IT'S ALL OVER? WHEN I'M LIKE YOU?
COME ON, WHAT ARE YOU WAITING FOR? SPILL THE BEANS.
NOT THAT IT MATTERS EITHER WAY. YOU CAN DO WHAT YOU WANT TO ME. WHATEVER HAPPENS, ALICE IS SAFE. THE TARDIS WILL GET HER HOME, FAR AWAY FROM YOU.

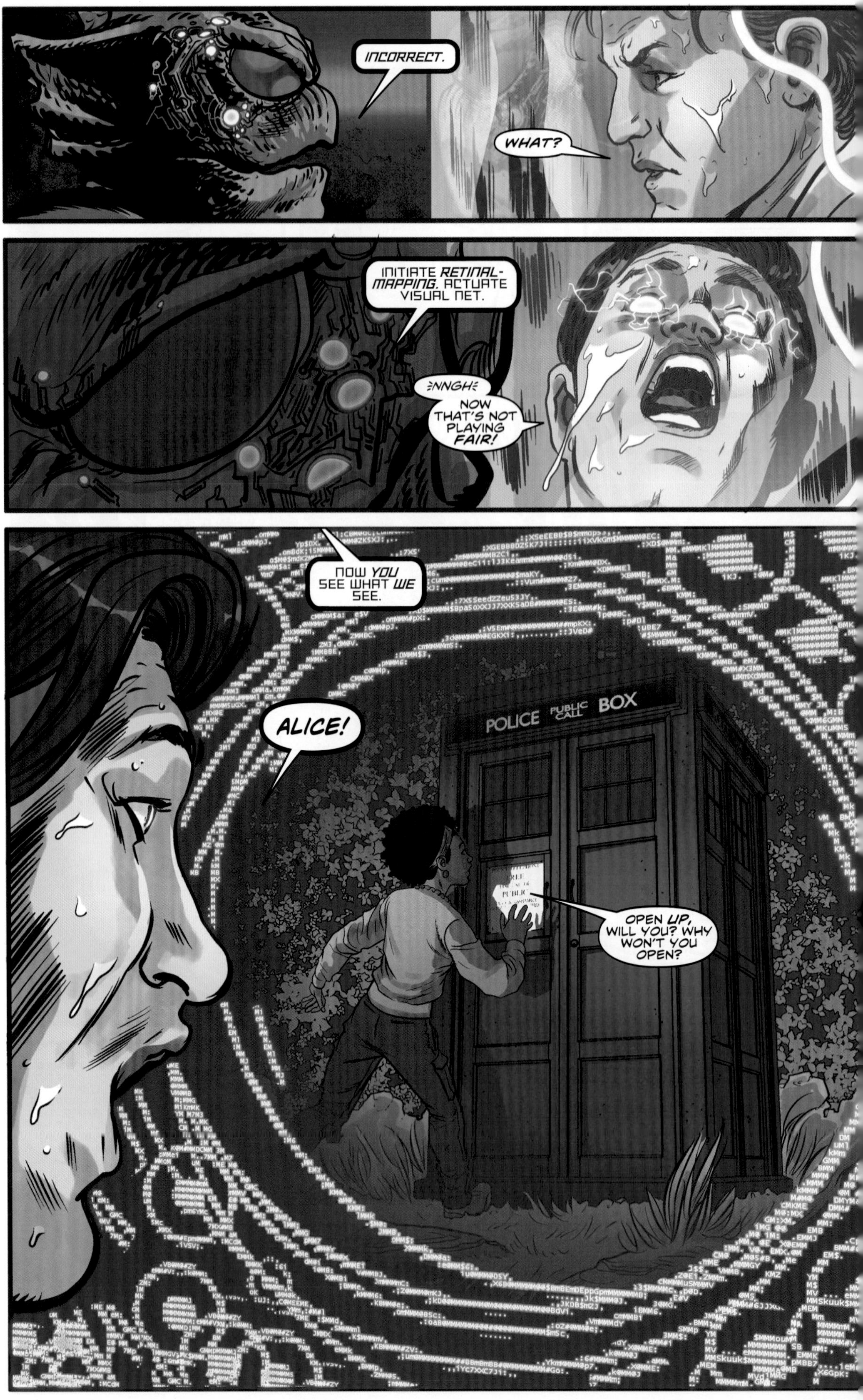
INCORRECT.
WHAT?
INITIATE RETINAL-MAPPING. ACTUATE VISUAL NET.
NNGH NOW THAT'S NOT PLAYING FAIR!
NOW YOU SEE WHAT WE SEE.
ALICE!
POLICE PUBLIC CALL BOX
OPEN UP, WILL YOU? WHY WON'T YOU OPEN?

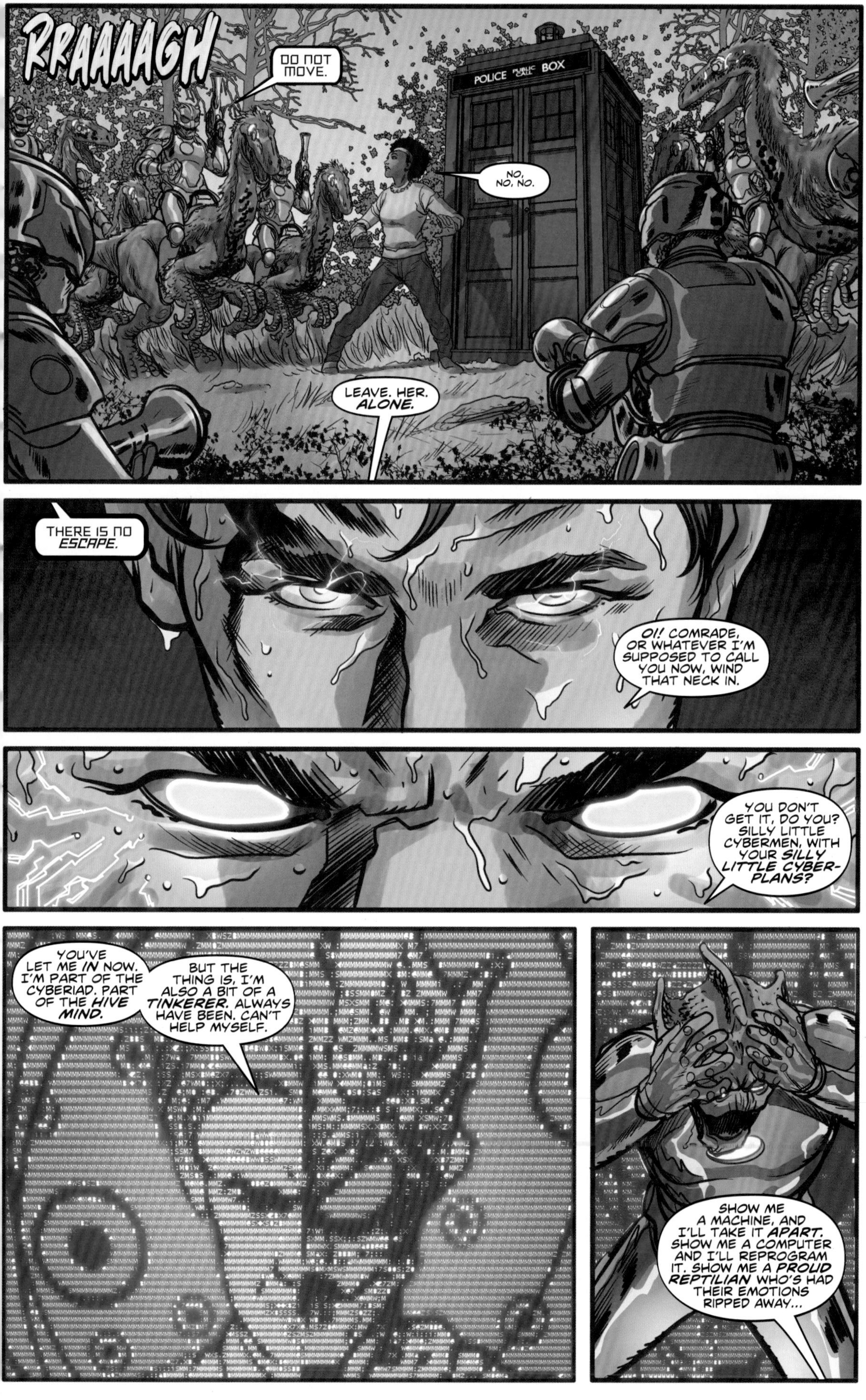

RRAAAAGH
DO NOT MOVE.
POLICE PUBLIC CALL BOX
NO, NO, NO.
LEAVE. HER. ALONE.
THERE IS NO ESCAPE.
OI! COMRADE, OR WHATEVER I'M SUPPOSED TO CALL YOU NOW, WIND THAT NECK IN.
YOU DON'T GET IT, DO YOU? SILLY LITTLE CYBERMEN, WITH YOUR SILLY LITTLE CYBER-PLANS?
YOU'VE LET ME IN NOW. I'M PART OF THE CYBERIAD. PART OF THE HIVE MIND.
BUT THE THING IS, I'M ALSO A BIT OF A TINKERER. ALWAYS HAVE BEEN. CAN'T HELP MYSELF.
SHOW ME A MACHINE, AND I'LL TAKE IT APART. SHOW ME A COMPUTER AND I'LL REPROGRAM IT. SHOW ME A PROUD REPTILIAN WHO'S HAD THEIR EMOTIONS RIPPED AWAY...

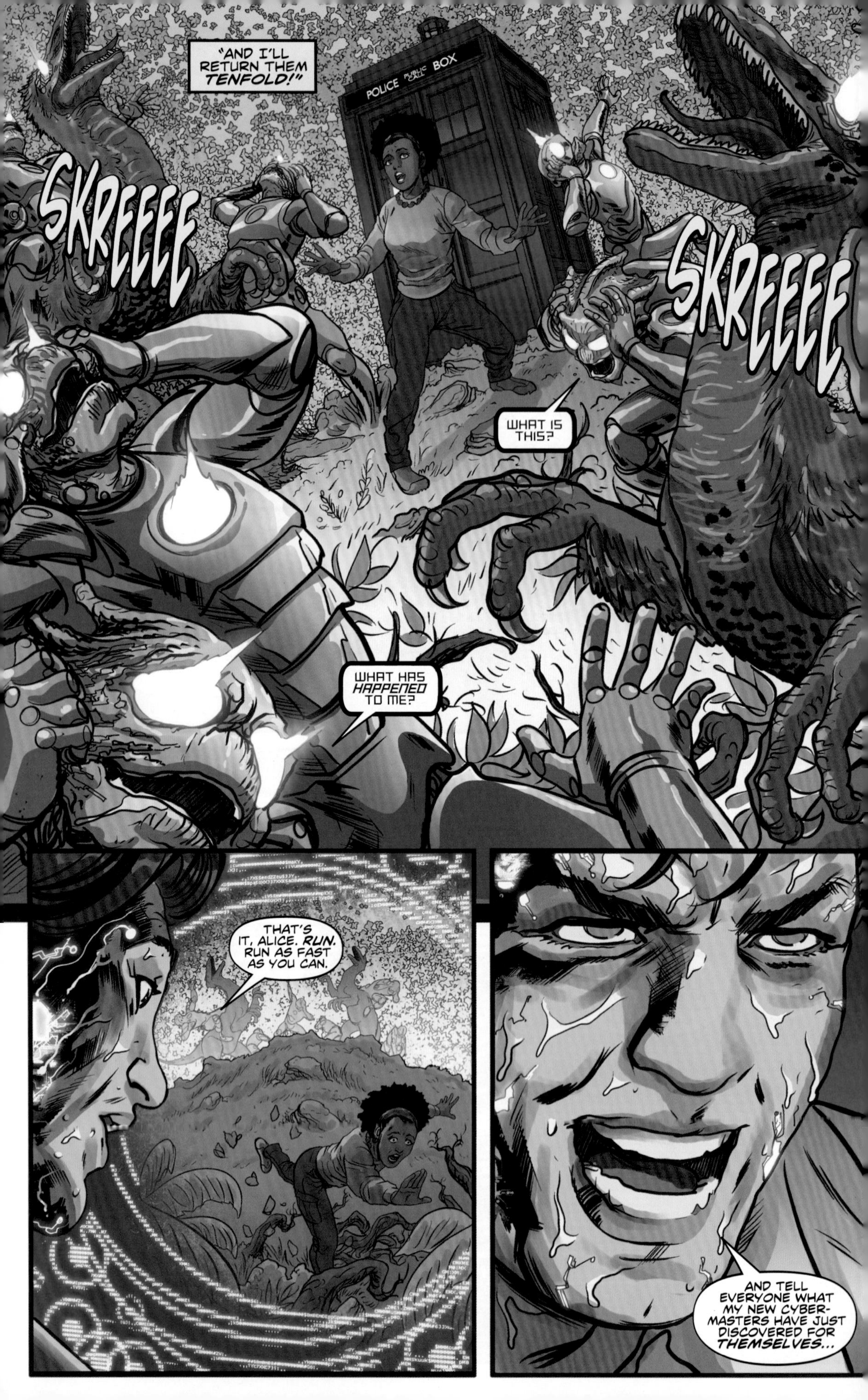
"AND I'LL RETURN THEM TENFOLD!"
SKREEEE
POLICE PUBLIC CALL BOX
SKREEEE
WHAT IS THIS?
WHAT HAS HAPPENED TO ME?
THAT'S IT, ALICE. RUN. RUN AS FAST AS YOU CAN.
AND TELL EVERYONE WHAT MY NEW CYBER-MASTERS HAVE JUST DISCOVERED FOR THEMSELVES...

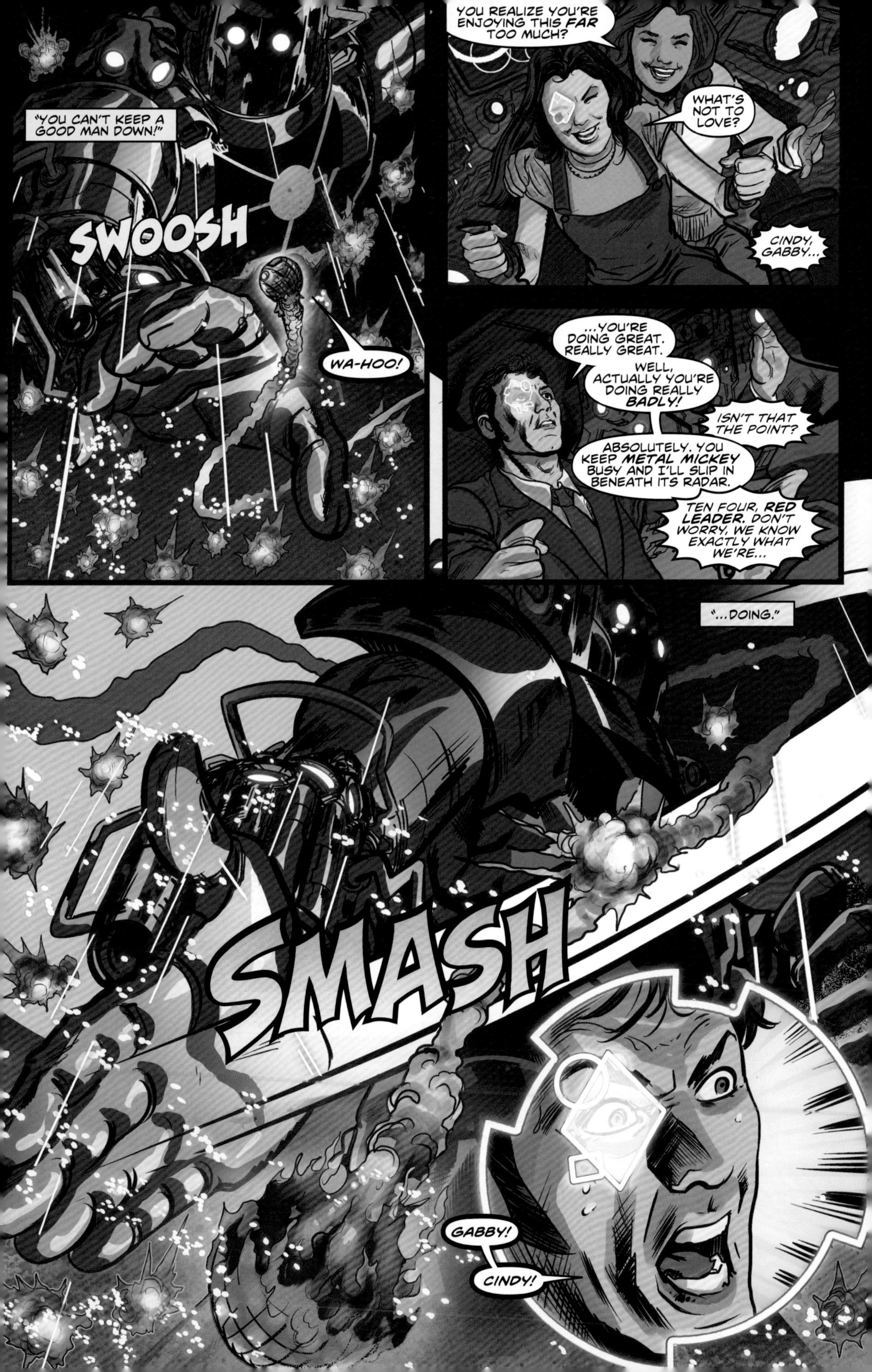
"YOU CAN'T KEEP A GOOD MAN DOWN!"
SWOOSH
WA-HOO!
YOU REALIZE YOU'RE ENJOYING THIS FAR TOO MUCH?
WHAT'S NOT TO LOVE?
CINDY, GABBY...
...YOU'RE DOING GREAT. REALLY GREAT.
WELL, ACTUALLY YOU'RE DOING REALLY BADLY!
ISN'T THAT THE POINT?
ABSOLUTELY. YOU KEEP METAL MICKEY BUSY AND I'LL SLIP IN BENEATH ITS RADAR.
TEN FOUR, RED LEADER. DON'T WORRY, WE KNOW EXACTLY WHAT WE'RE...
"...DOING."
SMASH
GABBY!
CINDY!

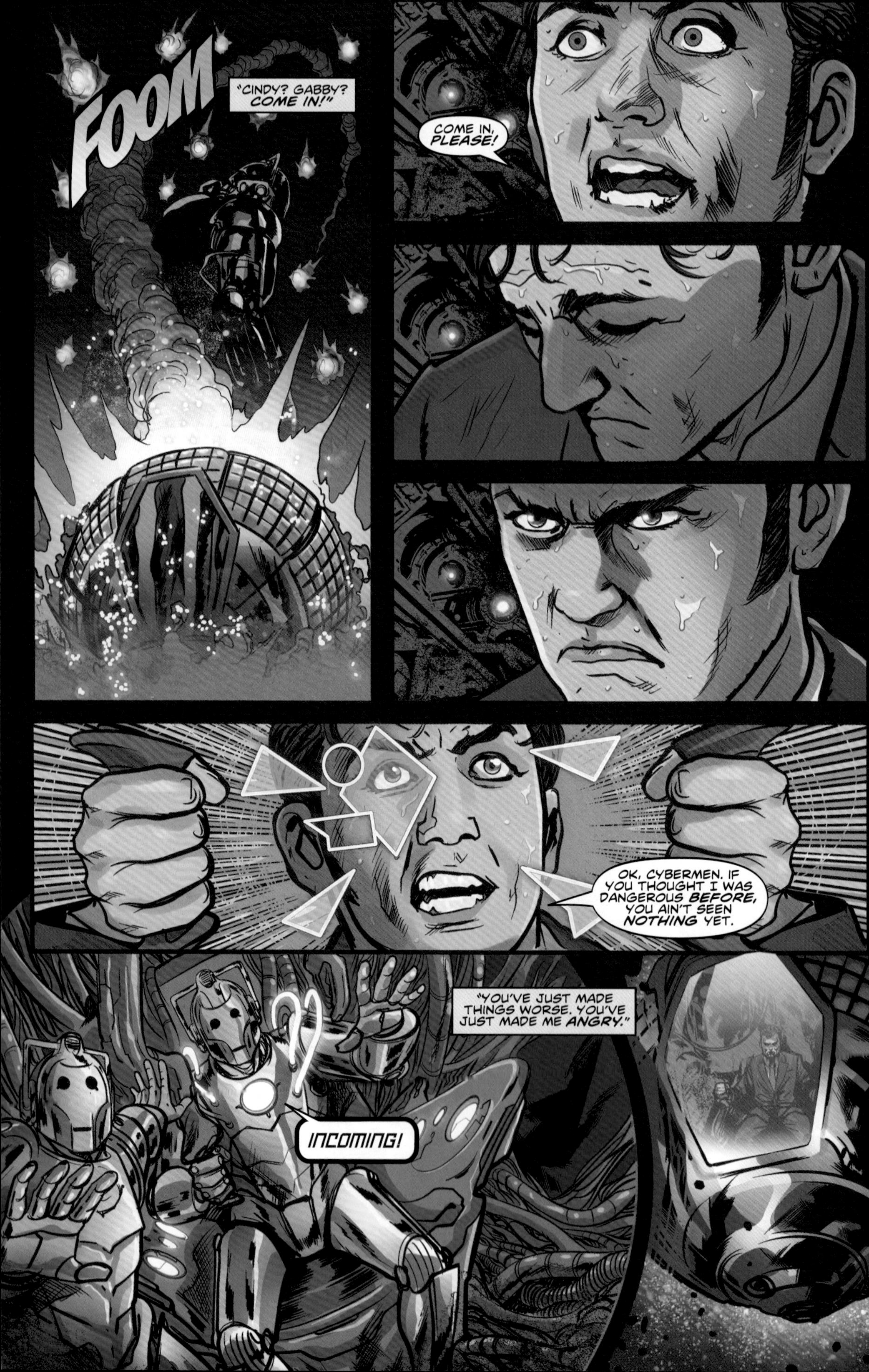
FOOM
"CINDY? GABBY? COME IN!"
COME IN, PLEASE!
OK, CYBERMEN. IF YOU THOUGHT I WAS DANGEROUS BEFORE, YOU AIN'T SEEN NOTHING YET.
"YOU'VE JUST MADE THINGS WORSE. YOU'VE JUST MADE ME ANGRY."
INCOMING!

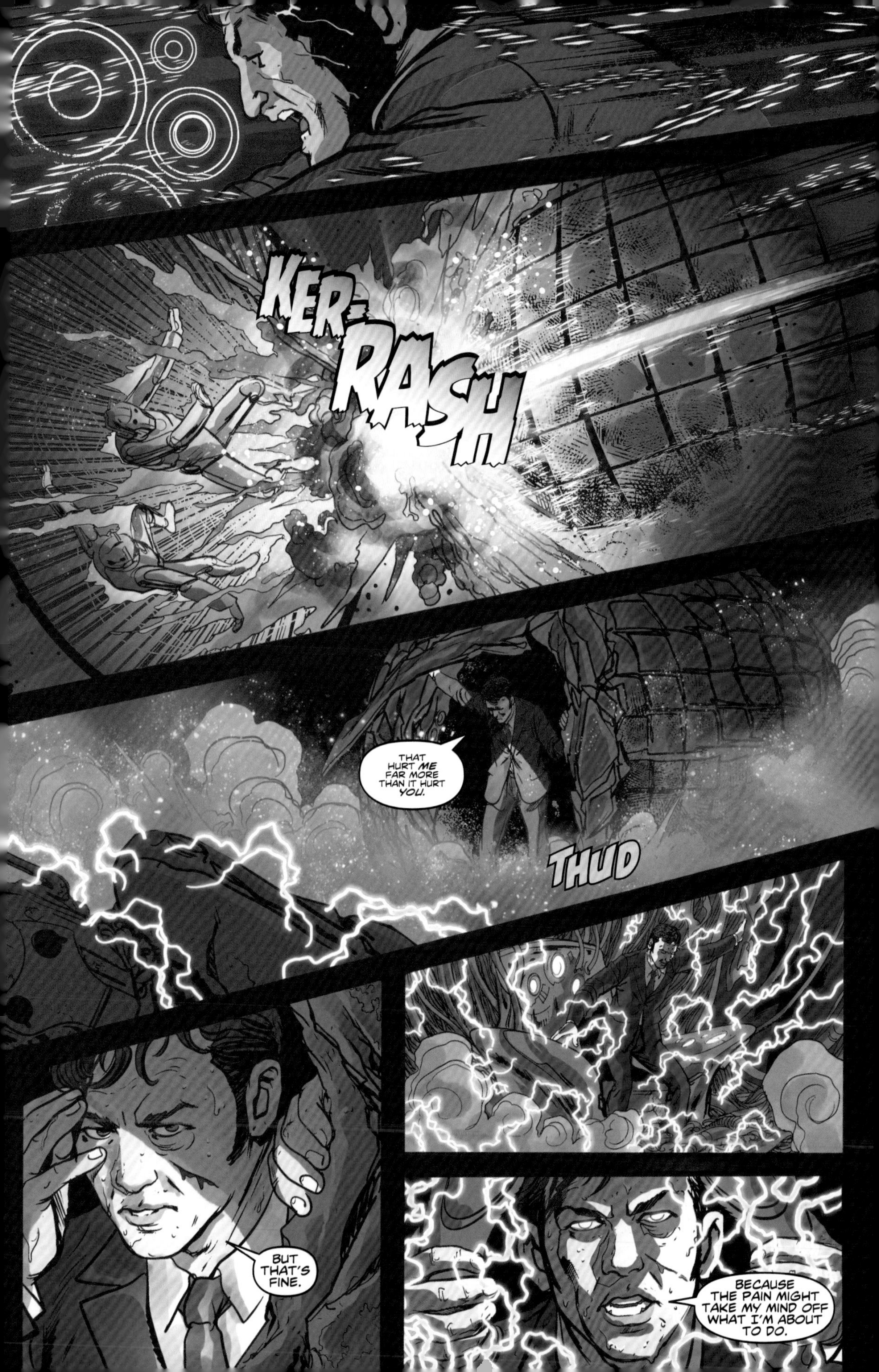
KER-RASH
THAT HURT ME FAR MORE THAN IT HURT YOU.
THUD
BUT THAT'S FINE.
BECAUSE THE PAIN MIGHT TAKE MY MIND OFF WHAT I'M ABOUT TO DO.

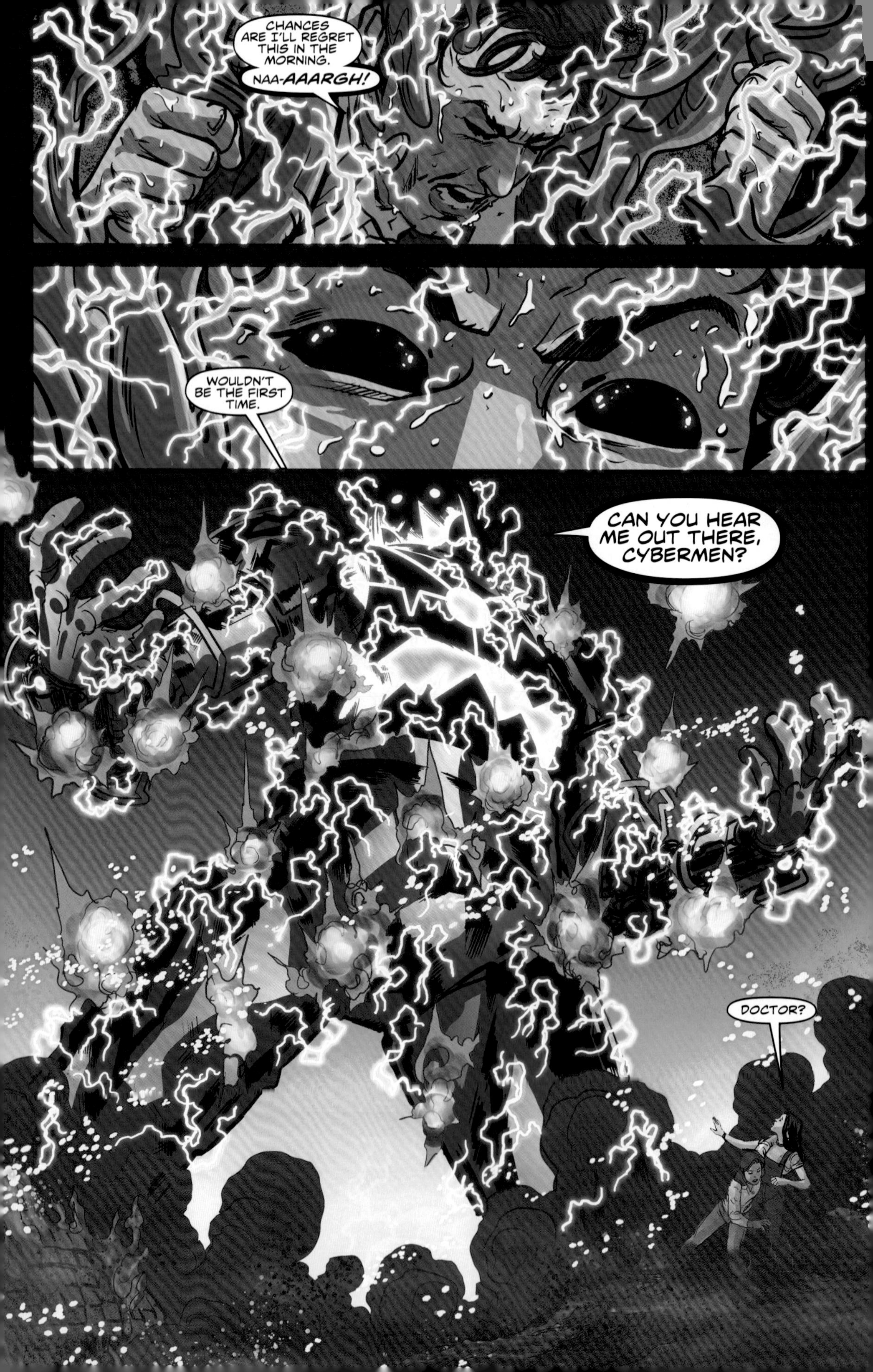
CHANCES ARE I'LL REGRET THIS IN THE MORNING.
NAA-AAARGH!
WOULDN'T BE THE FIRST TIME.
CAN YOU HEAR ME OUT THERE, CYBERMEN?
DOCTOR?

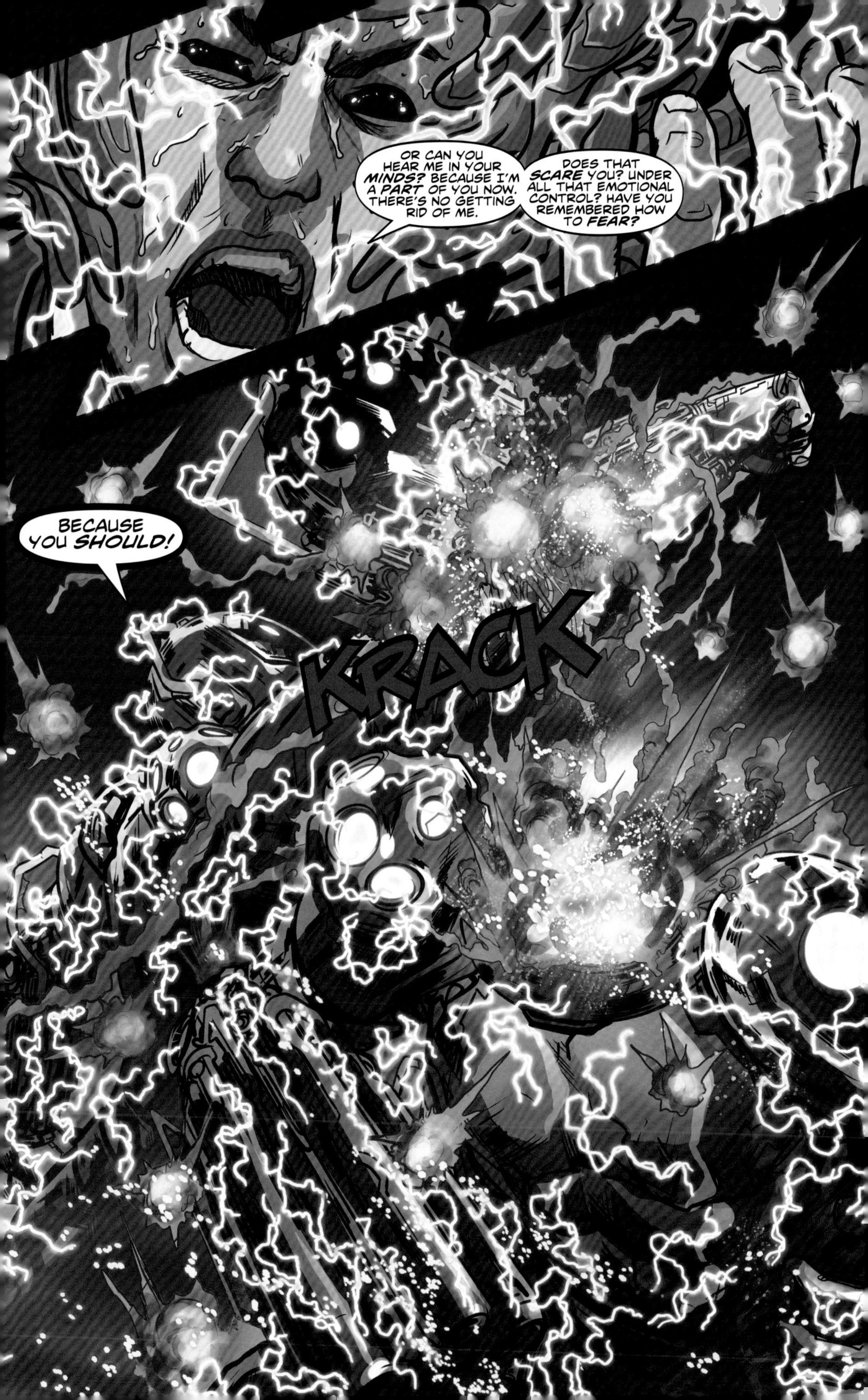
OR CAN YOU HEAR ME IN YOUR MINDS? BECAUSE I'M A PART OF YOU NOW. THERE'S NO GETTING RID OF ME.
DOES THAT SCARE YOU? UNDER ALL THAT EMOTIONAL CONTROL? HAVE YOU REMEMBERED HOW TO FEAR?
BECAUSE YOU SHOULD!
KRACK

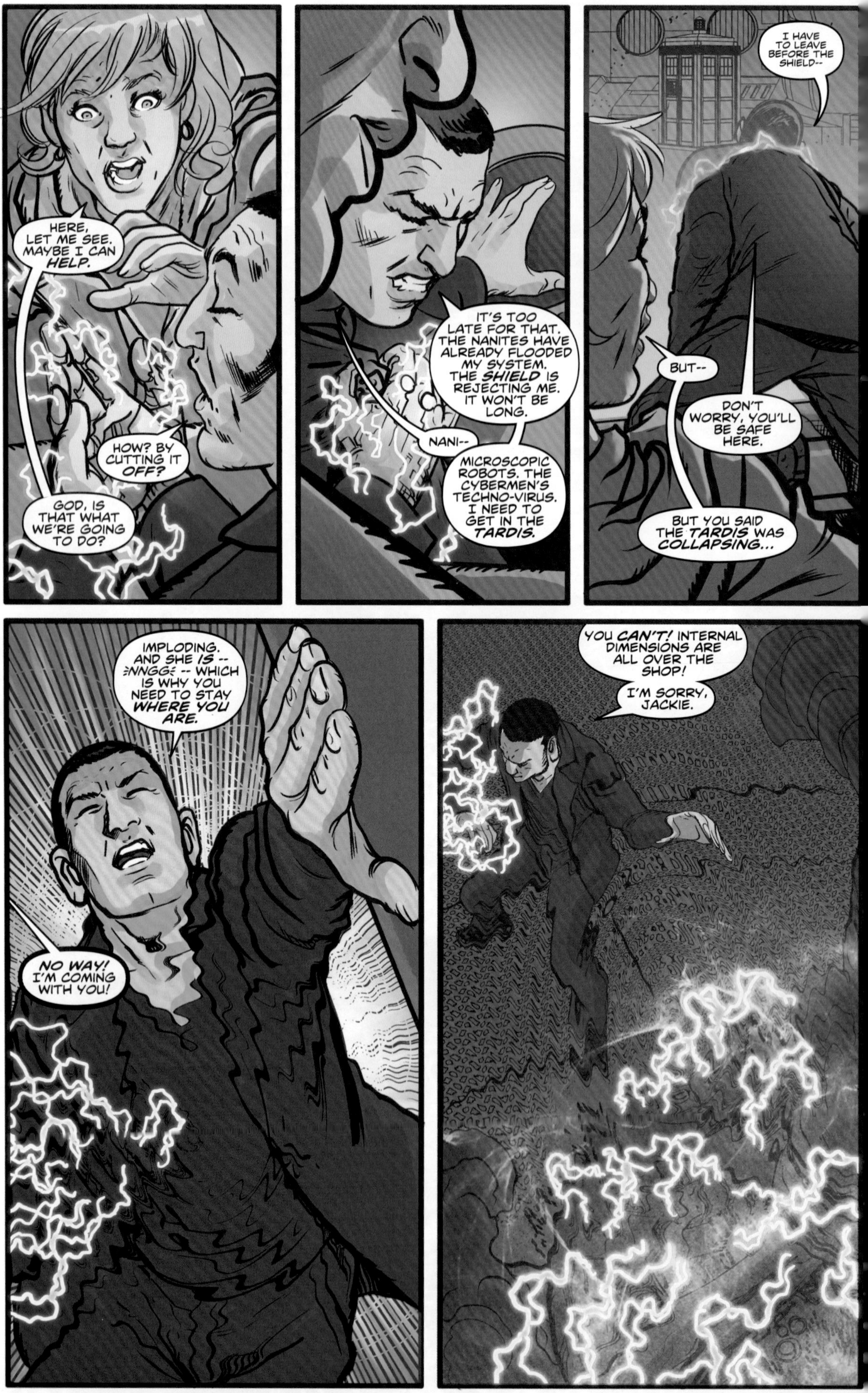
HERE, LET ME SEE. MAYBE I CAN HELP.
HOW? BY CUTTING IT OFF?
GOD, IS THAT WHAT WE'RE GOING TO DO?
IT'S TOO LATE FOR THAT. THE NANITES HAVE ALREADY FLOODED MY SYSTEM. THE SHIELD IS REJECTING ME. IT WON'T BE LONG.
NANI--
MICROSCOPIC ROBOTS. THE CYBERMEN'S TECHNO-VIRUS. I NEED TO GET IN THE TARDIS.
I HAVE TO LEAVE BEFORE THE SHIELD--
BUT--
DON'T WORRY, YOU'LL BE SAFE HERE.
BUT YOU SAID THE TARDIS WAS COLLAPSING...
IMPLODING. AND SHE IS -- NNGG -- WHICH IS WHY YOU NEED TO STAY WHERE YOU ARE.
NO WAY! I'M COMING WITH YOU!
YOU CAN'T! INTERNAL DIMENSIONS ARE ALL OVER THE SHOP!
I'M SORRY, JACKIE.

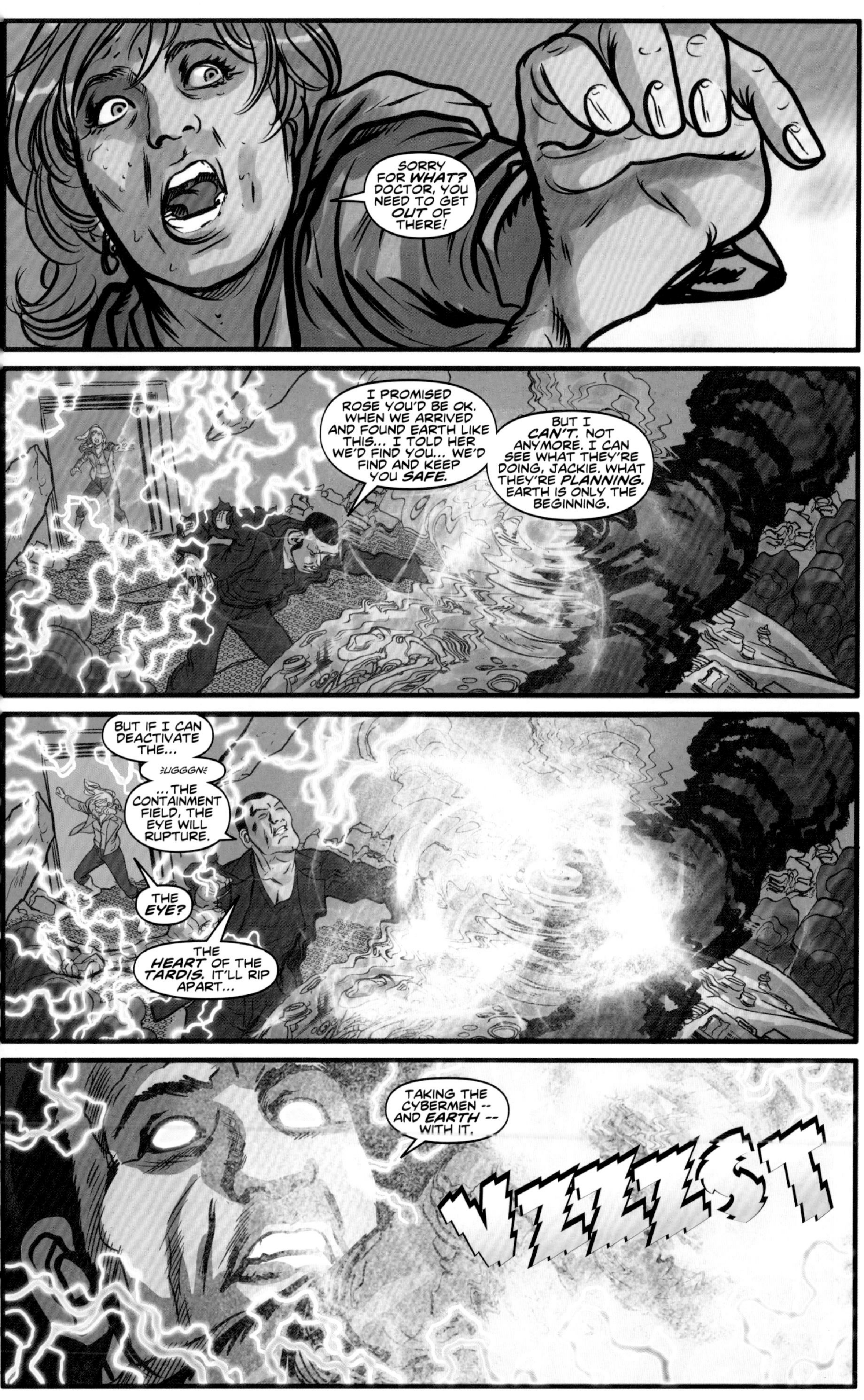
SORRY FOR WHAT? DOCTOR, YOU NEED TO GET OUT OF THERE!
I PROMISED ROSE YOU'D BE OK. WHEN WE ARRIVED AND FOUND EARTH LIKE THIS... I TOLD HER WE'D FIND YOU... WE'D FIND AND KEEP YOU SAFE.
BUT I CAN'T. NOT ANYMORE. I CAN SEE WHAT THEY'RE DOING, JACKIE. WHAT THEY'RE PLANNING. EARTH IS ONLY THE BEGINNING.
BUT IF I CAN DEACTIVATE THE...
UGGGN
...THE CONTAINMENT FIELD, THE EYE WILL RUPTURE.
THE EYE?
THE HEART OF THE TARDIS. IT'LL RIP APART...
TAKING THE CYBERMEN -- AND EARTH -- WITH IT.
VZZZST

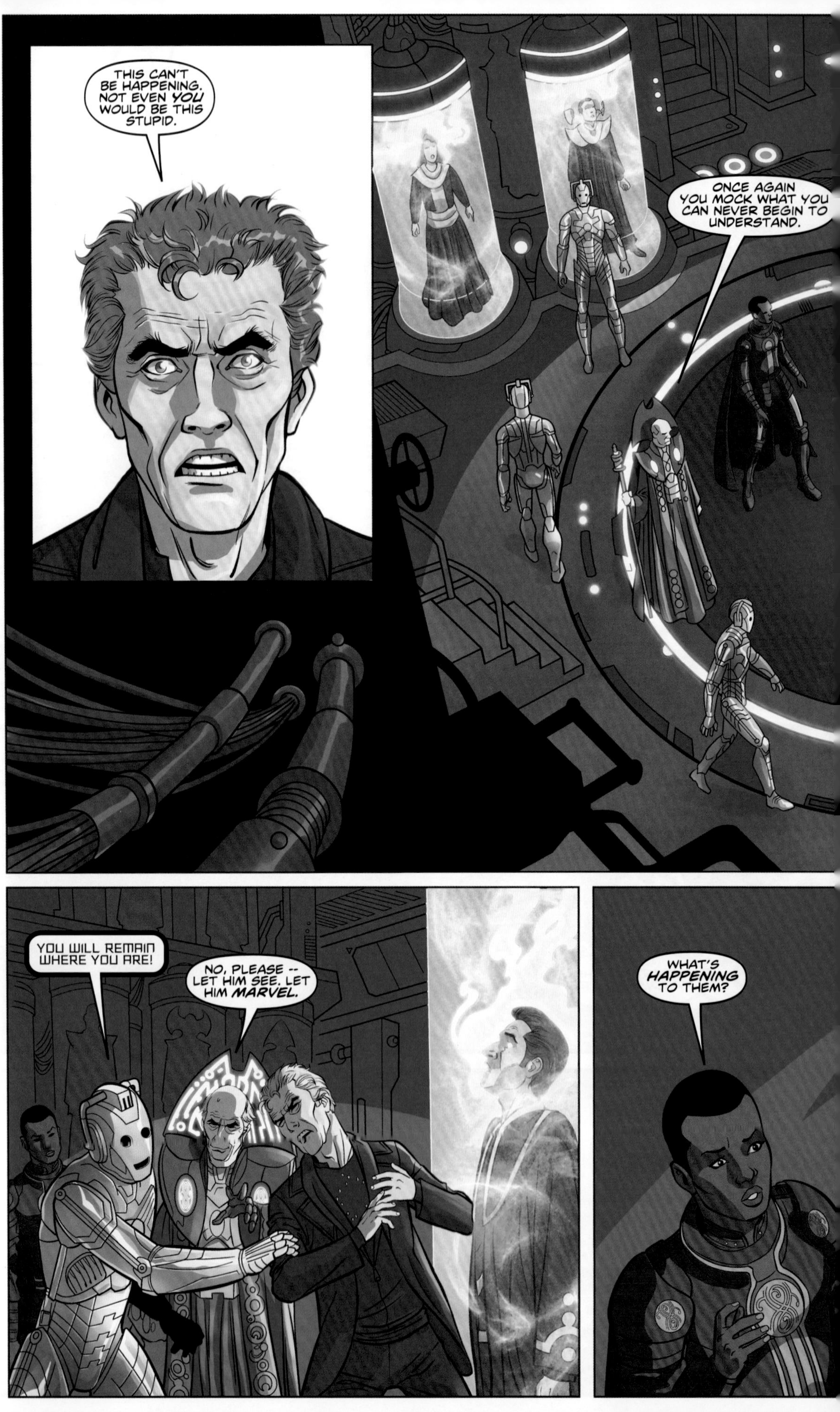
THIS CAN'T BE HAPPENING. NOT EVEN YOU WOULD BE THIS STUPID.
ONCE AGAIN YOU MOCK WHAT YOU CAN NEVER BEGIN TO UNDERSTAND.
YOU WILL REMAIN WHERE YOU ARE!
NO, PLEASE -- LET HIM SEE. LET HIM MARVEL.
WHAT'S HAPPENING TO THEM?

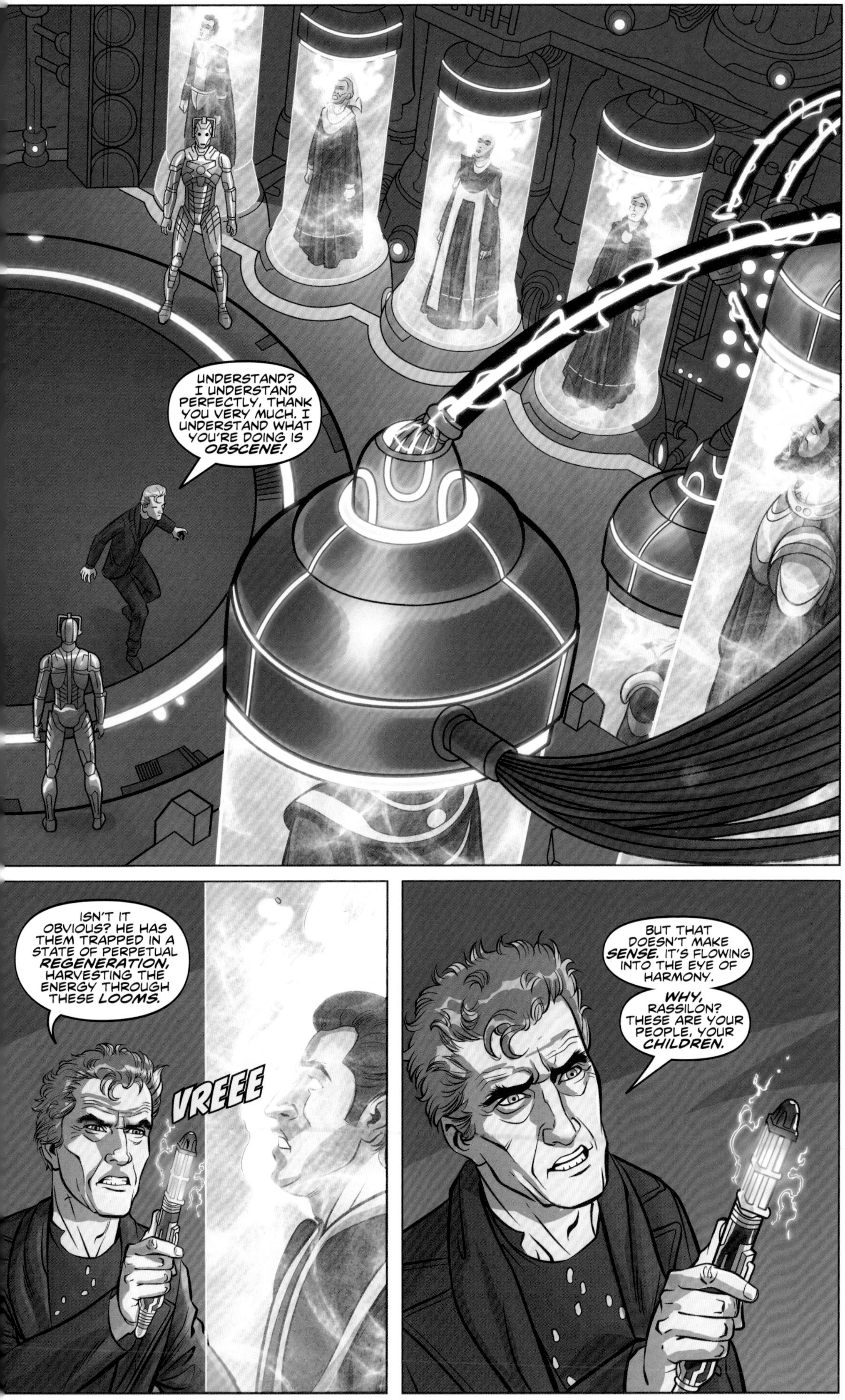
UNDERSTAND? I UNDERSTAND PERFECTLY, THANK YOU VERY MUCH. I UNDERSTAND WHAT YOU'RE DOING IS OBSCENE!
ISN'T IT OBVIOUS? HE HAS THEM TRAPPED IN A STATE OF PERPETUAL REGENERATION, HARVESTING THE ENERGY THROUGH THESE LOOMS.
VREEE
BUT THAT DOESN'T MAKE SENSE. IT'S FLOWING INTO THE EYE OF HARMONY.
WHY, RASSILON? THESE ARE YOUR PEOPLE, YOUR CHILDREN.

THE RENEGADE FINALLY SPEAKS SENSE. THEY *ARE* MY CHILDREN, DOCTOR. I CREATED THE TIME LORDS. THEY BELONG TO ME.

YOU BELONG TO ME.

GET YOUR HANDS *OFF* ME!

BUT WHO DO *YOU* BELONG TO, RASSILON? YOU CAN *STOP* ALL THIS, BEFORE IT'S TOO LATE.

GENERAL, YOU HAVE SERVED GALLIFREY FOR THOUSANDS OF YEARS. WE ARE *GRATEFUL*, AND HONOR THE SACRIFICE YOU ARE ABOUT TO MAKE.

NO. DON'T DO THIS. DON'T *DO...*

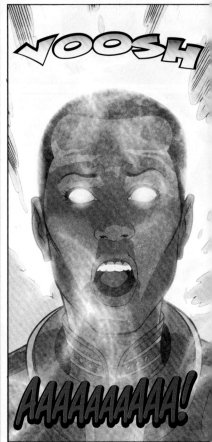

VOOSH

AAAAAAAAAA!

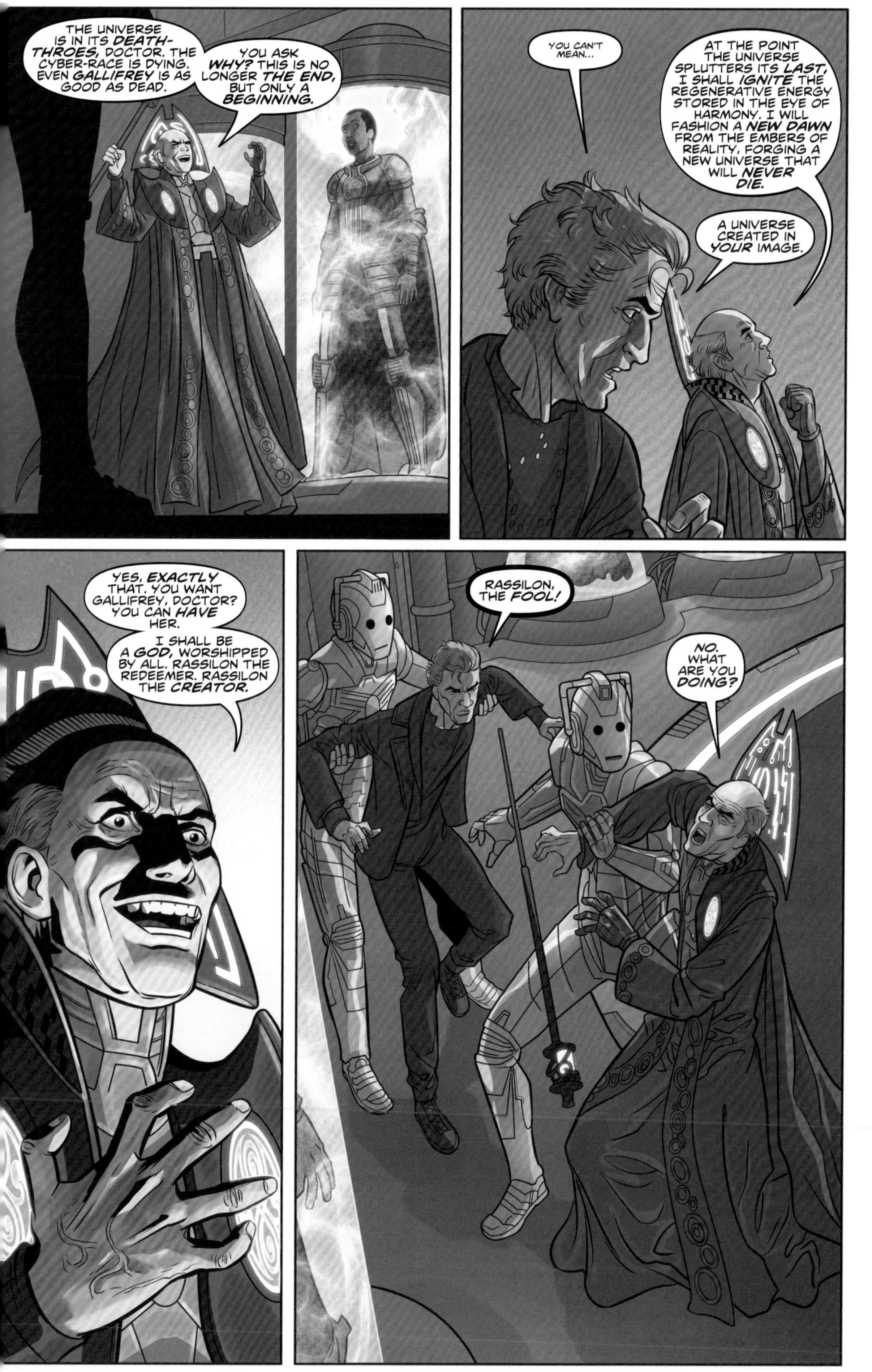
THE UNIVERSE IS IN ITS DEATH-THROES, DOCTOR. THE CYBER-RACE IS DYING. EVEN GALLIFREY IS AS GOOD AS DEAD.
YOU ASK WHY? THIS IS NO LONGER THE END, BUT ONLY A BEGINNING.
YOU CAN'T MEAN...
AT THE POINT THE UNIVERSE SPLUTTERS ITS LAST, I SHALL IGNITE THE REGENERATIVE ENERGY STORED IN THE EYE OF HARMONY. I WILL FASHION A NEW DAWN FROM THE EMBERS OF REALITY, FORGING A NEW UNIVERSE THAT WILL NEVER DIE.
A UNIVERSE CREATED IN YOUR IMAGE.
YES, EXACTLY THAT. YOU WANT GALLIFREY, DOCTOR? YOU CAN HAVE HER.
I SHALL BE A GOD, WORSHIPPED BY ALL. RASSILON THE REDEEMER. RASSILON THE CREATOR.
RASSILON, THE FOOL!
NO. WHAT ARE YOU DOING?

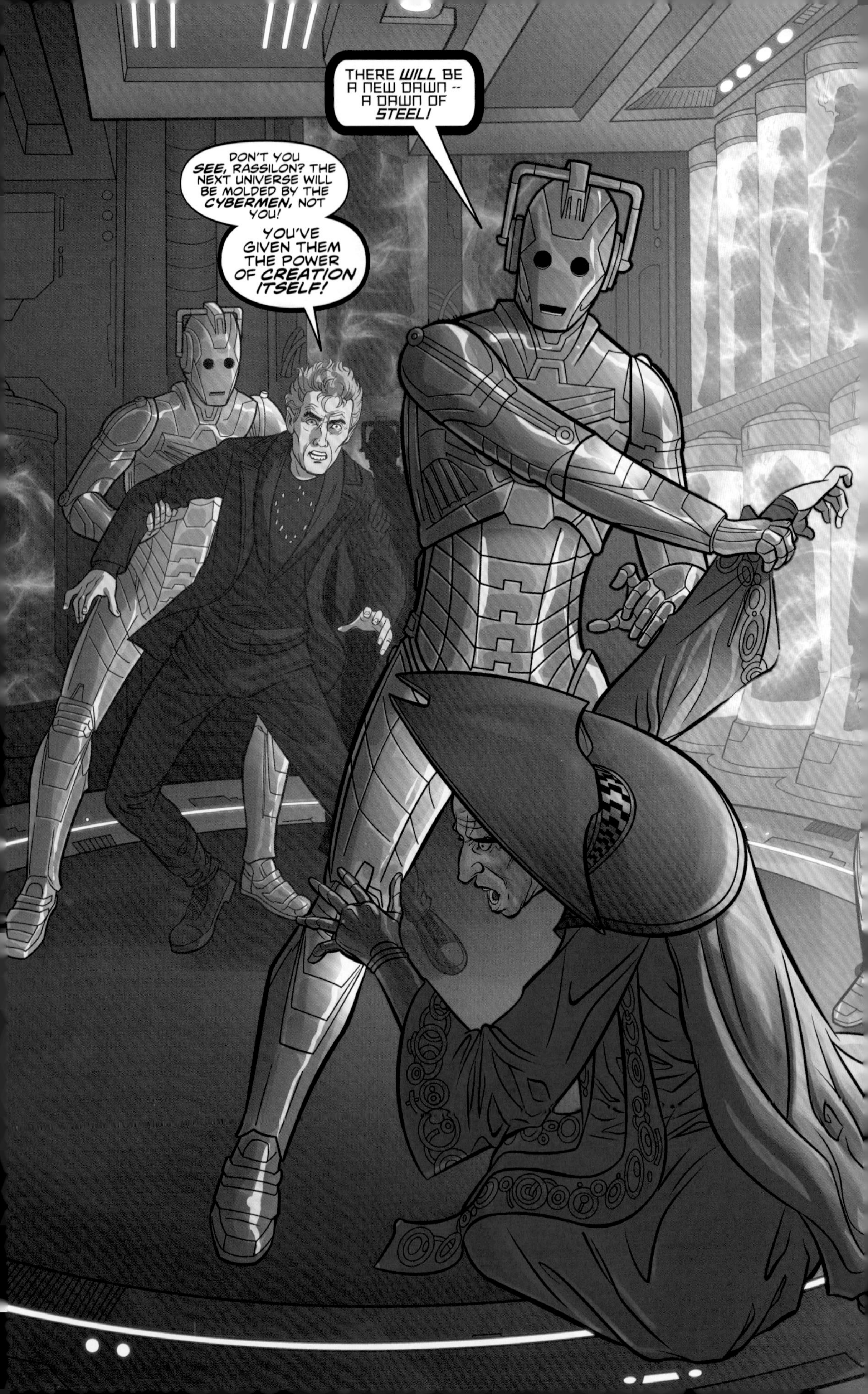
DON'T YOU SEE, RASSILON? THE NEXT UNIVERSE WILL BE MOLDED BY THE CYBERMEN, NOT YOU!
YOU'VE GIVEN THEM THE POWER OF CREATION ITSELF!
THERE WILL BE A NEW DAWN -- A DAWN OF STEEL!

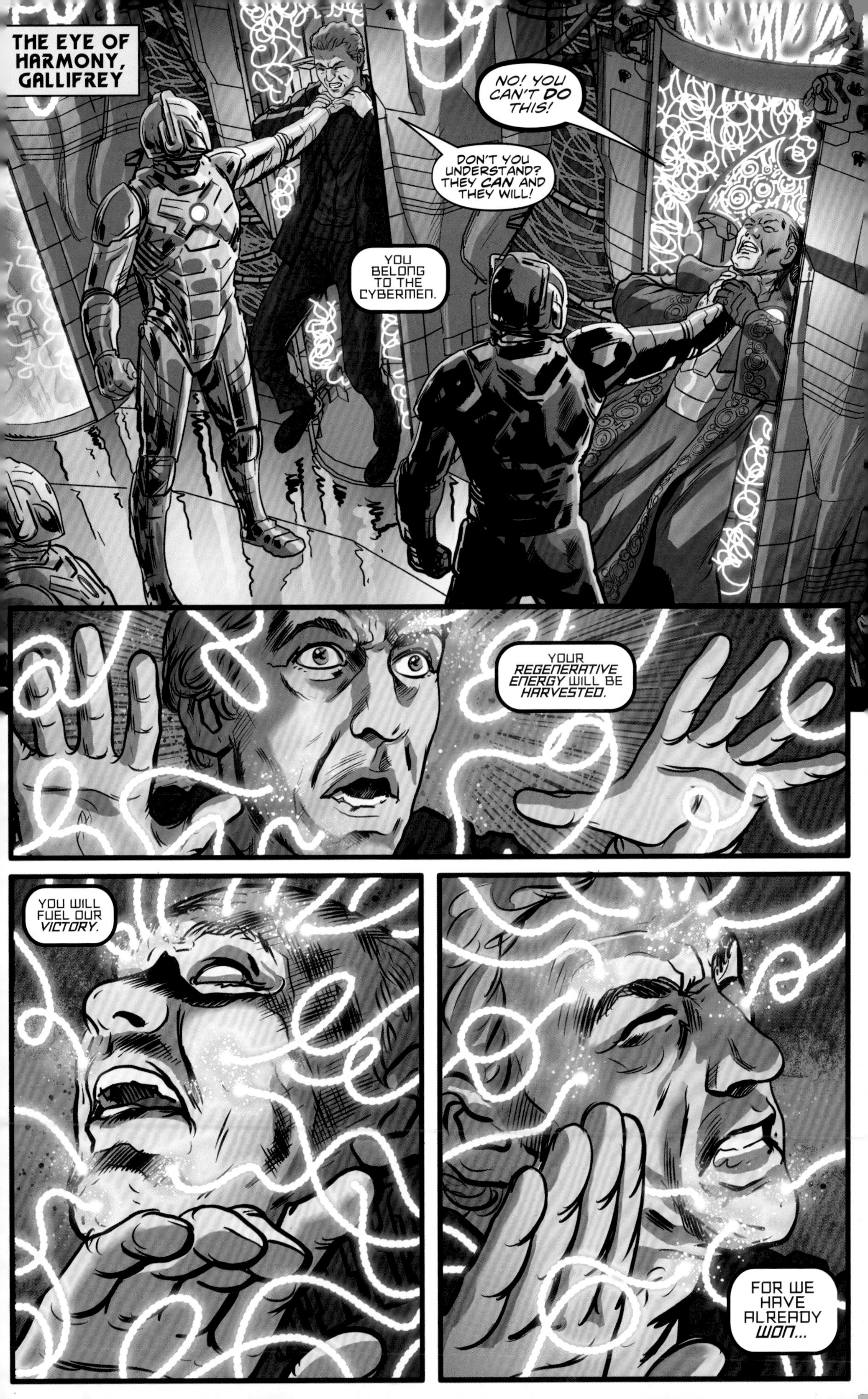
THE EYE OF HARMONY, GALLIFREY
NO! YOU CAN'T DO THIS!
DON'T YOU UNDERSTAND? THEY CAN AND THEY WILL!
YOU BELONG TO THE CYBERMEN.
YOUR REGENERATIVE ENERGY WILL BE HARVESTED.
YOU WILL FUEL OUR VICTORY.
FOR WE HAVE ALREADY WON...

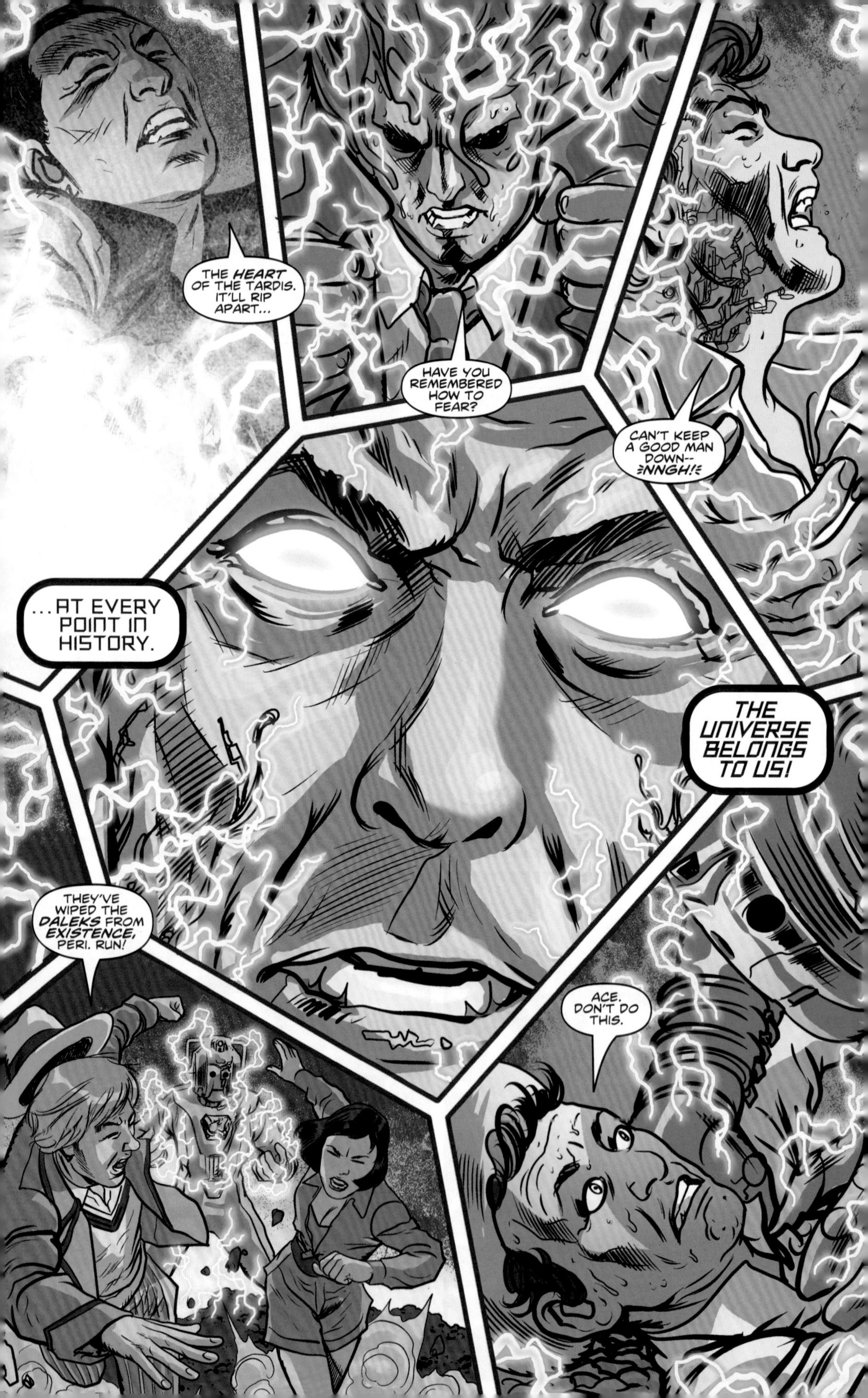
THE *HEART* OF THE TARDIS. IT'LL RIP APART...
HAVE YOU REMEMBERED HOW TO FEAR?
CAN'T KEEP A GOOD MAN DOWN-- *NNGH!*
...AT EVERY POINT IN HISTORY.
THE UNIVERSE BELONGS TO US!
THEY'VE WIPED THE *DALEKS* FROM *EXISTENCE,* PERI. RUN!
ACE. DON'T DO THIS.

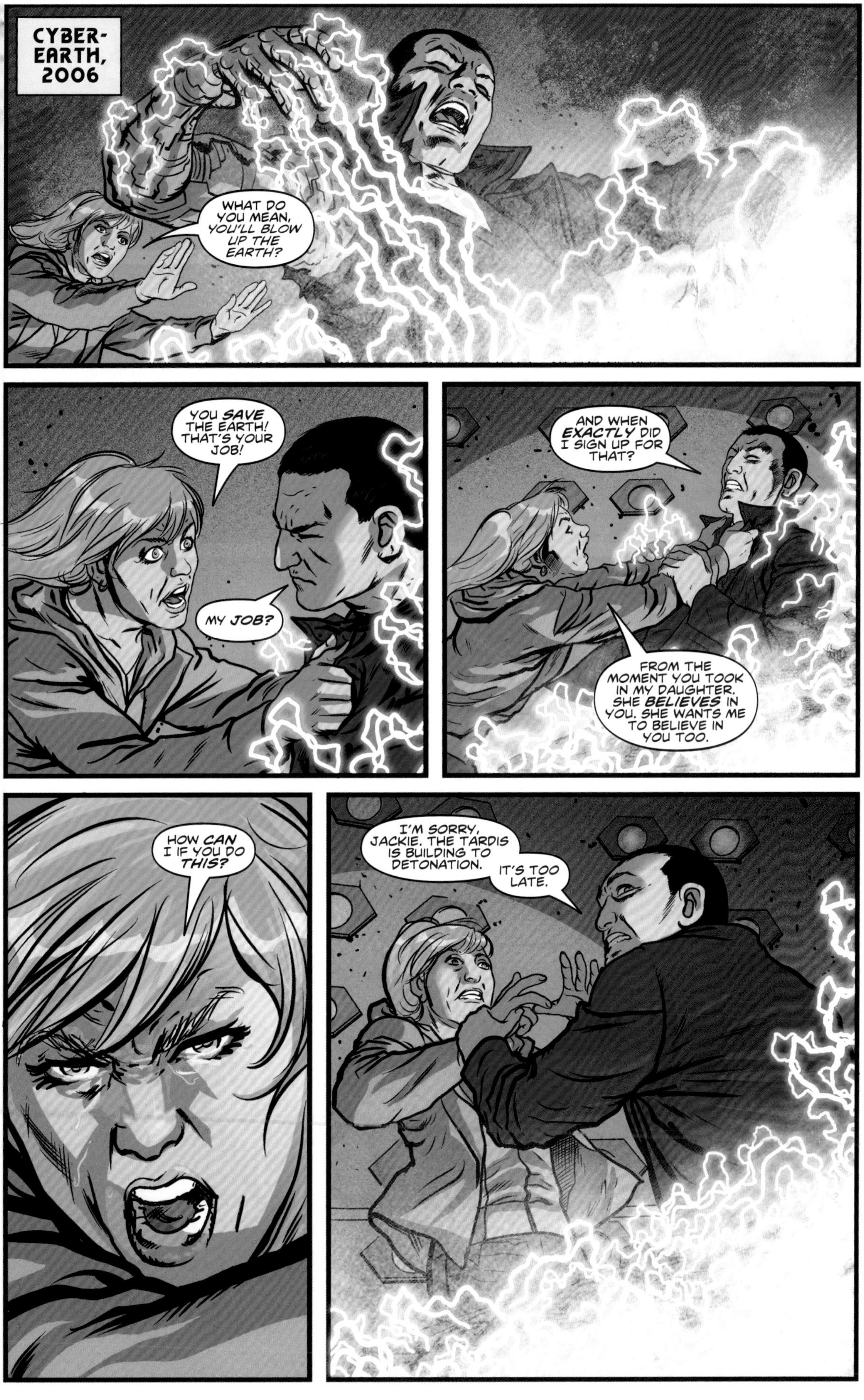
CYBER-EARTH, 2006
WHAT DO YOU MEAN, YOU'LL BLOW UP THE EARTH?
YOU SAVE THE EARTH! THAT'S YOUR JOB!
MY JOB?
AND WHEN EXACTLY DID I SIGN UP FOR THAT?
FROM THE MOMENT YOU TOOK IN MY DAUGHTER. SHE BELIEVES IN YOU. SHE WANTS ME TO BELIEVE IN YOU TOO.
HOW CAN I IF YOU DO THIS?
I'M SORRY, JACKIE. THE TARDIS IS BUILDING TO DETONATION.
IT'S TOO LATE.

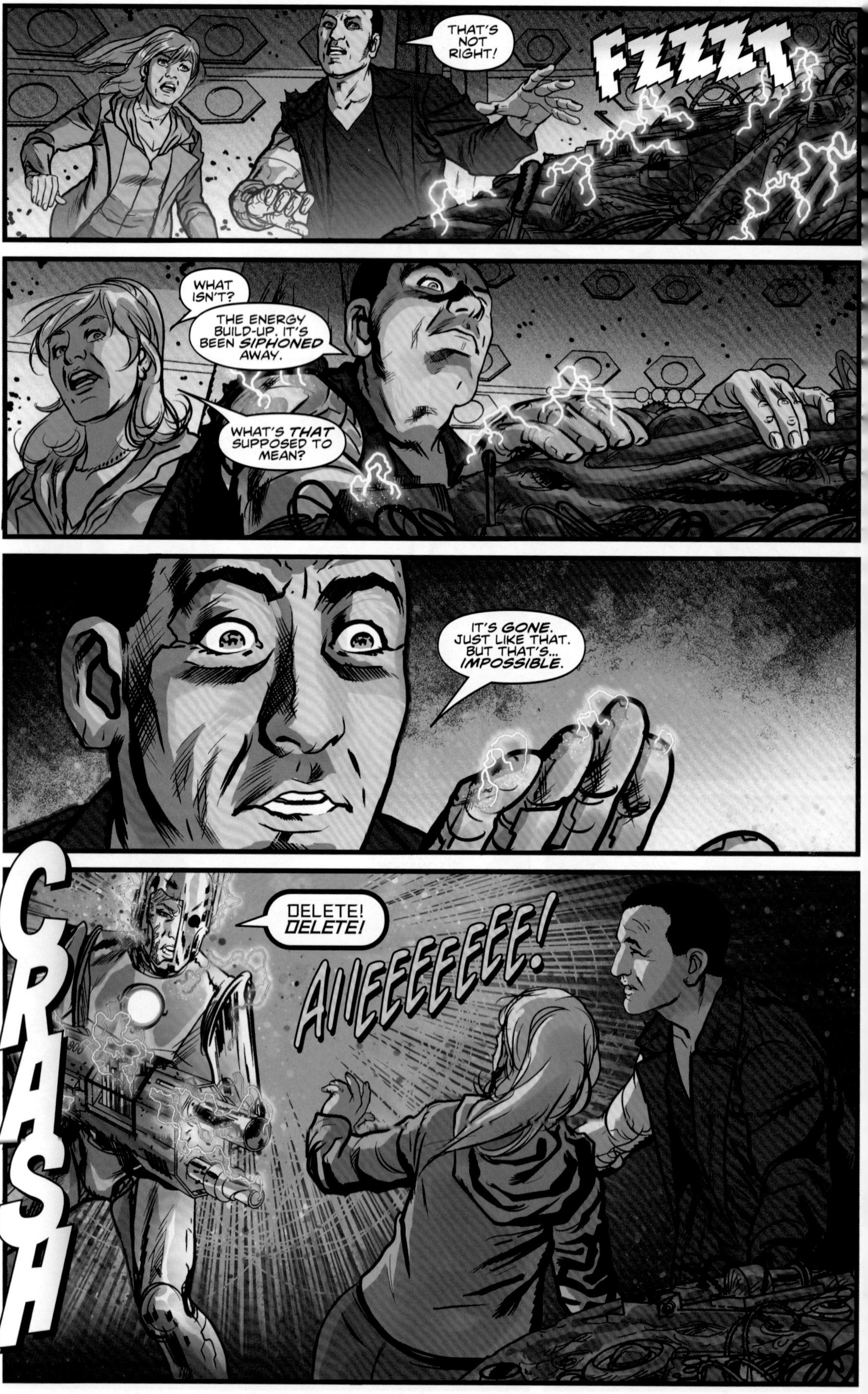
THAT'S NOT RIGHT!
FZZZZT
WHAT ISN'T?
THE ENERGY BUILD-UP. IT'S BEEN SIPHONED AWAY.
WHAT'S THAT SUPPOSED TO MEAN?
IT'S GONE. JUST LIKE THAT. BUT THAT'S... IMPOSSIBLE.
CRASH
DELETE! DELETE!
AIIEEEEEEEE!

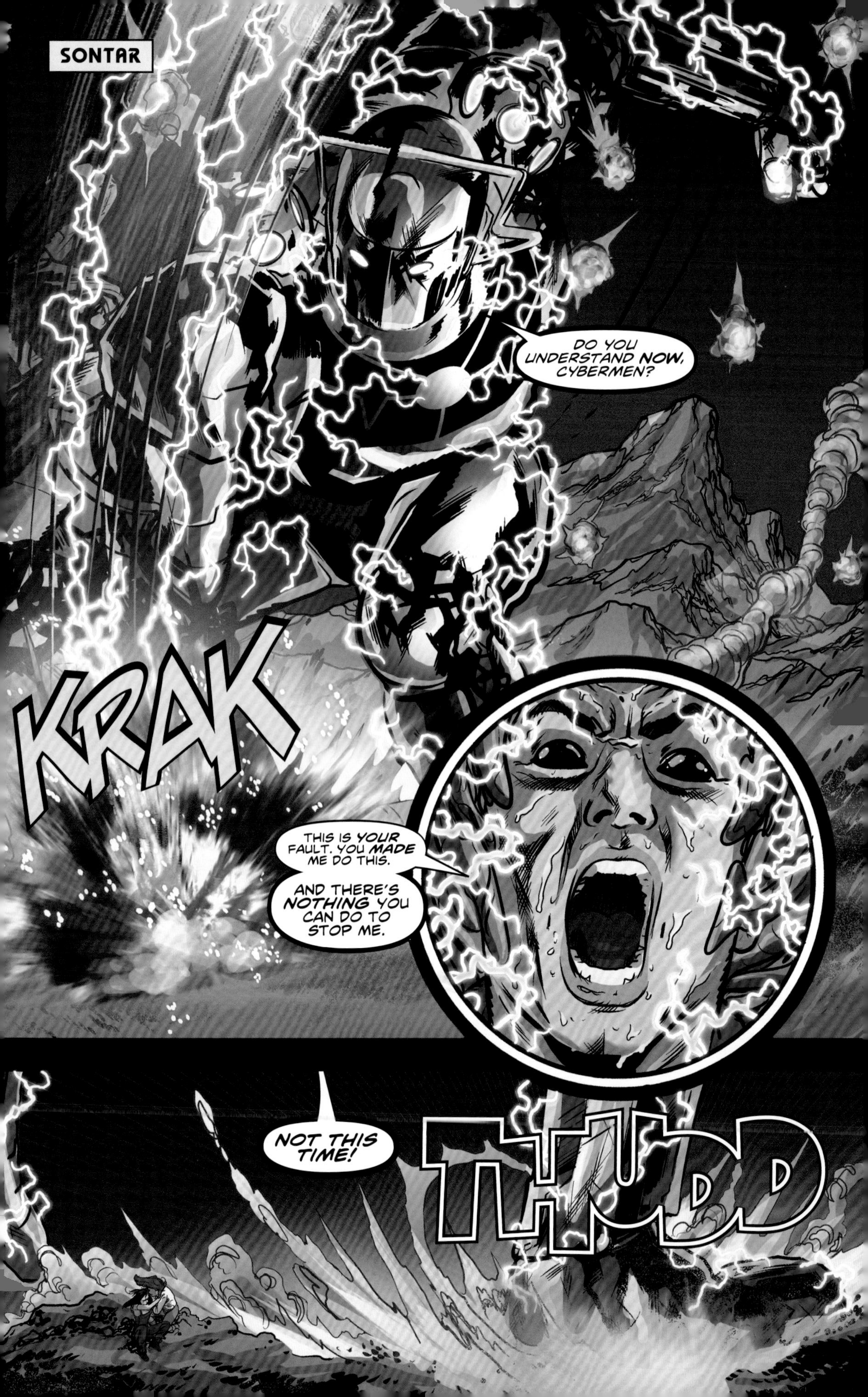
SONTAR
DO YOU UNDERSTAND NOW, CYBERMEN?
KRAK
THIS IS YOUR FAULT. YOU MADE ME DO THIS.
AND THERE'S NOTHING YOU CAN DO TO STOP ME.
NOT THIS TIME!
THUDD

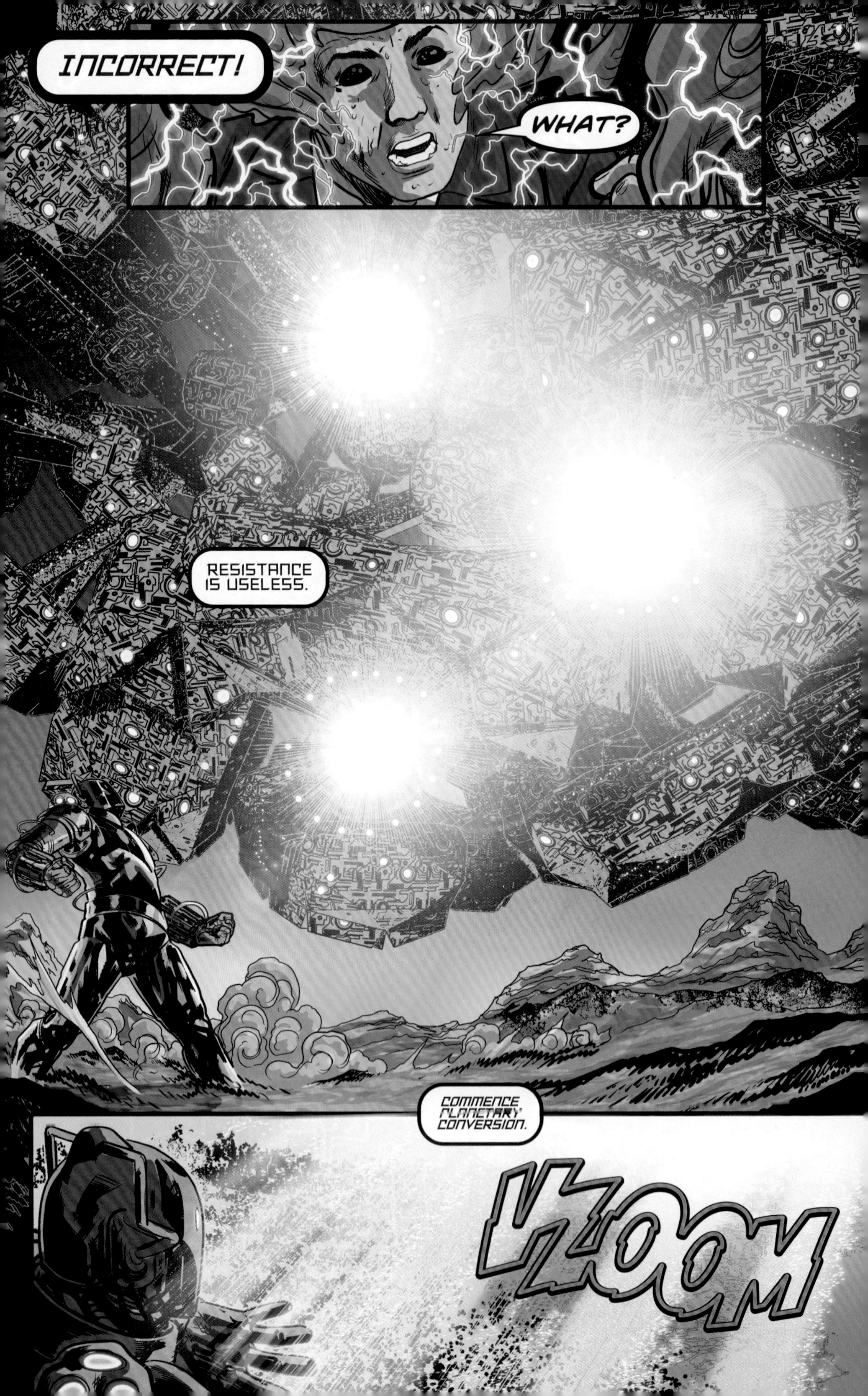
INCORRECT!
WHAT?
RESISTANCE IS USELESS.
COMMENCE PLANETARY CONVERSION.
VZOOM

PREHISTORIC EARTH.

IT'S OVER.

I'VE WON.

"SOON THOSE *PESKY* *EMOTIONS* WILL BE FLOWING THROUGHOUT THE CYBERIAD. EVERY LINKED MIND FINALLY *FREE*.

"DOCTOR: *ONE-BILLION*. CYBERMEN: *NIL!*"

WHAT... ARE THESE...?

DELETE

DO YOUR WORST!

NO. NOT YOU.

SAAARGH!

NO.

YOU *KILLED* THEM! YOUR *OWN* WARRIORS!

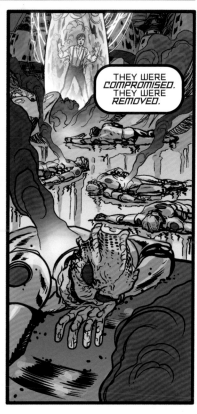

THEY WERE *COMPROMISED*. THEY WERE *REMOVED*.

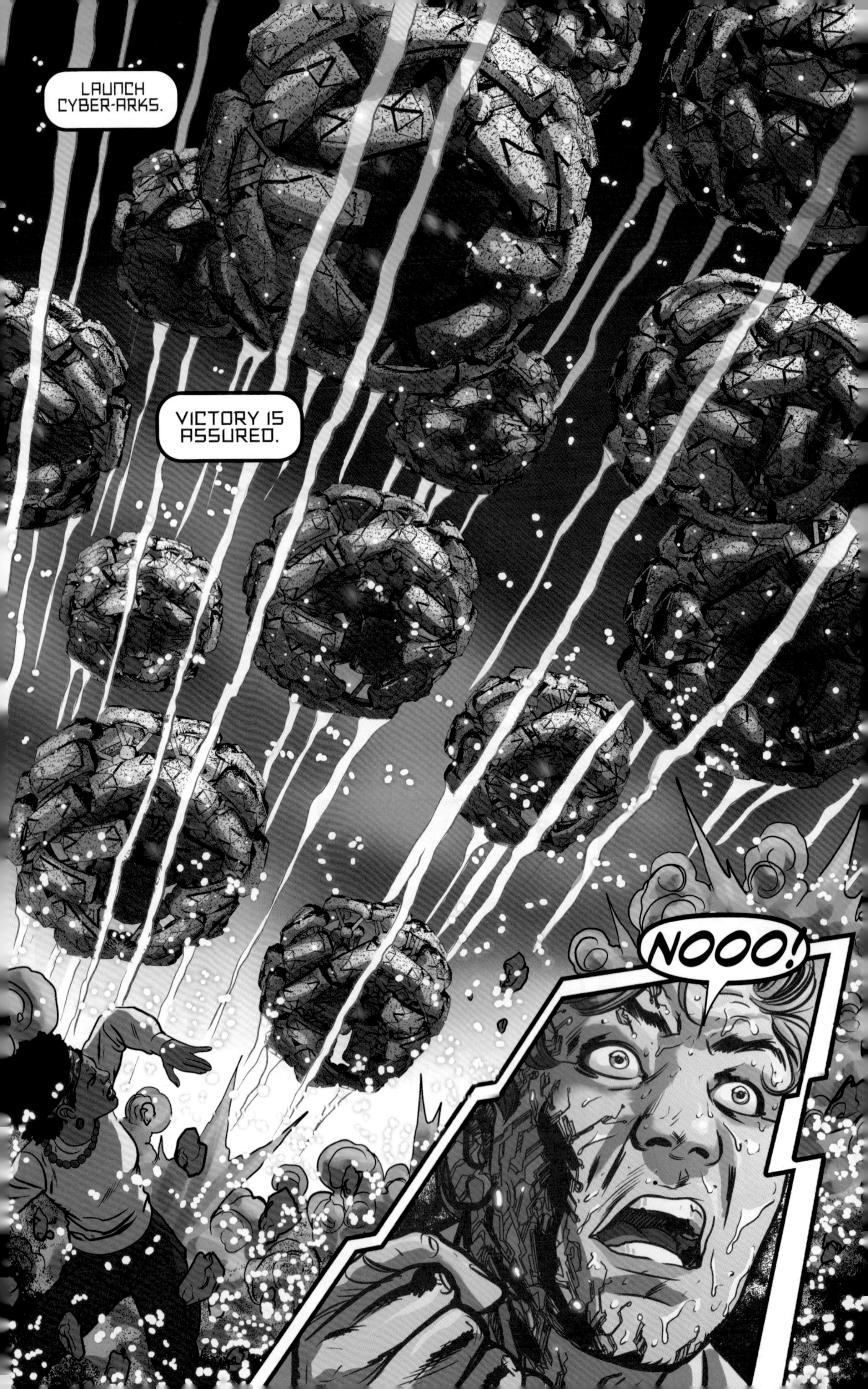
LAUNCH CYBER-ARKS.
VICTORY IS ASSURED.
NOOO!

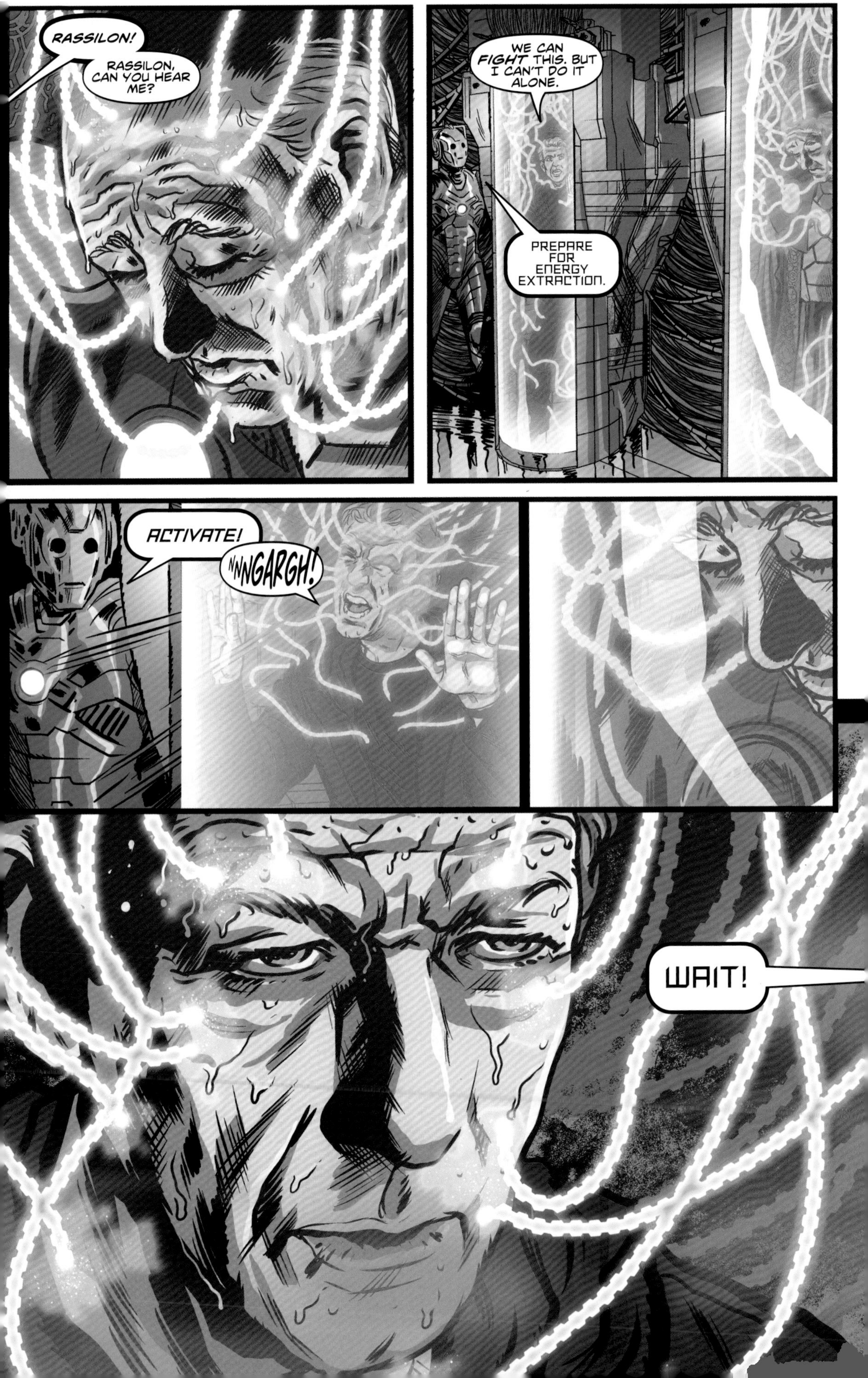
RASSILON!
RASSILON, CAN YOU HEAR ME?
WE CAN FIGHT THIS. BUT I CAN'T DO IT ALONE.
PREPARE FOR ENERGY EXTRACTION.
ACTIVATE!
NNNGARGH!
WAIT!

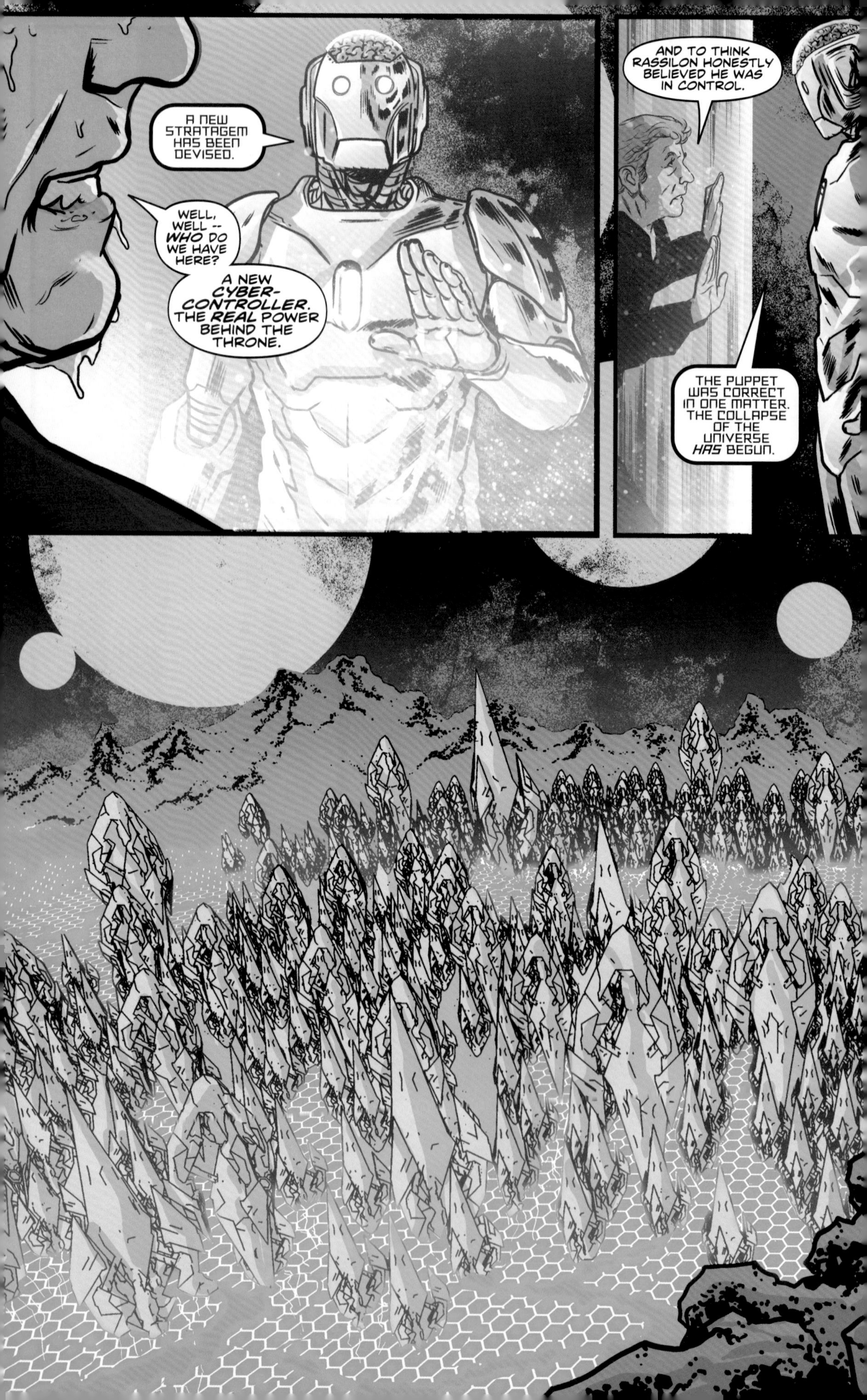
A NEW STRATAGEM HAS BEEN DEVISED.
WELL, WELL -- WHO DO WE HAVE HERE?
A NEW CYBER-CONTROLLER. THE REAL POWER BEHIND THE THRONE.
AND TO THINK RASSILON HONESTLY BELIEVED HE WAS IN CONTROL.
THE PUPPET WAS CORRECT IN ONE MATTER. THE COLLAPSE OF THE UNIVERSE HAS BEGUN.

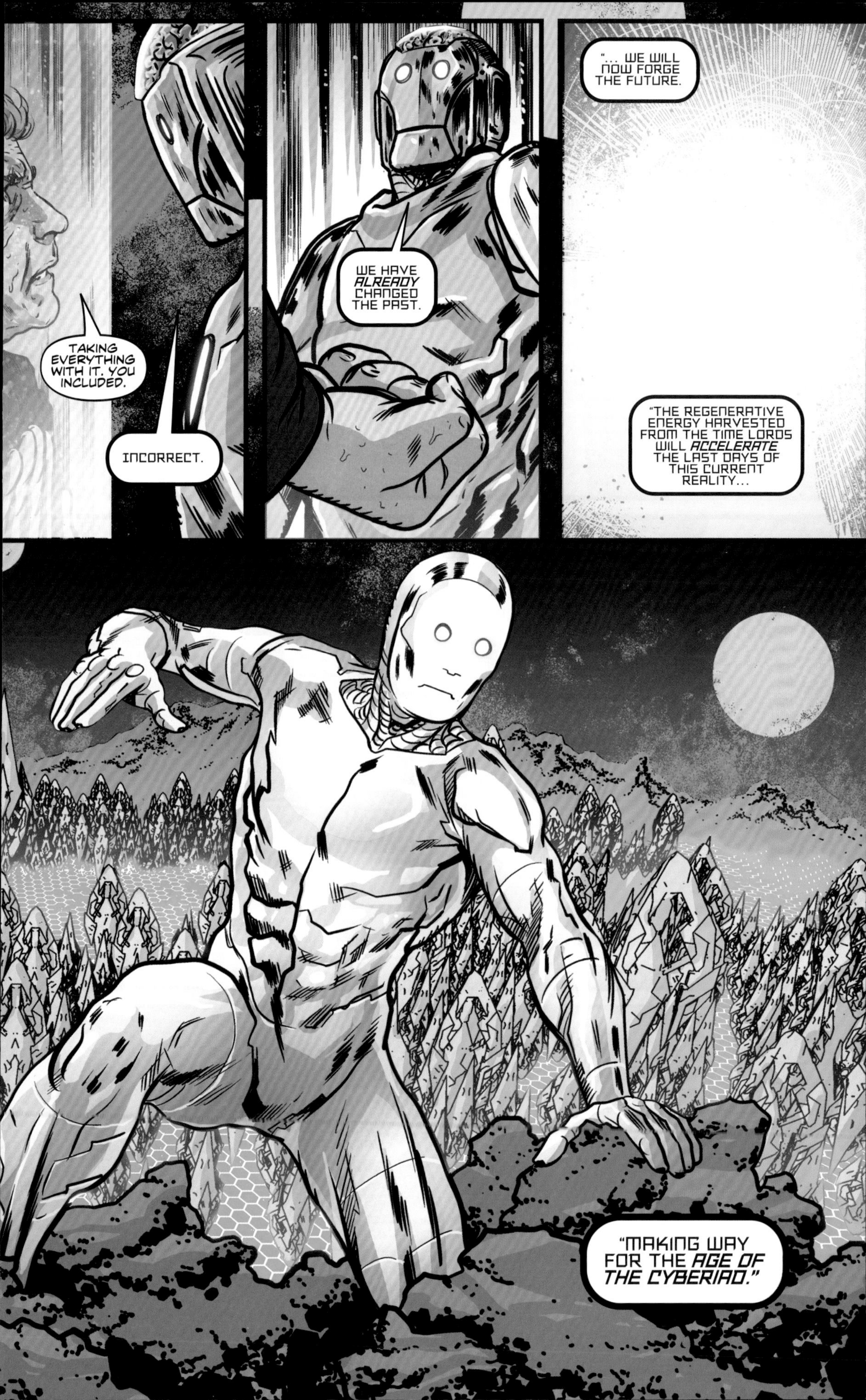
TAKING EVERYTHING WITH IT. YOU INCLUDED.
INCORRECT.
WE HAVE *ALREADY* CHANGED THE PAST.
"... WE WILL NOW FORGE THE FUTURE.
"THE REGENERATIVE ENERGY HARVESTED FROM THE TIME LORDS WILL *ACCELERATE* THE LAST DAYS OF THIS CURRENT REALITY...
"MAKING WAY FOR THE *AGE OF THE CYBERIAD.*"

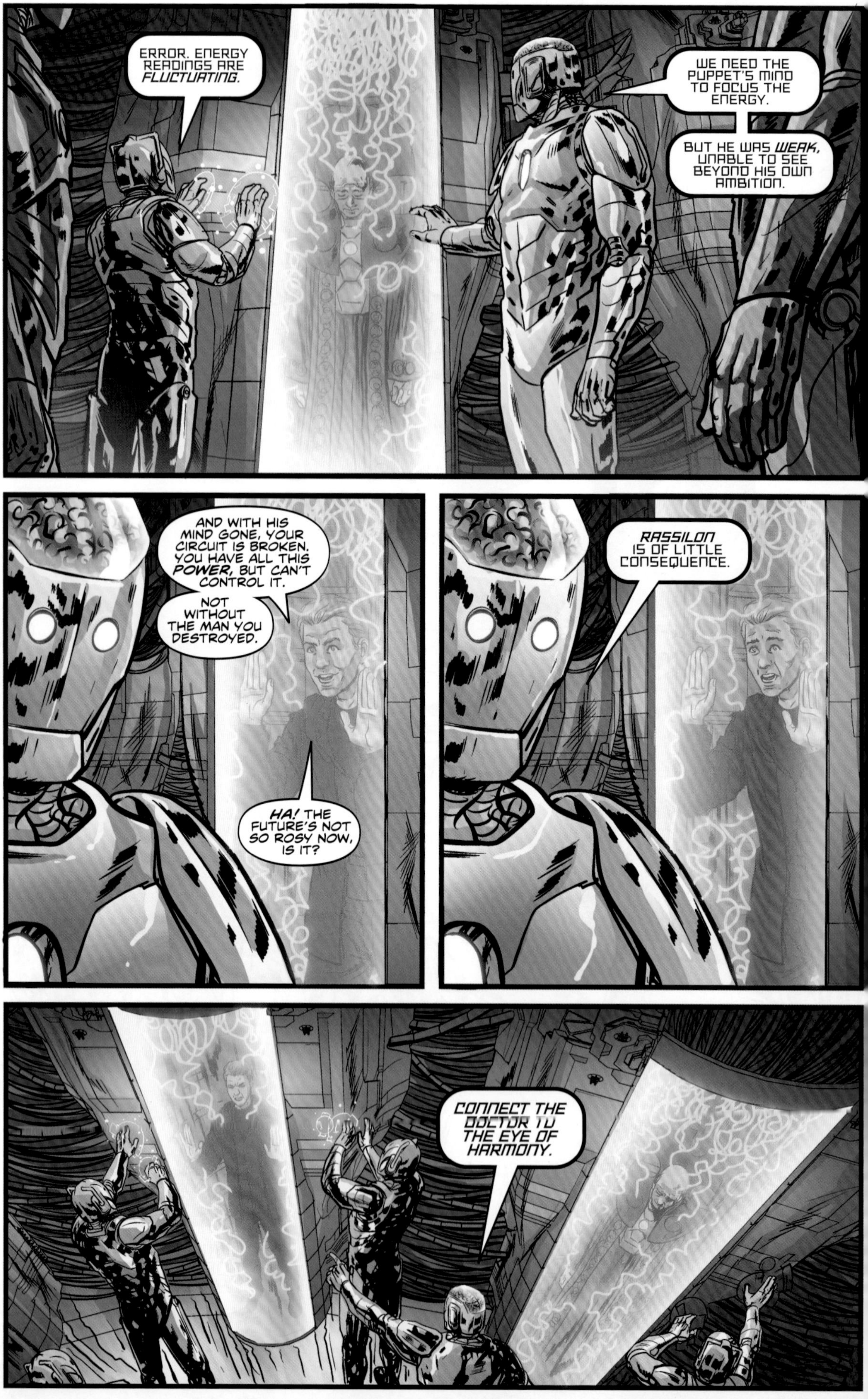
ERROR. ENERGY READINGS ARE *FLUCTUATING*.
WE NEED THE PUPPET'S MIND TO FOCUS THE ENERGY.
BUT HE WAS *WEAK*, UNABLE TO SEE BEYOND HIS OWN AMBITION.
AND WITH HIS MIND GONE, YOUR CIRCUIT IS BROKEN. YOU HAVE ALL THIS *POWER*, BUT CAN'T CONTROL IT.
NOT WITHOUT THE MAN YOU DESTROYED.
HA! THE FUTURE'S NOT SO ROSY NOW, IS IT?
RASSILON IS OF LITTLE CONSEQUENCE.
CONNECT THE DOCTOR TO THE EYE OF HARMONY.

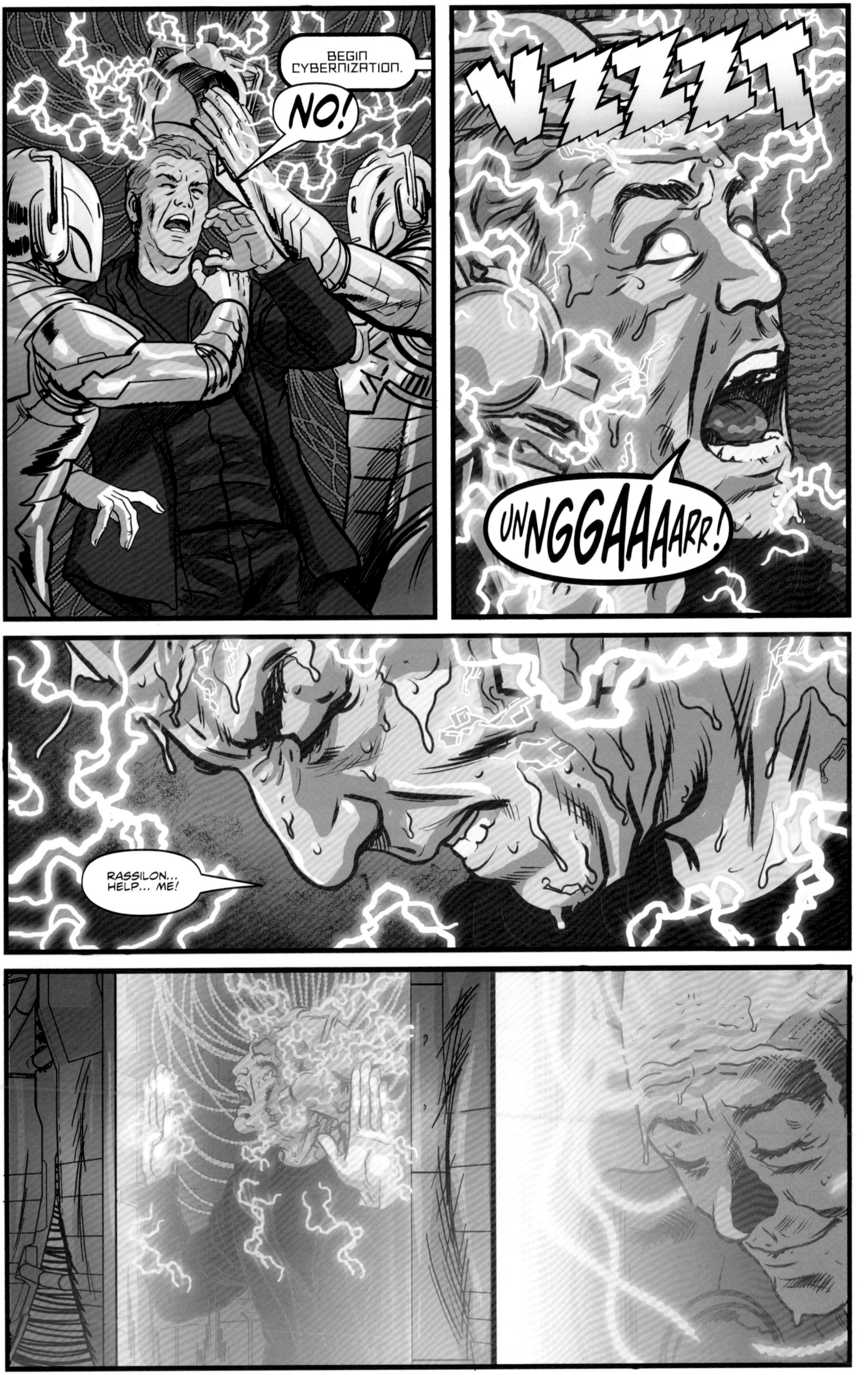
BEGIN CYBERNIZATION.
NO!
VZZZT
UNNGGAAAARR!
RASSILON... HELP... ME!

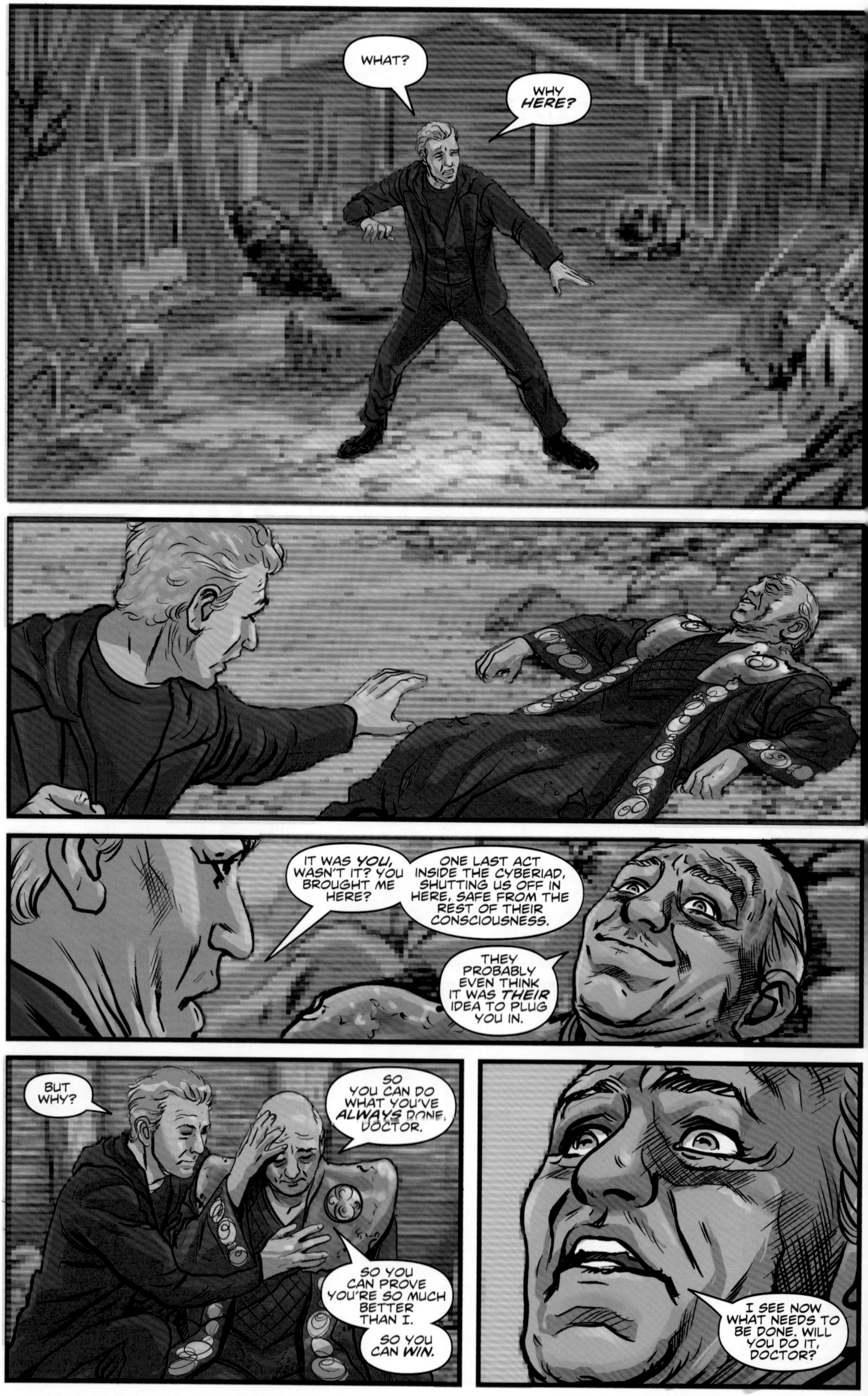
WHAT?
WHY HERE?
IT WAS YOU, WASN'T IT? YOU BROUGHT ME HERE?
ONE LAST ACT INSIDE THE CYBERIAD, SHUTTING US OFF IN HERE, SAFE FROM THE REST OF THEIR CONSCIOUSNESS.
THEY PROBABLY EVEN THINK IT WAS THEIR IDEA TO PLUG YOU IN.
BUT WHY?
SO YOU CAN DO WHAT YOU'VE ALWAYS DONE, DOCTOR.
SO YOU CAN PROVE YOU'RE SO MUCH BETTER THAN I.
SO YOU CAN WIN.
I SEE NOW WHAT NEEDS TO BE DONE. WILL YOU DO IT, DOCTOR?

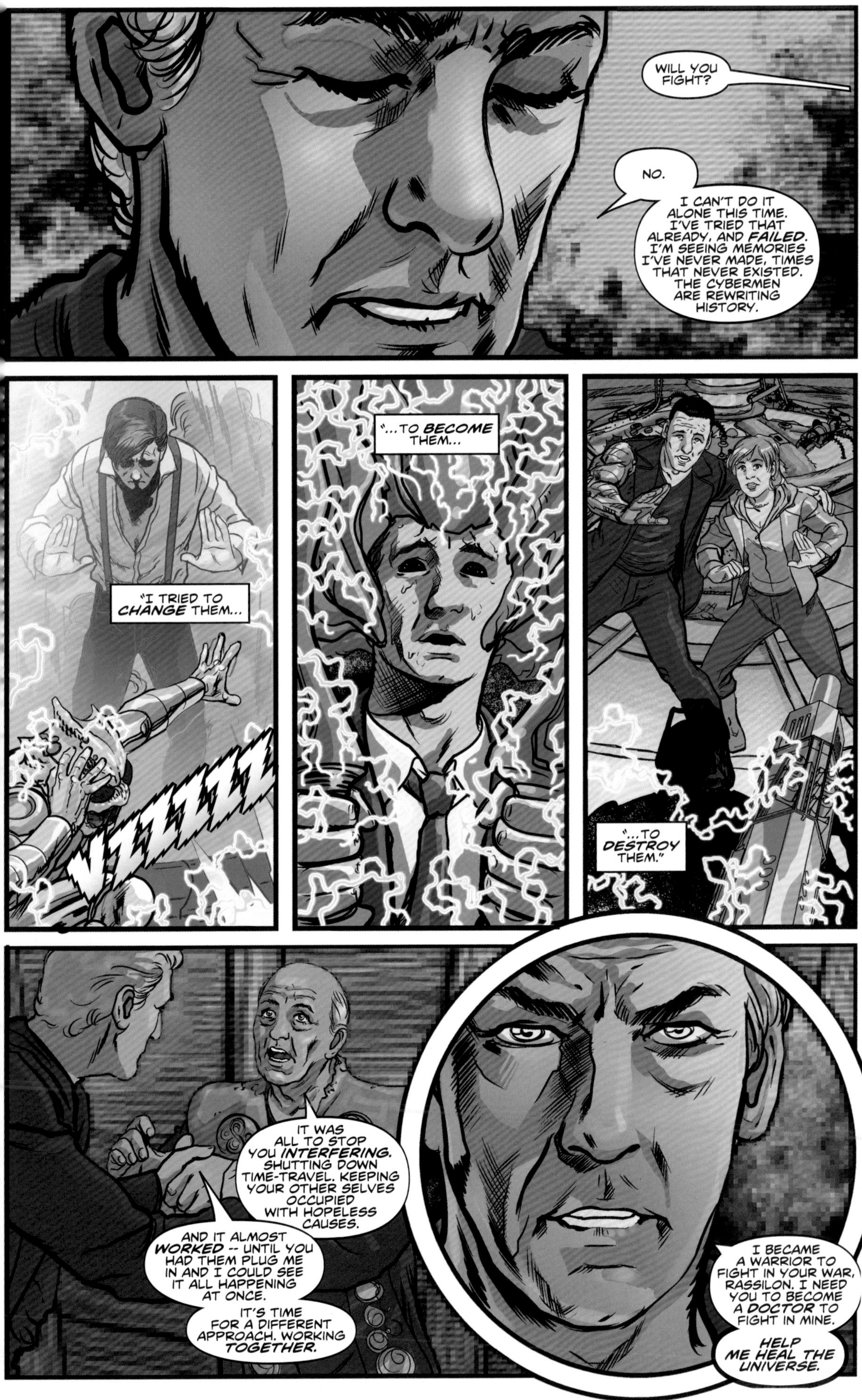
WILL YOU FIGHT?
NO.
I CAN'T DO IT ALONE THIS TIME. I'VE TRIED THAT ALREADY, AND *FAILED*. I'M SEEING MEMORIES I'VE NEVER MADE, TIMES THAT NEVER EXISTED. THE CYBERMEN ARE REWRITING HISTORY.
"I TRIED TO *CHANGE* THEM...
VZZZZZZ
"...TO *BECOME* THEM...
"...TO *DESTROY* THEM."
IT WAS ALL TO STOP YOU *INTERFERING*. SHUTTING DOWN TIME-TRAVEL. KEEPING YOUR OTHER SELVES OCCUPIED WITH HOPELESS CAUSES.
AND IT ALMOST *WORKED* -- UNTIL YOU HAD THEM PLUG ME IN AND I COULD SEE IT ALL HAPPENING AT ONCE.
IT'S TIME FOR A DIFFERENT APPROACH. WORKING *TOGETHER*.
I BECAME A WARRIOR TO FIGHT IN YOUR WAR, RASSILON. I NEED YOU TO BECOME A *DOCTOR* TO FIGHT IN MINE.
HELP ME HEAL THE UNIVERSE.

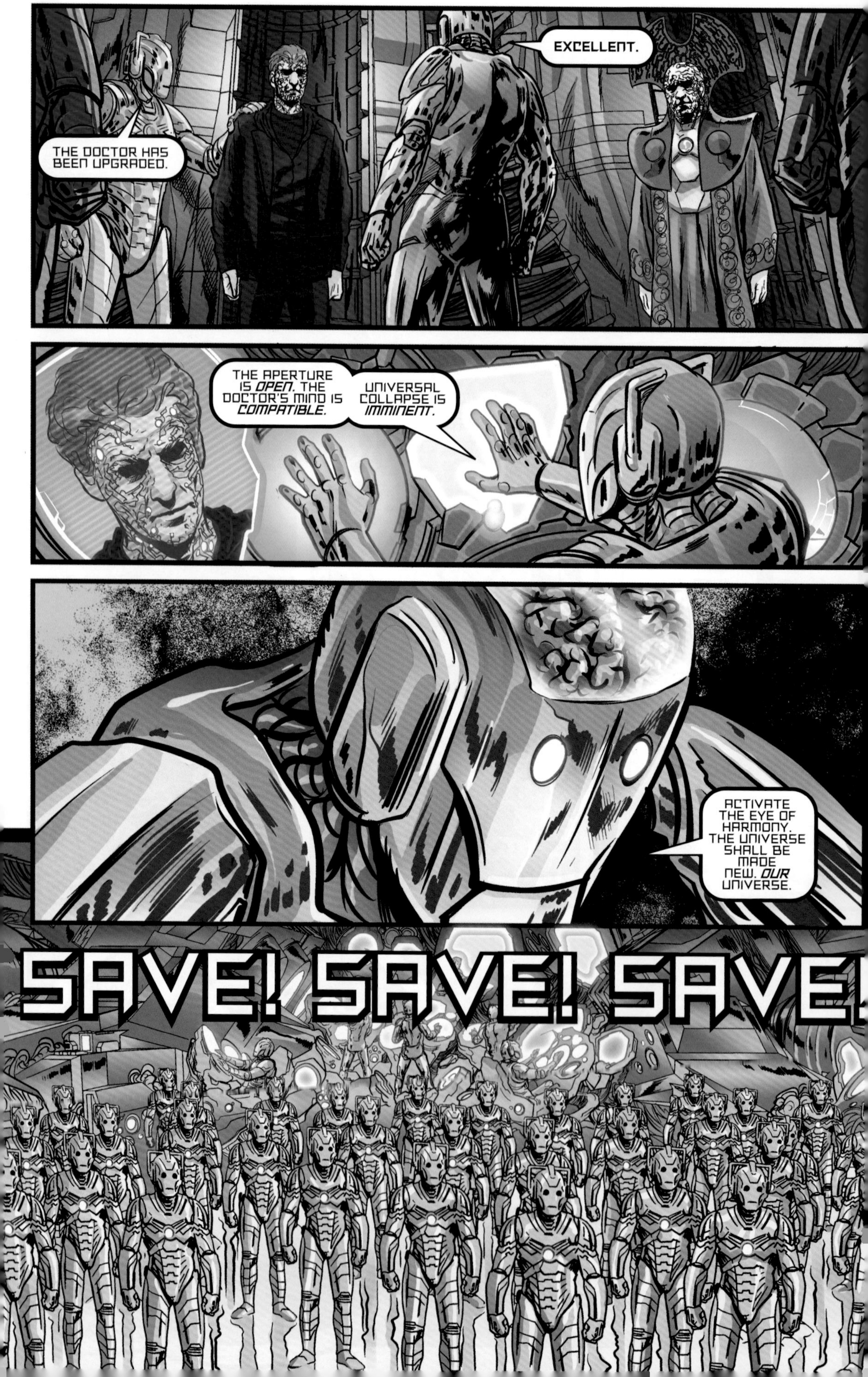
EXCELLENT.
THE DOCTOR HAS BEEN UPGRADED.
THE APERTURE IS OPEN. THE DOCTOR'S MIND IS COMPATIBLE.
UNIVERSAL COLLAPSE IS IMMINENT.
ACTIVATE THE EYE OF HARMONY. THE UNIVERSE SHALL BE MADE NEW. OUR UNIVERSE.
SAVE! SAVE! SAVE!

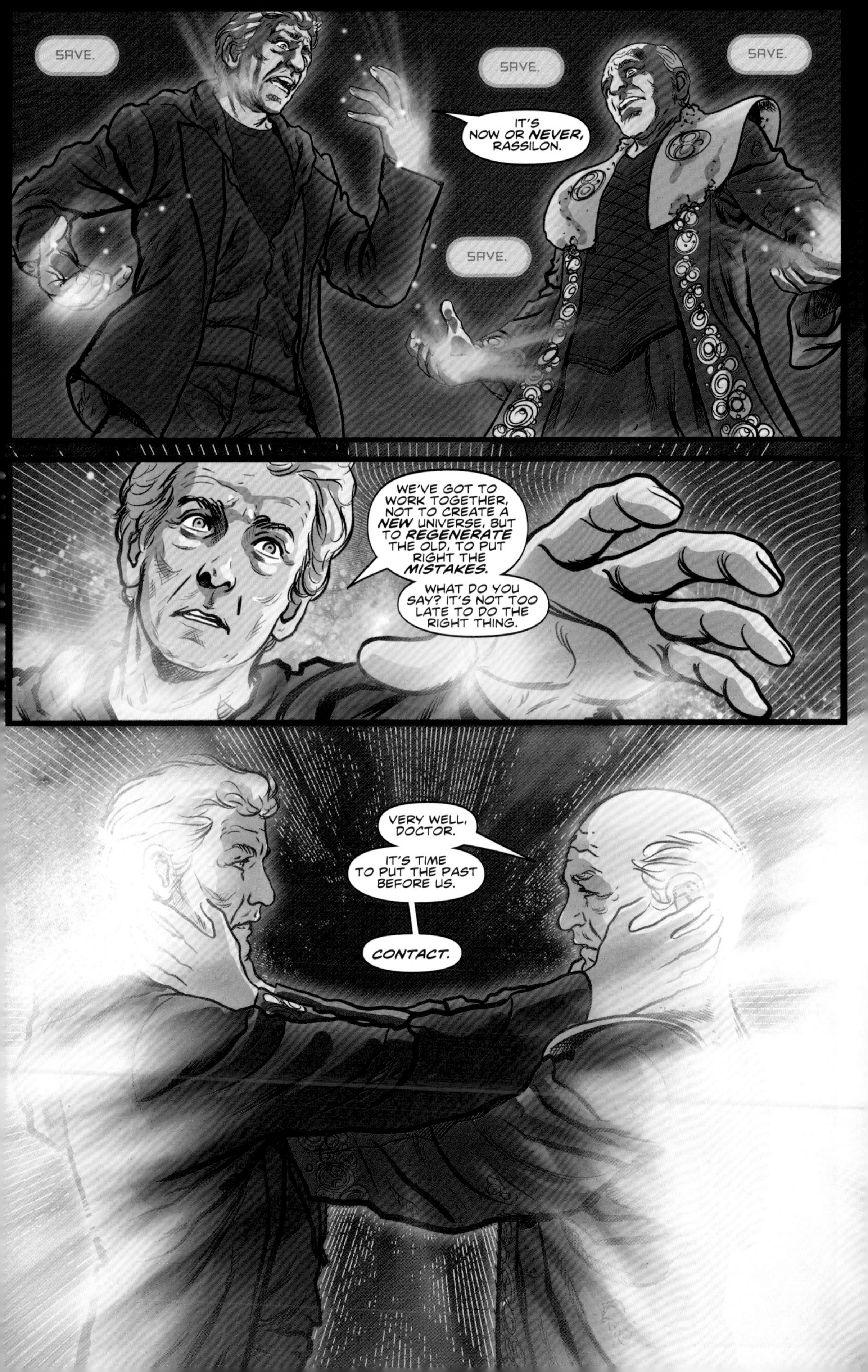
SAVE.
SAVE.
SAVE.
IT'S NOW OR NEVER, RASSILON.
SAVE.
WE'VE GOT TO WORK TOGETHER, NOT TO CREATE A NEW UNIVERSE, BUT TO REGENERATE THE OLD, TO PUT RIGHT THE MISTAKES.
WHAT DO YOU SAY? IT'S NOT TOO LATE TO DO THE RIGHT THING.
VERY WELL, DOCTOR.
IT'S TIME TO PUT THE PAST BEFORE US.
CONTACT.

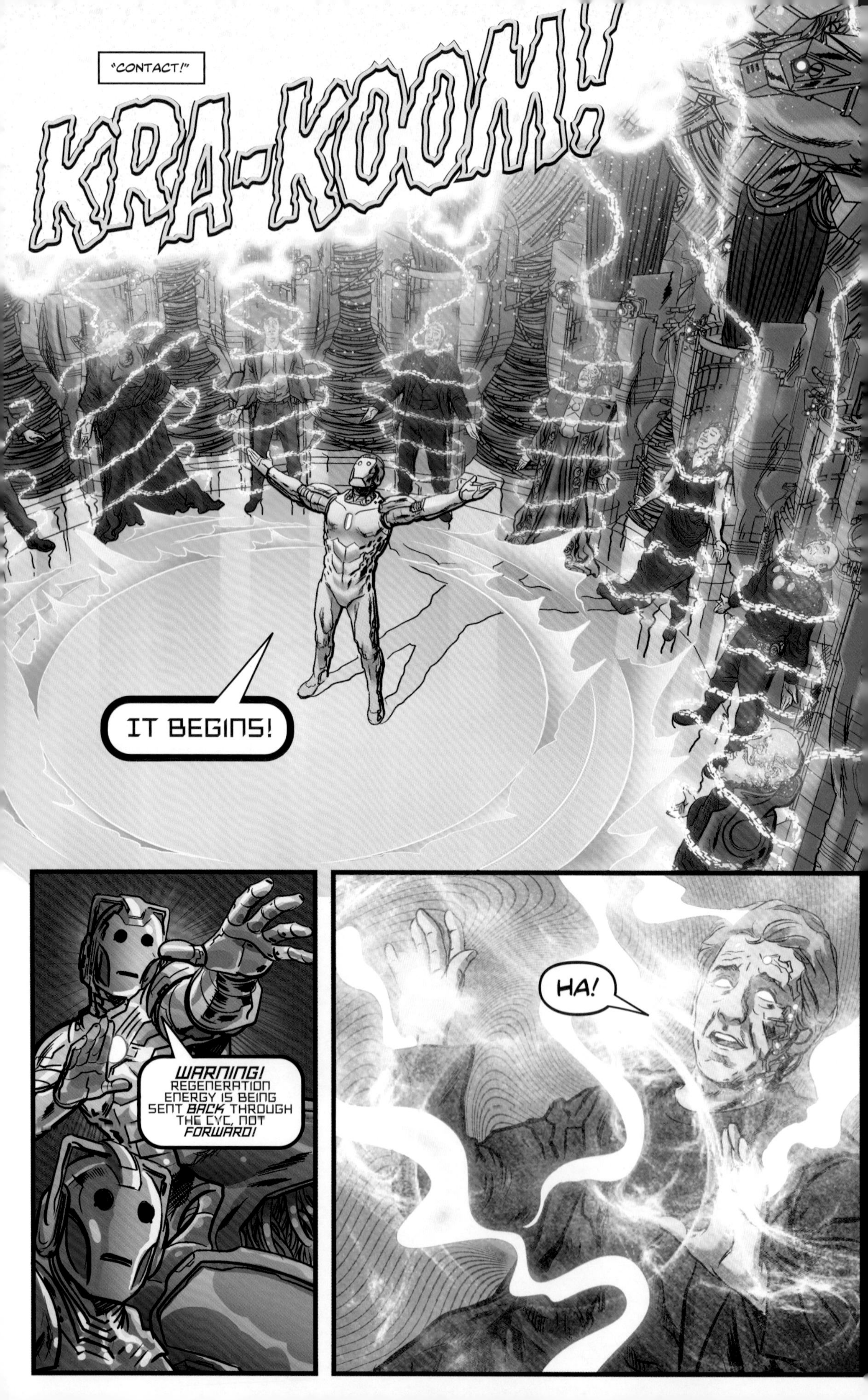
"CONTACT!"
KRA-KOOM!
IT BEGINS!
WARNING! REGENERATION ENERGY IS BEING SENT BACK THROUGH THE CYC, NOT FORWARD!
HA!

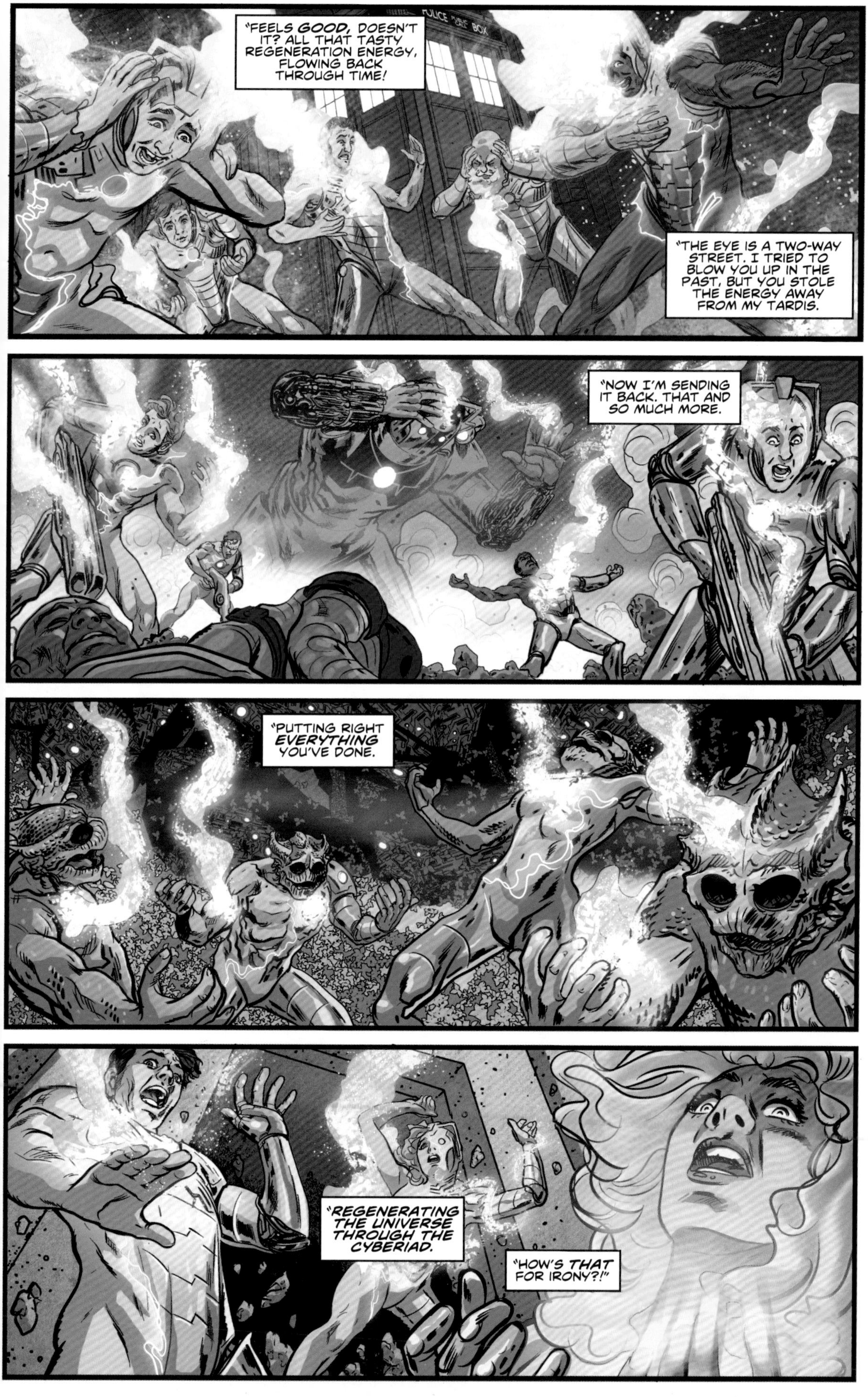
"FEELS GOOD, DOESN'T IT? ALL THAT TASTY REGENERATION ENERGY, FLOWING BACK THROUGH TIME!
POLICE BOX
"THE EYE IS A TWO-WAY STREET. I TRIED TO BLOW YOU UP IN THE PAST, BUT YOU STOLE THE ENERGY AWAY FROM MY TARDIS.
"NOW I'M SENDING IT BACK. THAT AND SO MUCH MORE.
"PUTTING RIGHT EVERYTHING YOU'VE DONE.
"REGENERATING THE UNIVERSE THROUGH THE CYBERIAD.
"HOW'S THAT FOR IRONY?!"

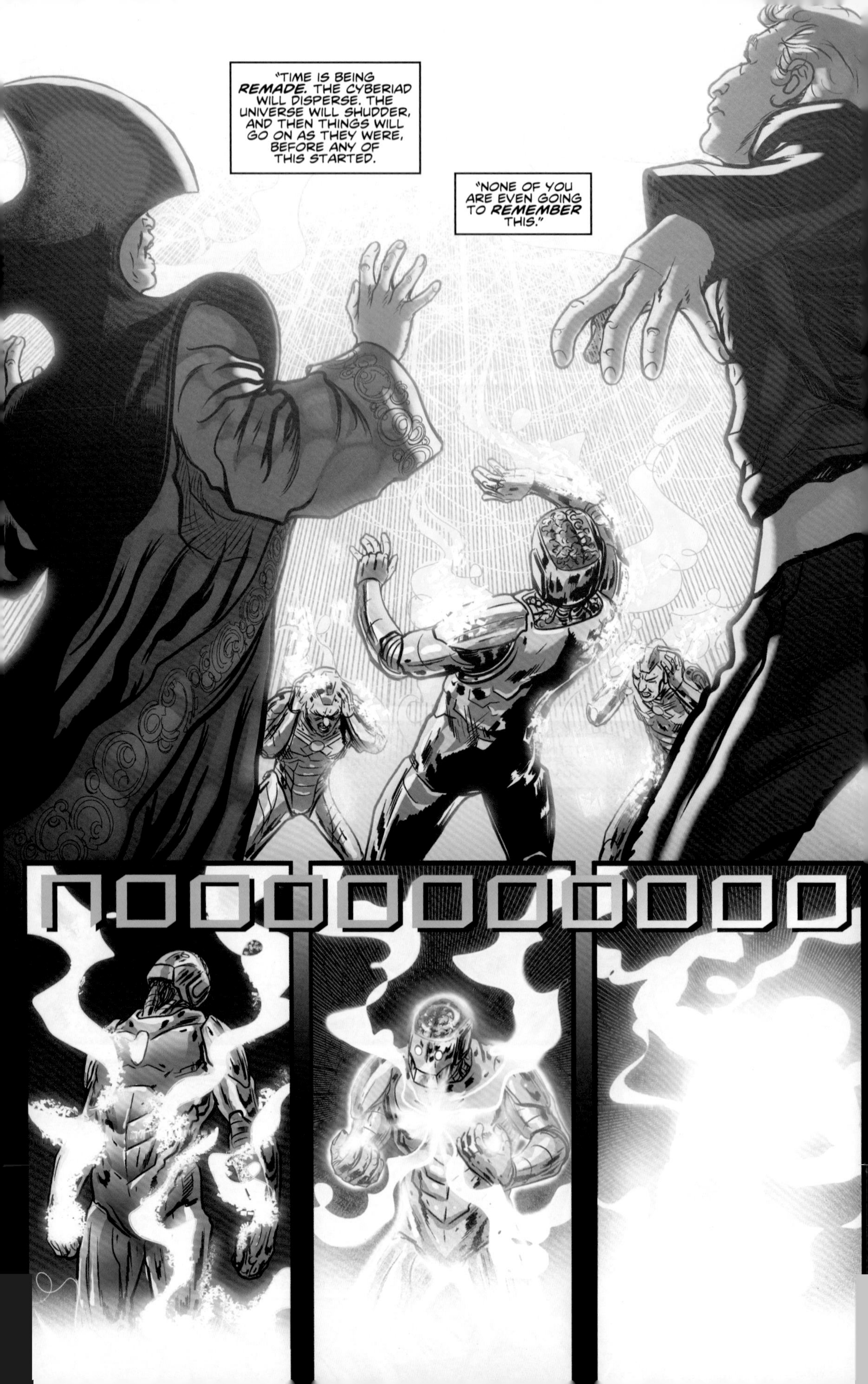
"TIME IS BEING REMADE. THE CYBERIAD WILL DISPERSE. THE UNIVERSE WILL SHUDDER, AND THEN THINGS WILL GO ON AS THEY WERE, BEFORE ANY OF THIS STARTED.
"NONE OF YOU ARE EVEN GOING TO REMEMBER THIS."
NOOOOOOOOOOO

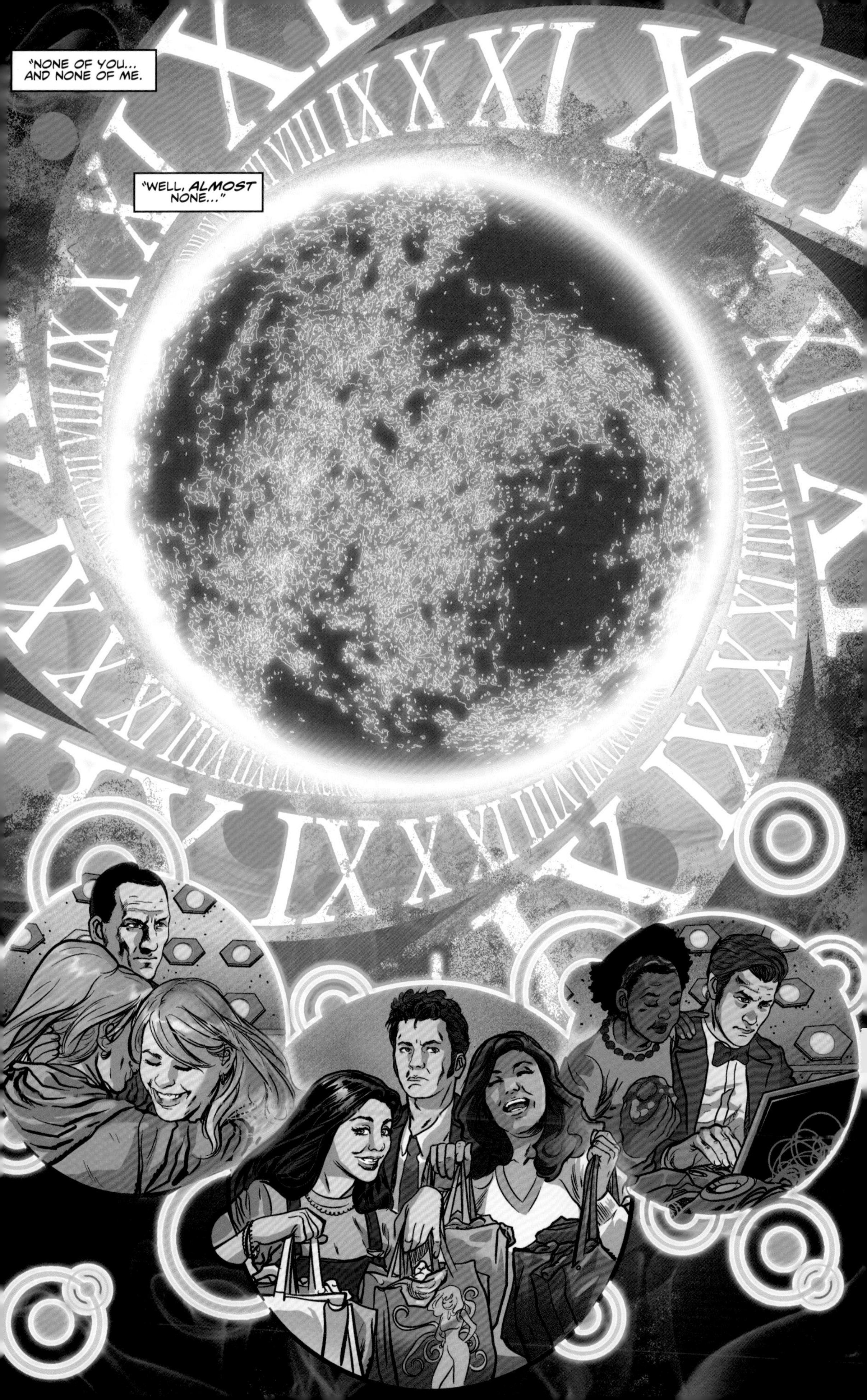
"NONE OF YOU...
AND NONE OF ME.
"WELL, *ALMOST*
NONE..."

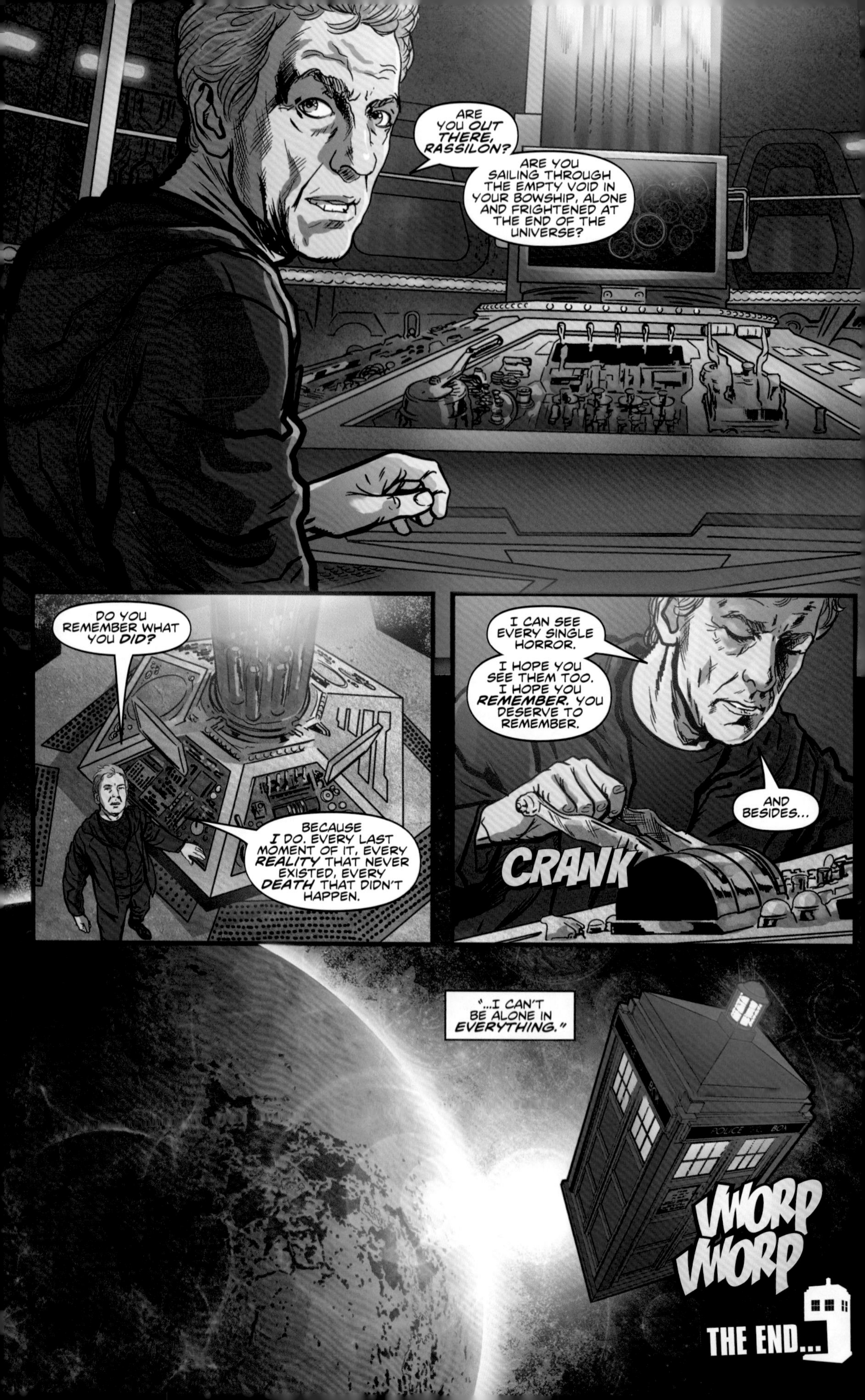
ARE YOU OUT THERE, RASSILON?
ARE YOU SAILING THROUGH THE EMPTY VOID IN YOUR BOWSHIP, ALONE AND FRIGHTENED AT THE END OF THE UNIVERSE?
DO YOU REMEMBER WHAT YOU DID?
BECAUSE I DO. EVERY LAST MOMENT OF IT, EVERY REALITY THAT NEVER EXISTED, EVERY DEATH THAT DIDN'T HAPPEN.
I CAN SEE EVERY SINGLE HORROR.
I HOPE YOU SEE THEM TOO. I HOPE YOU REMEMBER. YOU DESERVE TO REMEMBER.
AND BESIDES...
CRANK
"...I CAN'T BE ALONE IN EVERYTHING."
POLICE BOX
VWORP VWORP
THE END...

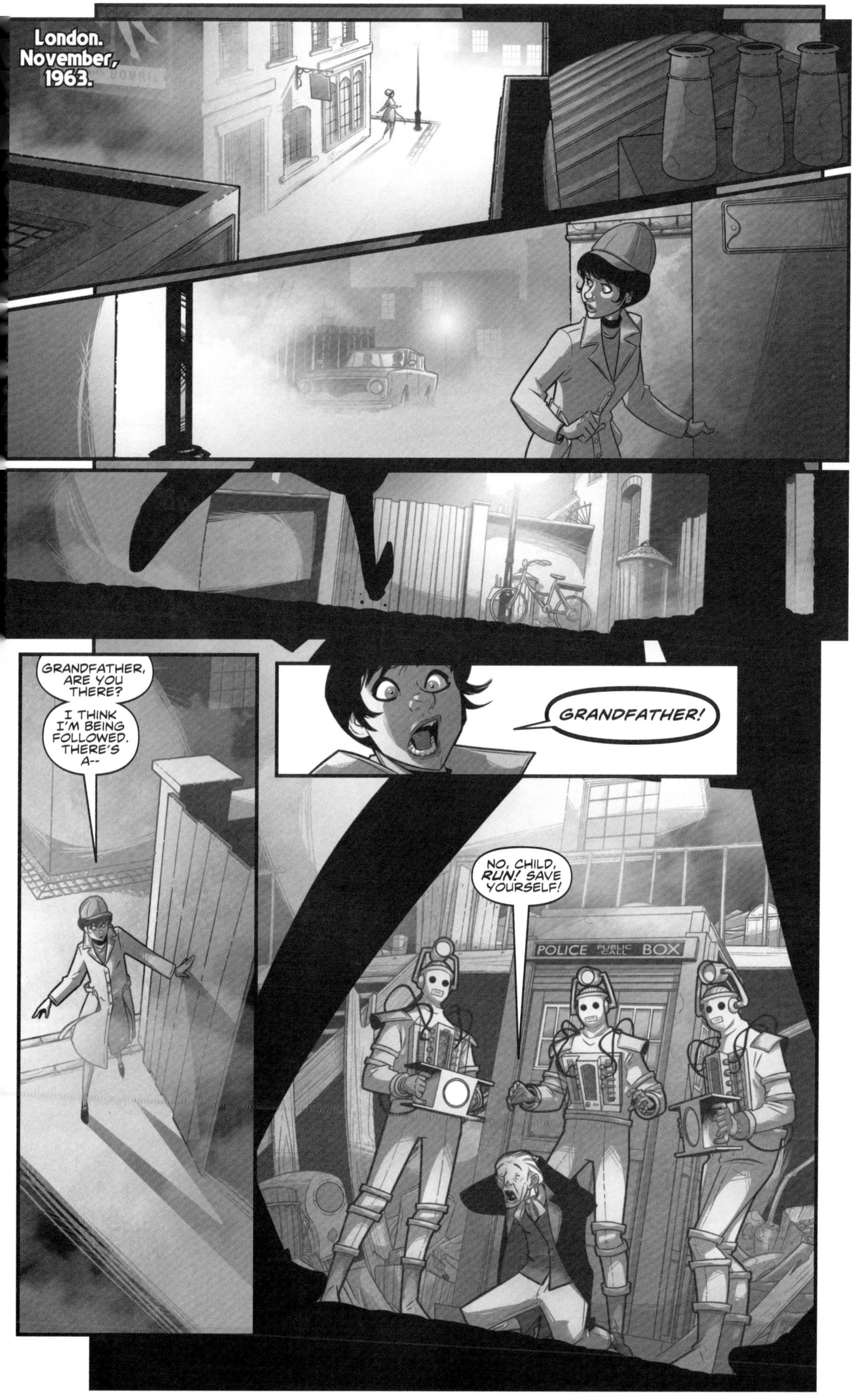
London. November, 1963.
GRANDFATHER, ARE YOU THERE?
I THINK I'M BEING FOLLOWED. THERE'S A--
GRANDFATHER!
POLICE PUBLIC CALL BOX
NO, CHILD, RUN! SAVE YOURSELF!

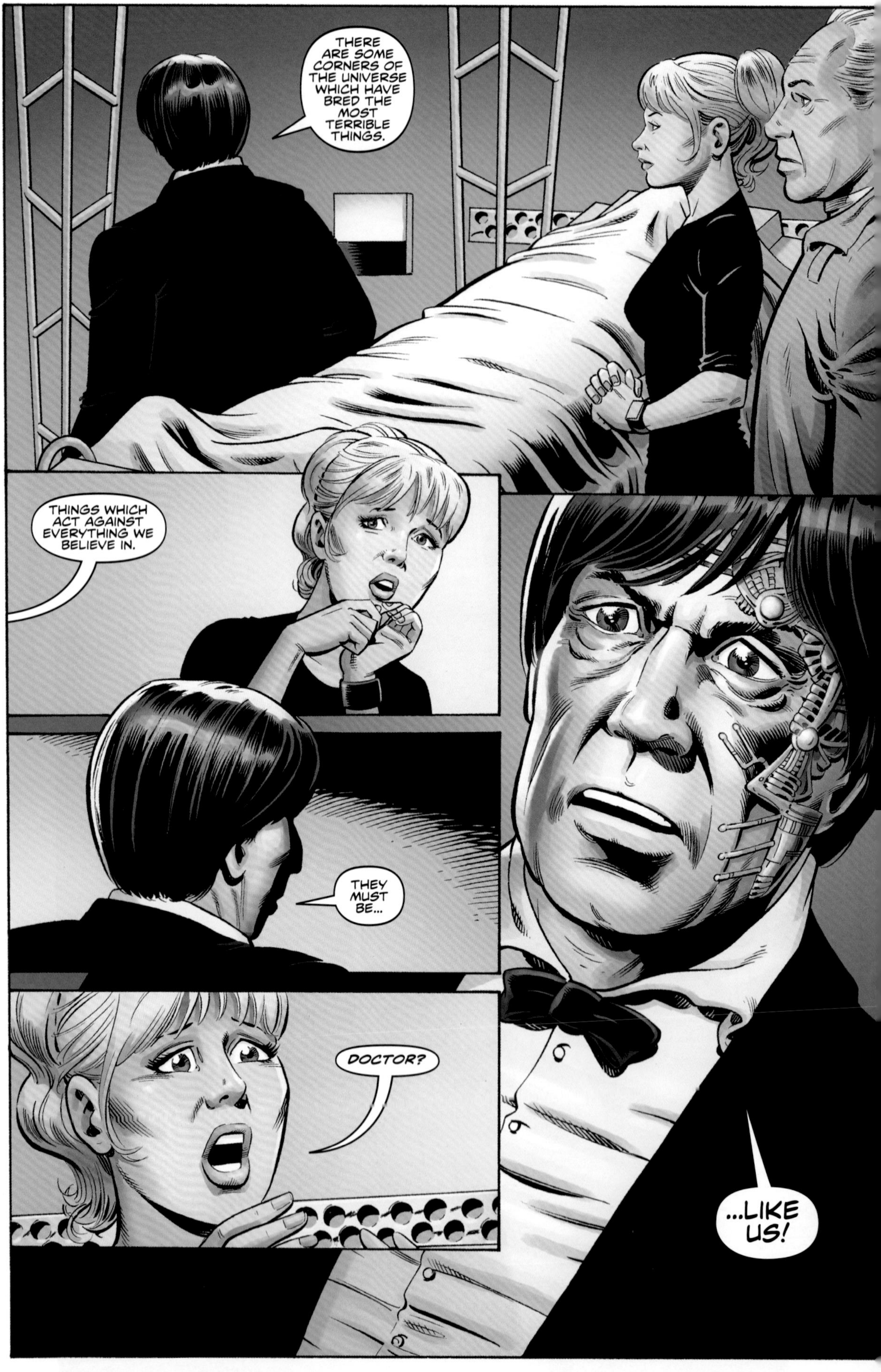
THERE ARE SOME CORNERS OF THE UNIVERSE WHICH HAVE BRED THE MOST TERRIBLE THINGS.
THINGS WHICH ACT AGAINST EVERYTHING WE BELIEVE IN.
THEY MUST BE...
DOCTOR?
...LIKE US!

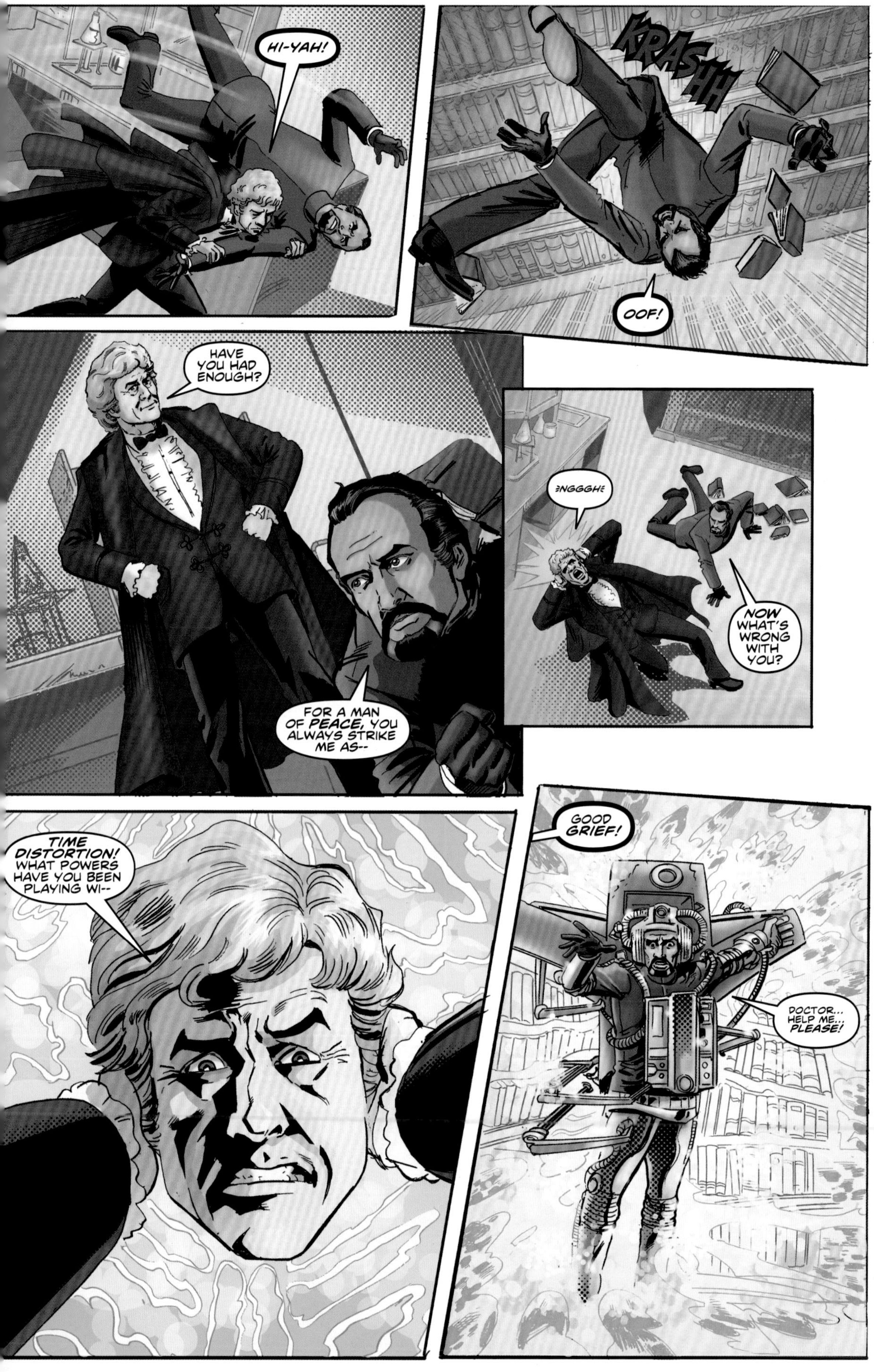

HI-YAH!
KRASHH
OOF!
HAVE YOU HAD ENOUGH?
FOR A MAN OF PEACE, YOU ALWAYS STRIKE ME AS--
NGGGH
NOW WHAT'S WRONG WITH YOU?
TIME DISTORTION! WHAT POWERS HAVE YOU BEEN PLAYING WI--
GOOD GRIEF!
DOCTOR... HELP ME... PLEASE!

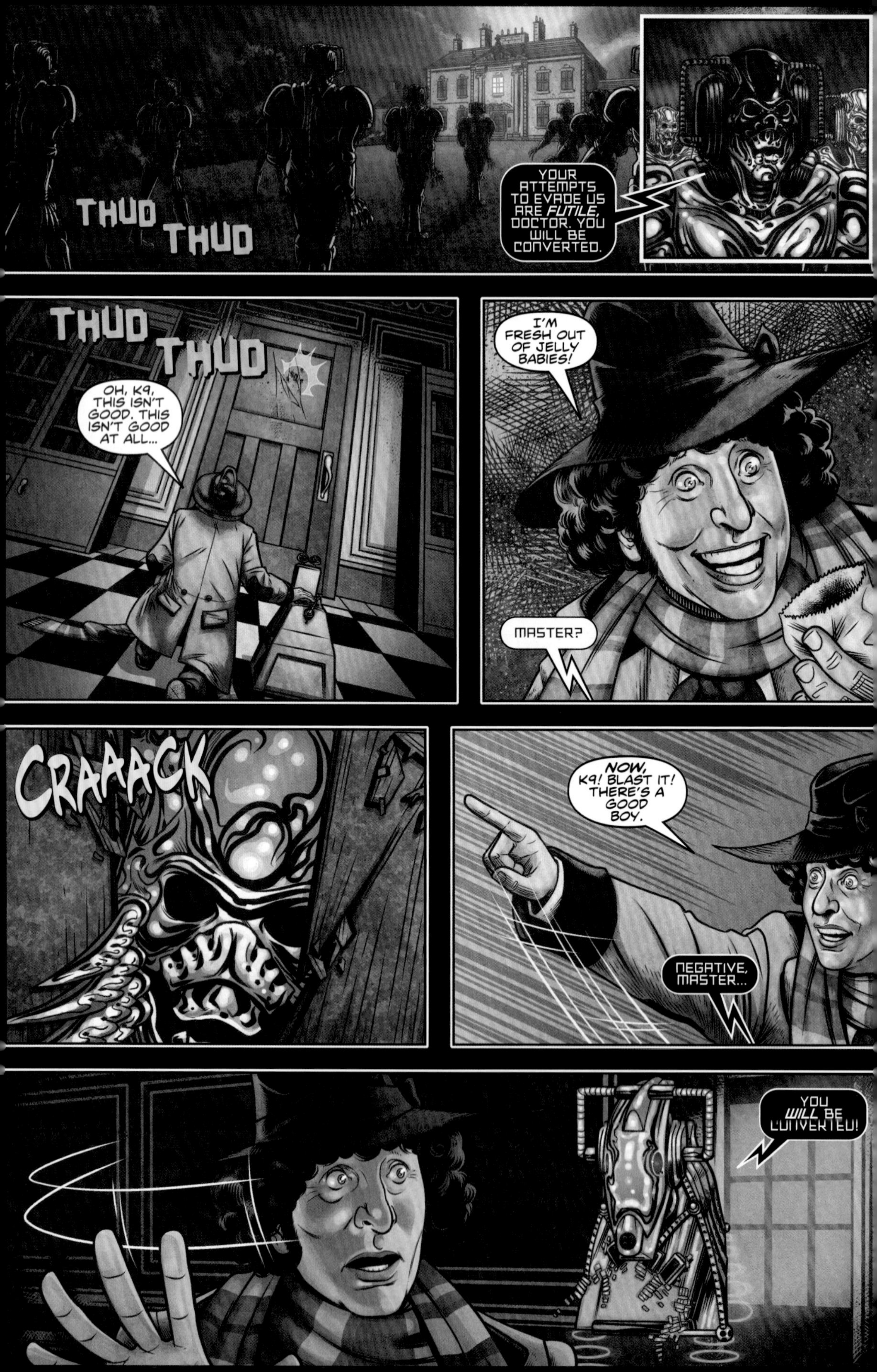
THUD THUD
YOUR ATTEMPTS TO EVADE US ARE FUTILE, DOCTOR. YOU WILL BE CONVERTED.
THUD THUD
OH, K9, THIS ISN'T GOOD. THIS ISN'T GOOD AT ALL...
I'M FRESH OUT OF JELLY BABIES!
MASTER?
CRAAACK
NOW, K9! BLAST IT! THERE'S A GOOD BOY.
NEGATIVE, MASTER...
YOU WILL BE CONVERTED!

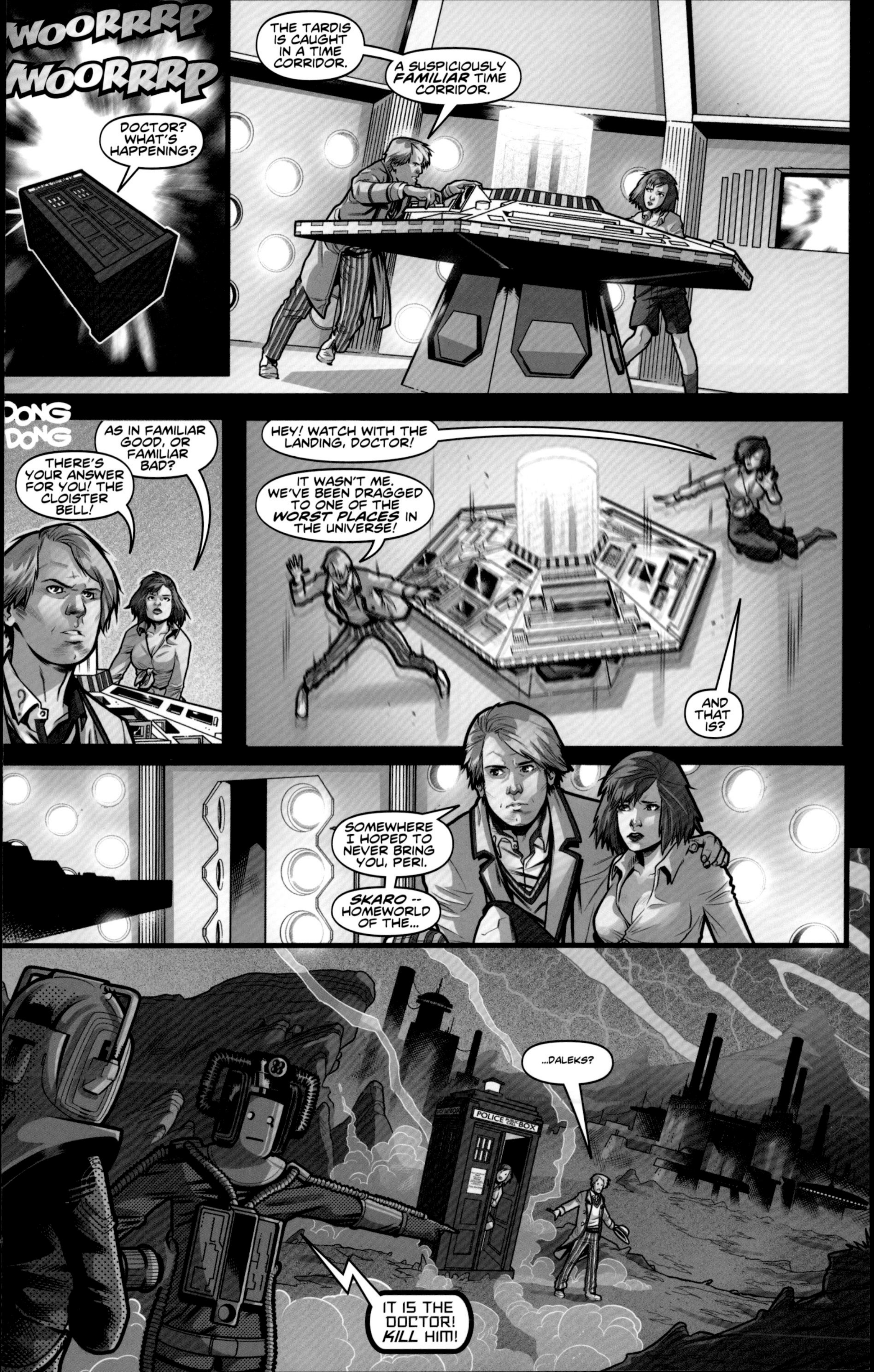
WOORRRP
WOORRRP
DOCTOR? WHAT'S HAPPENING?
THE TARDIS IS CAUGHT IN A TIME CORRIDOR.
A SUSPICIOUSLY FAMILIAR TIME CORRIDOR.
DONG
DONG
AS IN FAMILIAR GOOD, OR FAMILIAR BAD?
THERE'S YOUR ANSWER FOR YOU! THE CLOISTER BELL!
HEY! WATCH WITH THE LANDING, DOCTOR!
IT WASN'T ME. WE'VE BEEN DRAGGED TO ONE OF THE WORST PLACES IN THE UNIVERSE!
AND THAT IS?
SOMEWHERE I HOPED TO NEVER BRING YOU, PERI.
SKARO -- HOMEWORLD OF THE...
...DALEKS?
POLICE PUBLIC CALL BOX
IT IS THE DOCTOR! KILL HIM!

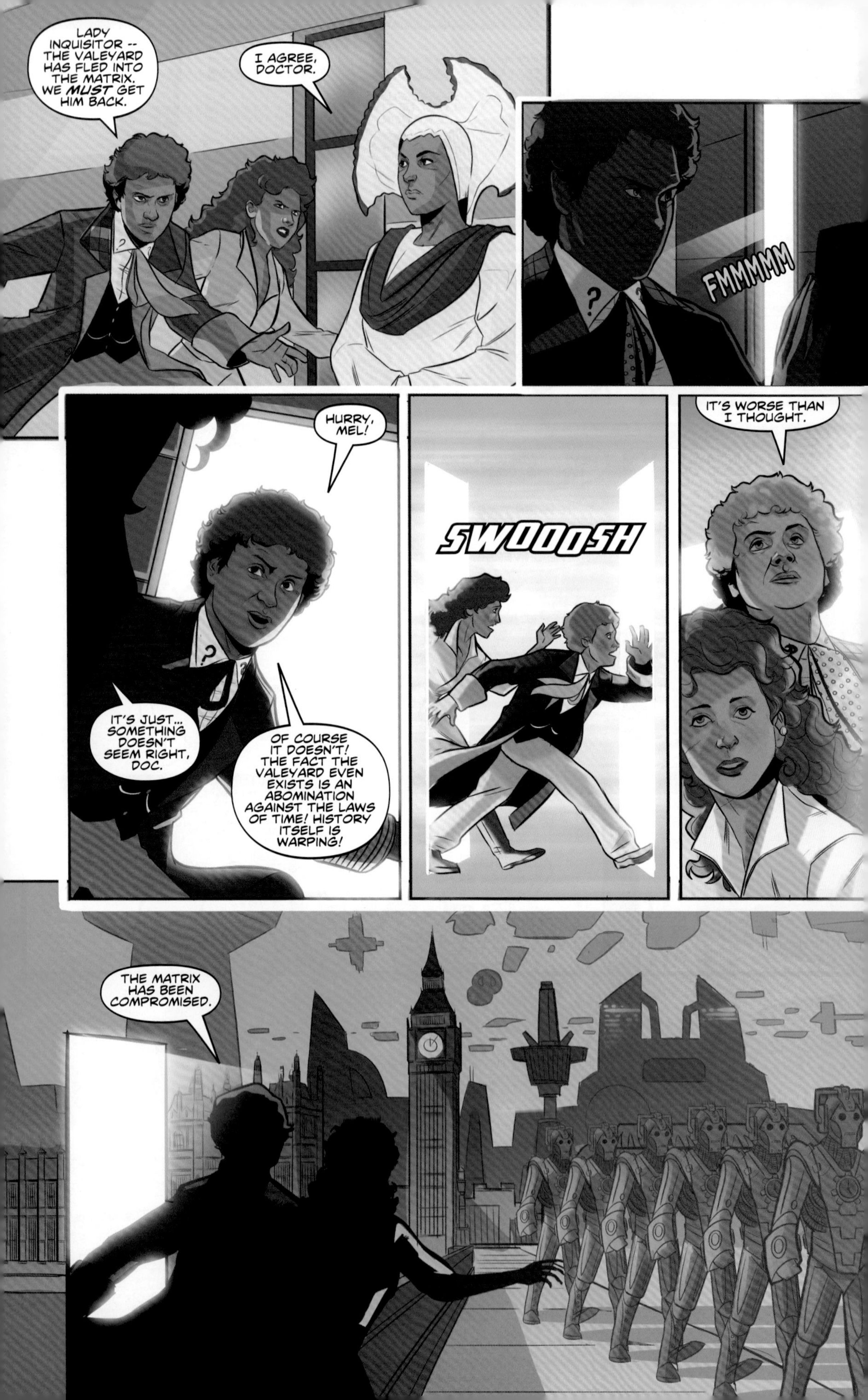
LADY INQUISITOR -- THE VALEYARD HAS FLED INTO THE MATRIX. WE *MUST* GET HIM BACK.
I AGREE, DOCTOR.
FMMMMM
HURRY, MEL!
IT'S JUST... SOMETHING DOESN'T SEEM RIGHT, DOC.
OF COURSE IT DOESN'T! THE FACT THE VALEYARD EVEN EXISTS IS AN ABOMINATION AGAINST THE LAWS OF TIME! HISTORY ITSELF IS WARPING!
SWOOOSH
IT'S WORSE THAN I THOUGHT.
THE MATRIX HAS BEEN COMPROMISED.

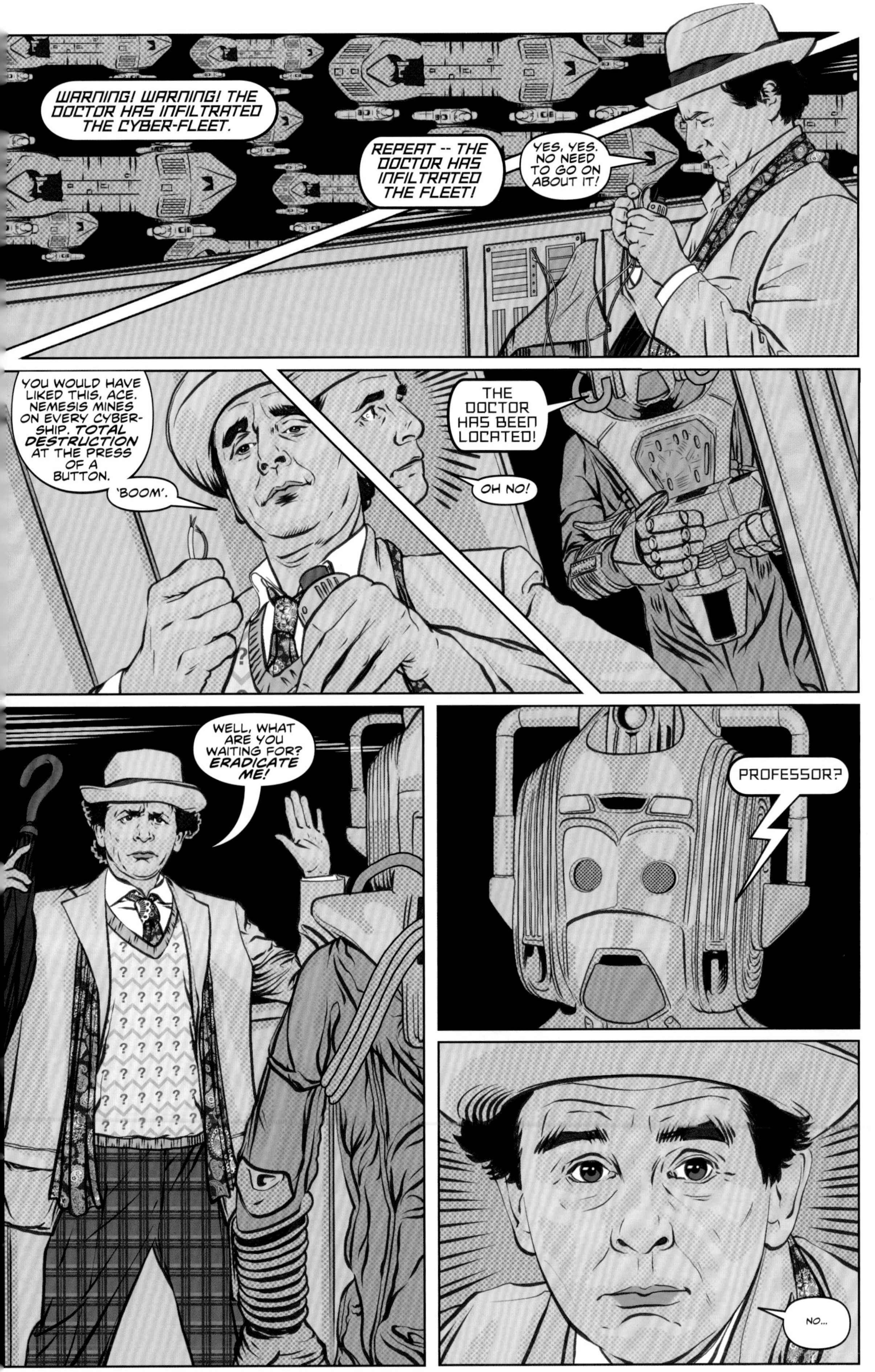
WARNING! WARNING! THE DOCTOR HAS INFILTRATED THE CYBER-FLEET.
REPEAT -- THE DOCTOR HAS INFILTRATED THE FLEET!
YES, YES. NO NEED TO GO ON ABOUT IT!
YOU WOULD HAVE LIKED THIS, ACE. NEMESIS MINES ON EVERY CYBER-SHIP. TOTAL DESTRUCTION AT THE PRESS OF A BUTTON.
'BOOM'.
THE DOCTOR HAS BEEN LOCATED!
OH NO!
WELL, WHAT ARE YOU WAITING FOR? ERADICATE ME!
PROFESSOR?
NO...

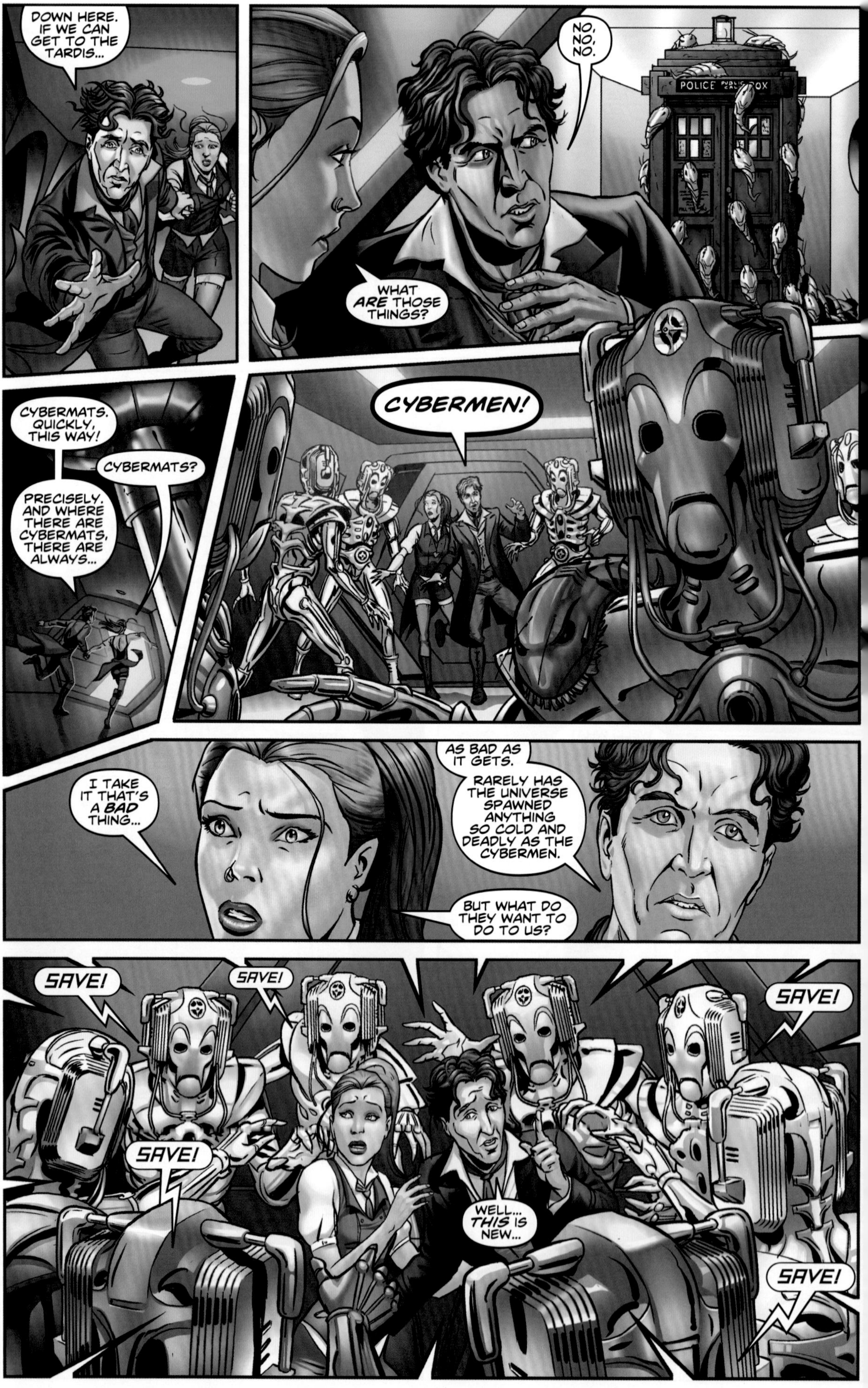
DOWN HERE. IF WE CAN GET TO THE TARDIS...
NO, NO, NO.
POLICE PUBLIC CALL BOX
WHAT *ARE* THOSE THINGS?
CYBERMATS. QUICKLY, THIS WAY!
CYBERMATS?
PRECISELY. AND WHERE THERE ARE CYBERMATS, THERE ARE ALWAYS...
CYBERMEN!
I TAKE IT THAT'S A *BAD* THING...
AS BAD AS IT GETS.
RARELY HAS THE UNIVERSE SPAWNED ANYTHING SO COLD AND DEADLY AS THE CYBERMEN.
BUT WHAT DO THEY WANT TO DO TO US?
SAVE!
SAVE!
SAVE!
SAVE!
WELL... *THIS* IS NEW...
SAVE!

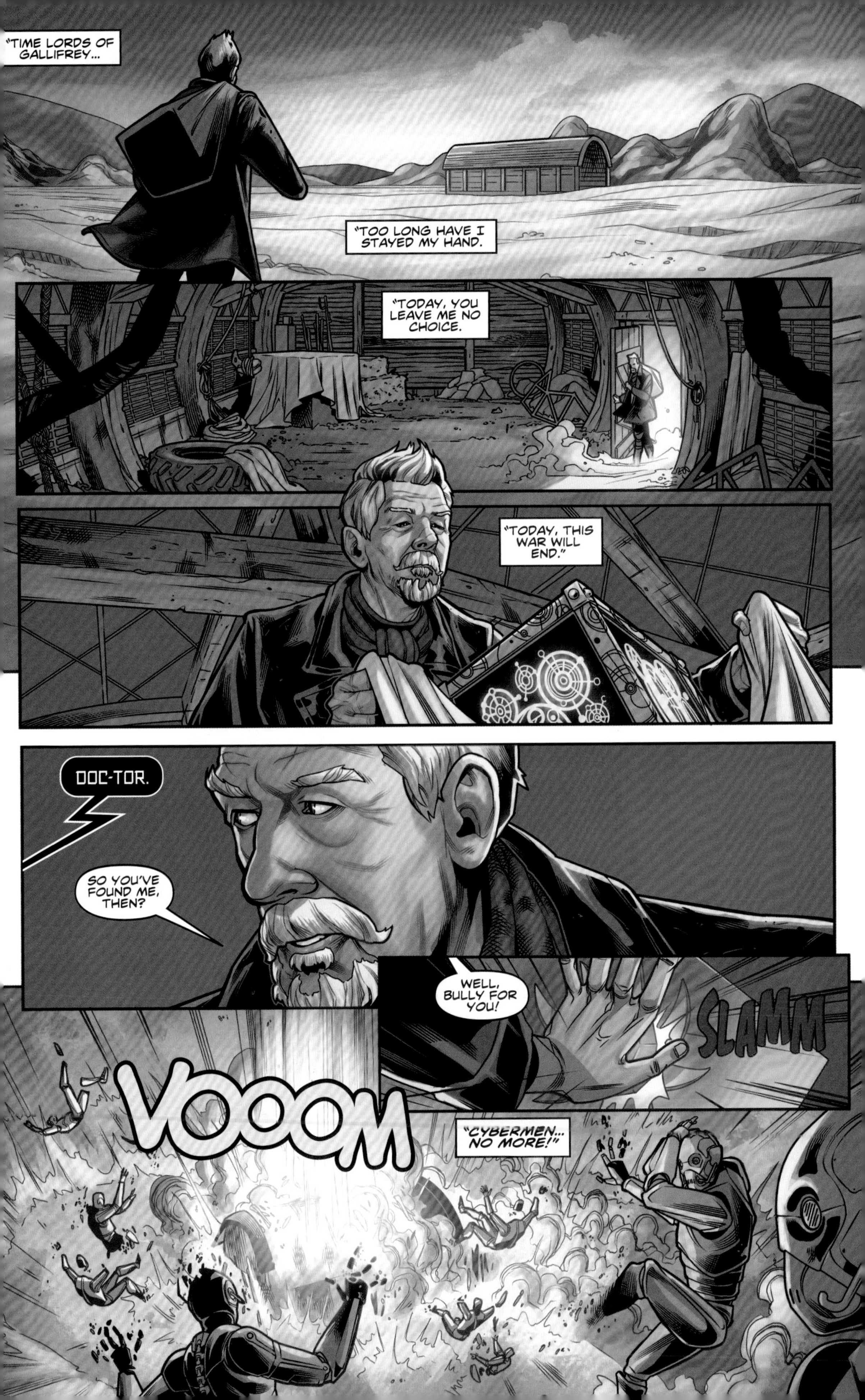
"TIME LORDS OF GALLIFREY...
"TOO LONG HAVE I STAYED MY HAND.
"TODAY, YOU LEAVE ME NO CHOICE.
"TODAY, THIS WAR WILL END."
DOC-TOR.
SO YOU'VE FOUND ME, THEN?
WELL, BULLY FOR YOU!
SLAMM
VOOOM
"CYBERMEN... NO MORE!"

COVER A
BY ALESSANDRO VITTI & NICOLA RIGHI

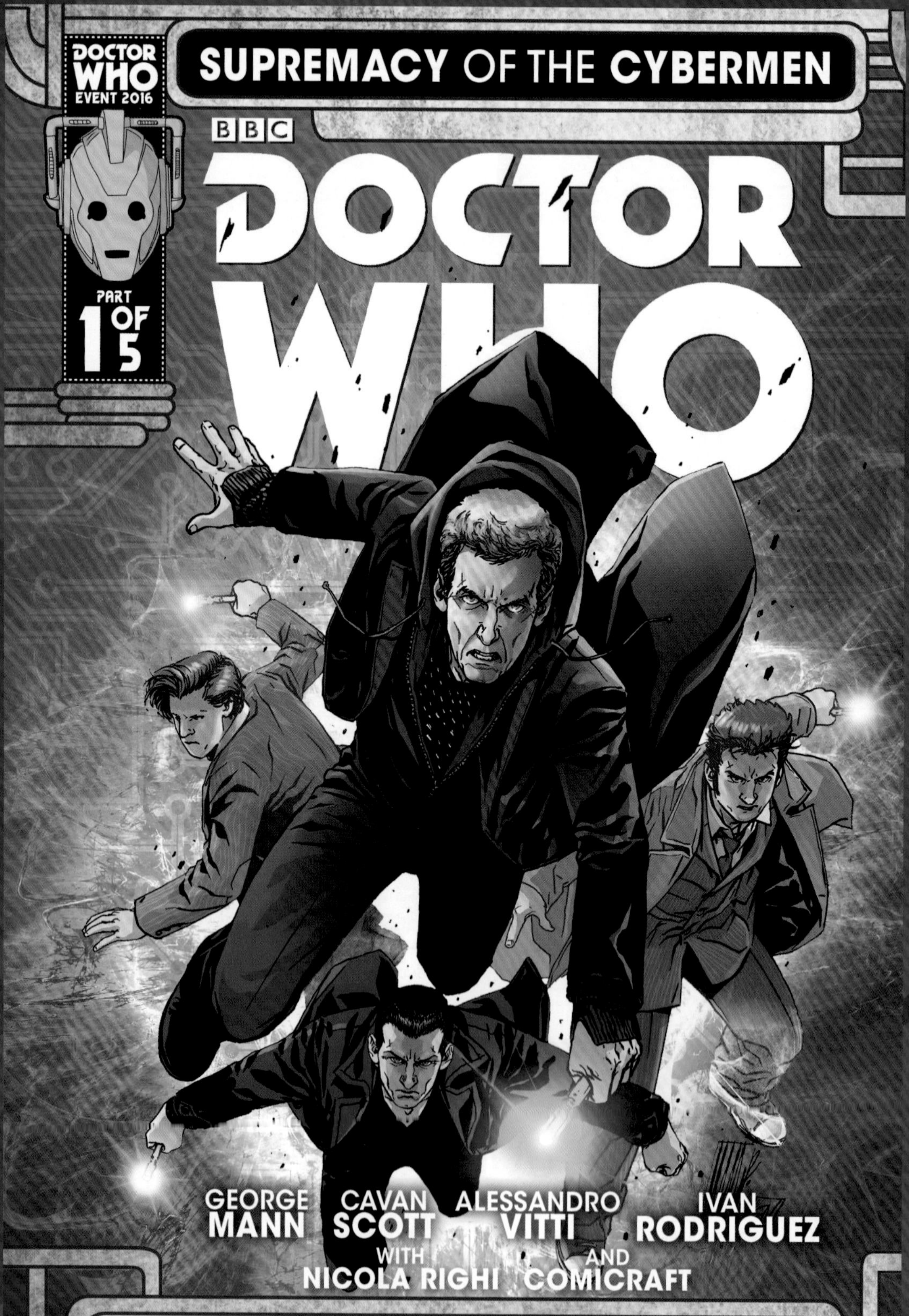

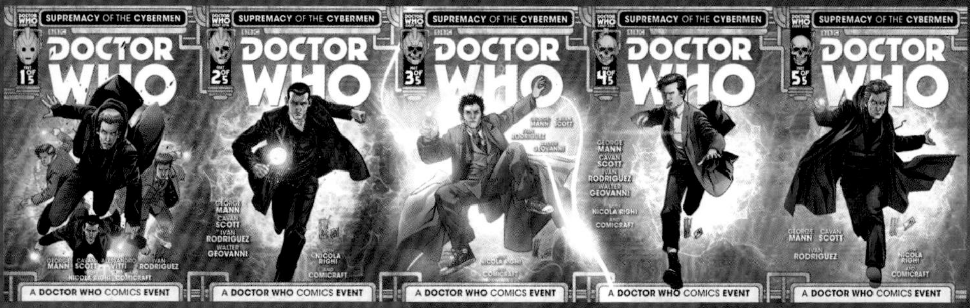
SUPREMACY OF THE CYBERMEN
DOCTOR WHO
A DOCTOR WHO COMICS EVENT

Collect all 5 covers!

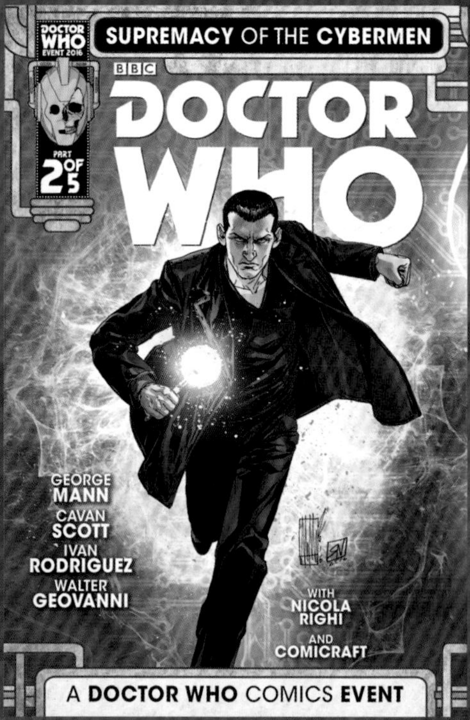
DOCTOR WHO EVENT 2016
SUPREMACY OF THE CYBERMEN
BBC
DOCTOR WHO
PART 2 OF 5
GEORGE MANN
CAVAN SCOTT
IVAN RODRIGUEZ
WALTER GEOVANNI
WITH NICOLA RIGHI AND COMICRAFT
A DOCTOR WHO COMICS EVENT

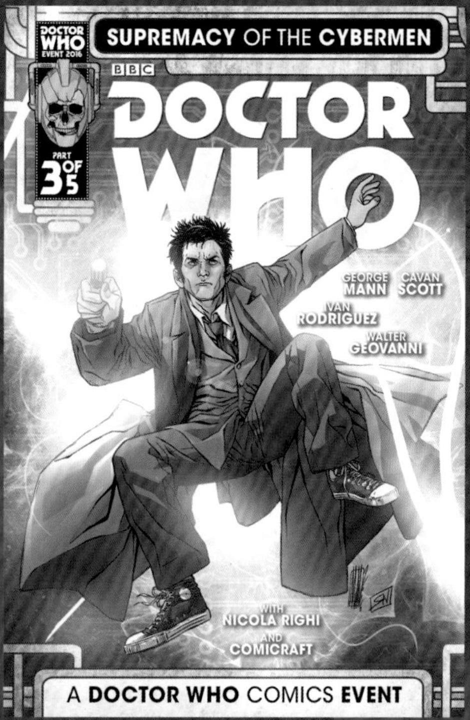
DOCTOR WHO EVENT 2016
SUPREMACY OF THE CYBERMEN
BBC
DOCTOR WHO
PART 3 OF 5
GEORGE MANN
CAVAN SCOTT
IVAN RODRIGUEZ
WALTER GEOVANNI
WITH NICOLA RIGHI AND COMICRAFT
A DOCTOR WHO COMICS EVENT

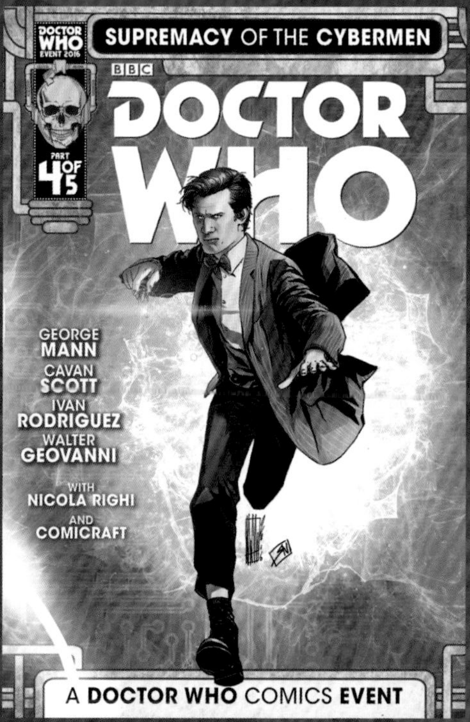
DOCTOR WHO EVENT 2016
SUPREMACY OF THE CYBERMEN
BBC
DOCTOR WHO
PART 4 OF 5
GEORGE MANN
CAVAN SCOTT
IVAN RODRIGUEZ
WALTER GEOVANNI
WITH NICOLA RIGHI AND COMICRAFT
A DOCTOR WHO COMICS EVENT

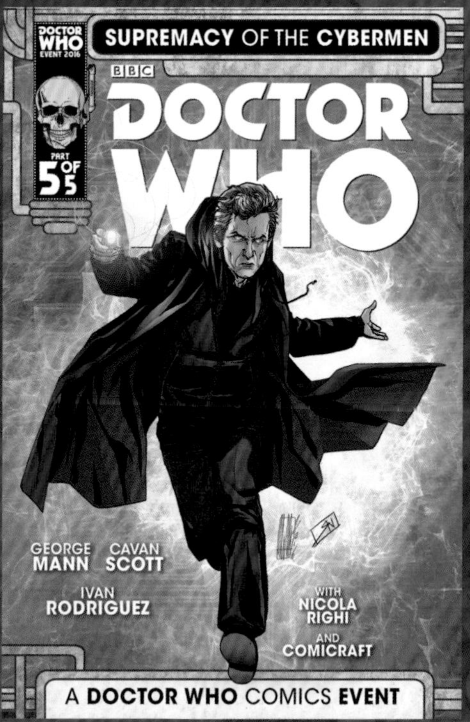
DOCTOR WHO EVENT 2016
SUPREMACY OF THE CYBERMEN
BBC
DOCTOR WHO
PART 5 OF 5
GEORGE MANN
CAVAN SCOTT
IVAN RODRIGUEZ
WITH NICOLA RIGHI AND COMICRAFT
A DOCTOR WHO COMICS EVENT

COVER B
PHOTO COVER

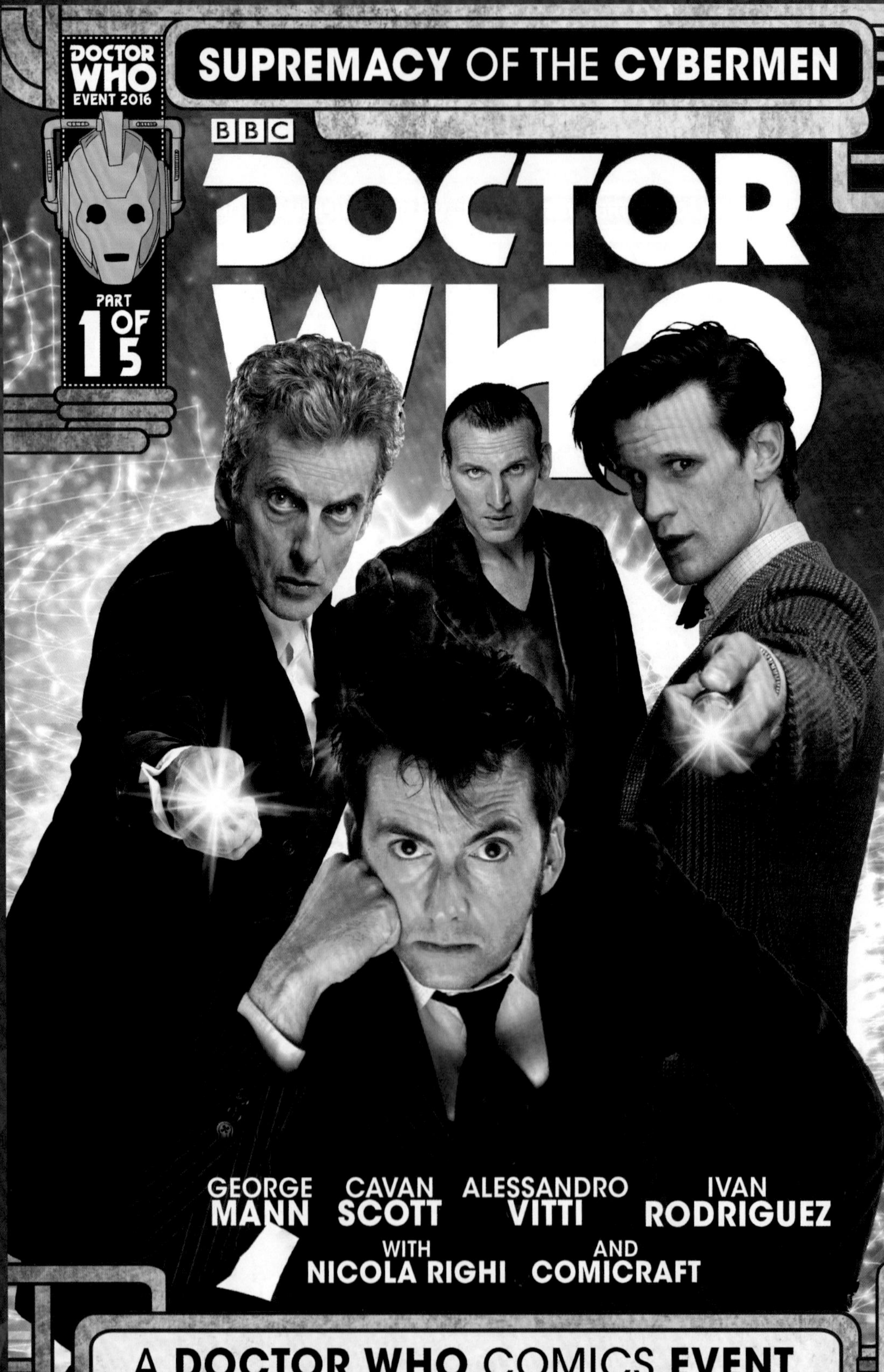
DOCTOR WHO
EVENT 2016
SUPREMACY OF THE CYBERMEN
BBC
DOCTOR WHO
PART 1 OF 5
GEORGE MANN
CAVAN SCOTT
ALESSANDRO VITTI
IVAN RODRIGUEZ
WITH NICOLA RIGHI
AND COMICRAFT
A DOCTOR WHO COMICS EVENT

Collect all 5 covers!

COVER C
BY FABIO LISTRANI

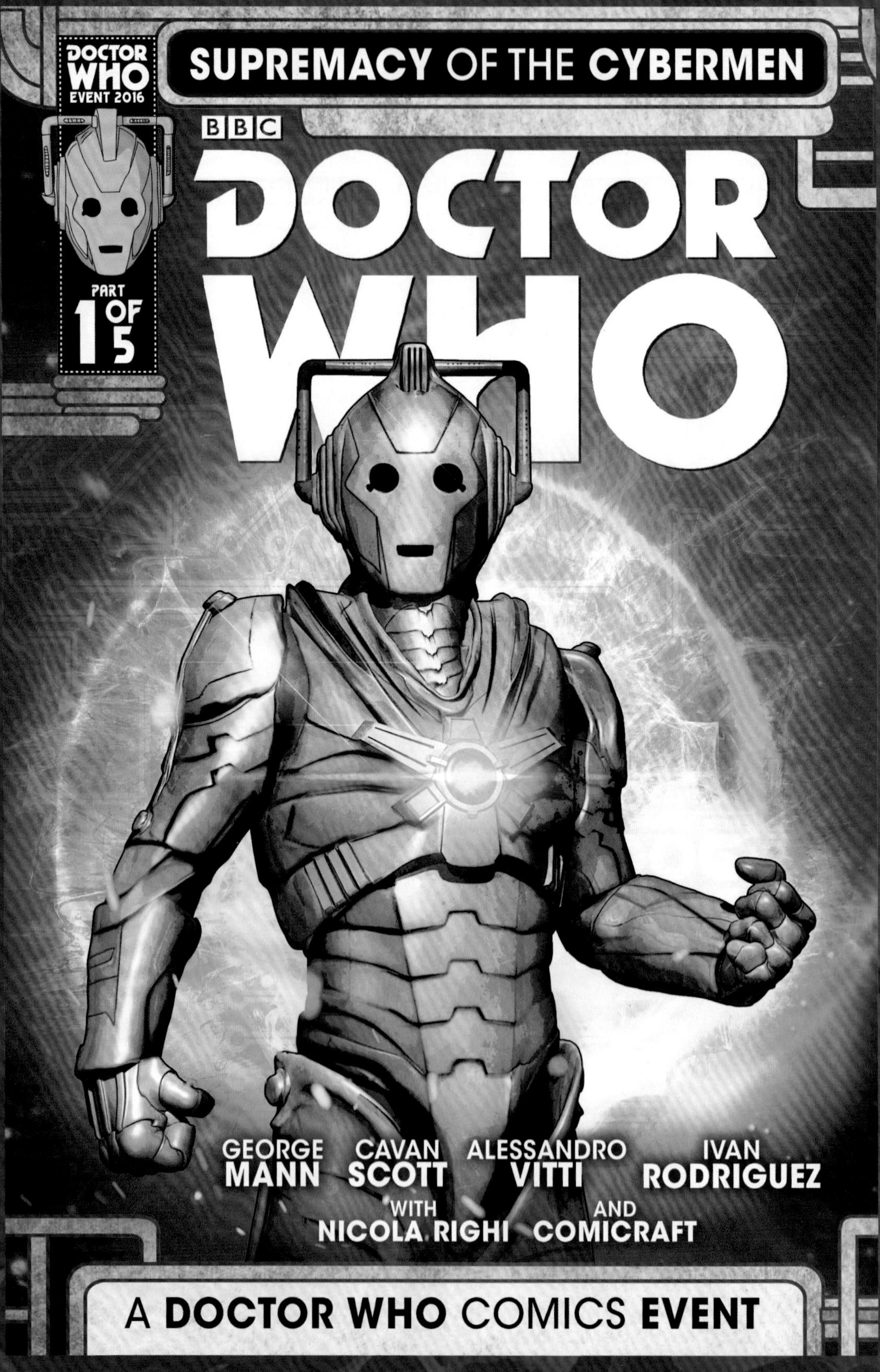

SUPREMACY OF THE CYBERMEN
DOCTOR WHO EVENT 2016
PART 1 OF 5
BBC
DOCTOR WHO
GEORGE MANN
CAVAN SCOTT
ALESSANDRO VITTI
IVAN RODRIGUEZ
WITH NICOLA RIGHI
AND COMICRAFT
A DOCTOR WHO COMICS EVENT

FOLLOW YOUR FAVORITE INCARNATIONS ACROSS THESE FANTASTIC COLLECTIONS!

DOCTOR WHO: THE TWELFTH DOCTOR VOL. 1: TERRORFORMER

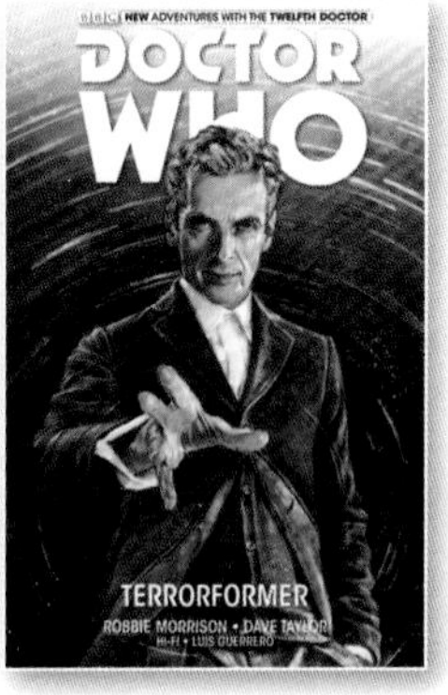
DOCTOR WHO
TERRORFORMER
ROBBIE MORRISON • DAVE TAYLOR

ISBN: 9781782761778
ON SALE NOW - $19.99 / $22.95 CAN / £10.99
(UK EDITION ISBN: 9781782763864)

DOCTOR WHO: THE TWELFTH DOCTOR VOL. 2: FRACTURES

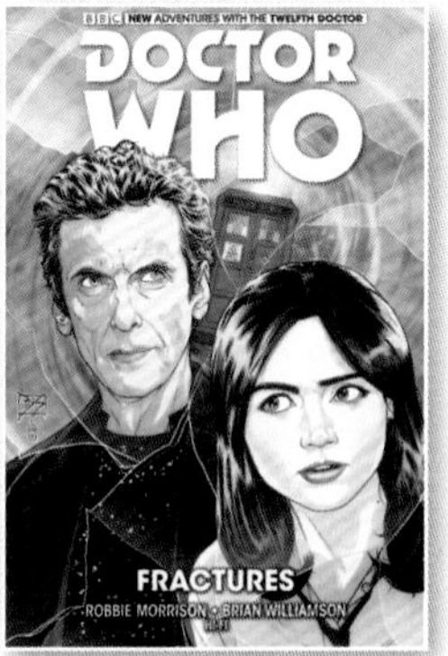
DOCTOR WHO
FRACTURES
ROBBIE MORRISON • BRIAN WILLIAMSON

ISBN: 9781782763017
ON SALE NOW - $19.99 / $25.99 CAN / £10.99
(UK EDITION ISBN: 9781782766599)

DOCTOR WHO: THE TWELFTH DOCTOR VOL. 3: HYPERION

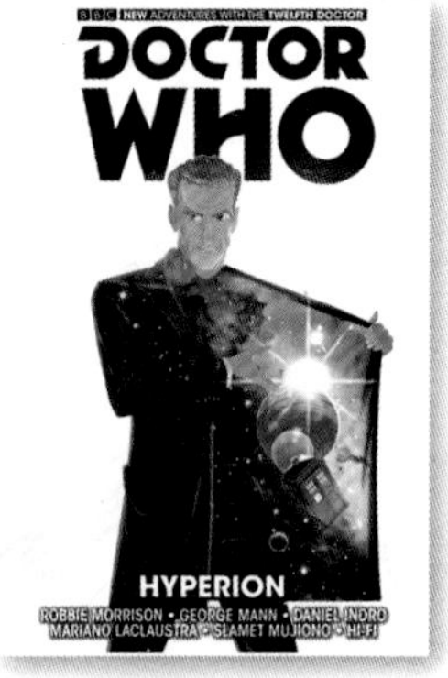
DOCTOR WHO
HYPERION

ISBN: 9781782767473
ON SALE NOW- $19.99 / $25.99 CAN / £10.99
(UK EDITION ISBN: 9781782767442)

DOCTOR WHO: THE TWELFTH DOCTOR VOL. 4: THE SCHOOL OF DEATH

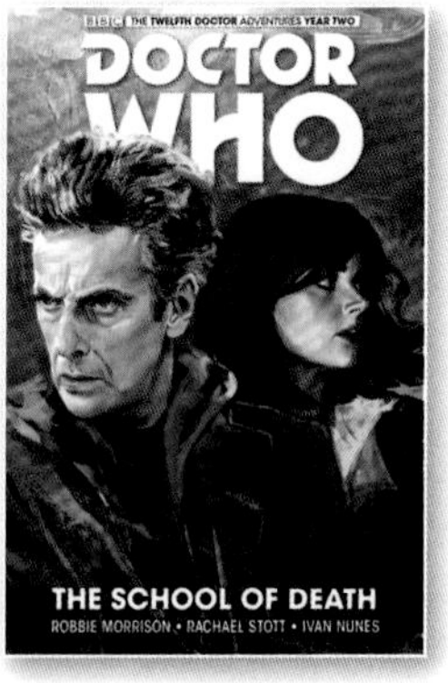
DOCTOR WHO
THE SCHOOL OF DEATH
ROBBIE MORRISON • RACHAEL STOTT • IVAN NUNES

ISBN: 9781785851087
COMING SOON - $19.99 / $25.99 CAN / £10.99
(UK EDITION ISBN: 9781785851070)

DOCTOR WHO: THE ELEVENTH DOCTOR VOL. 1: AFTER LIFE

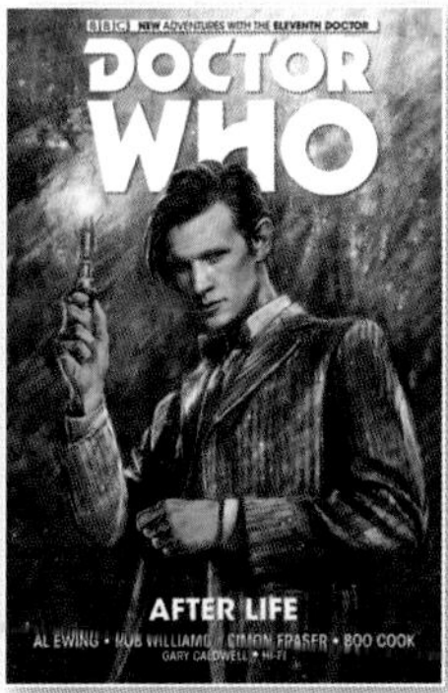
DOCTOR WHO
AFTER LIFE

ISBN: 9781782761747
ON SALE NOW - $19.99 / $22.95 CAN / £10.99
(UK EDITION ISBN: 9781782763857)

DOCTOR WHO: THE ELEVENTH DOCTOR VOL. 2: SERVE YOU

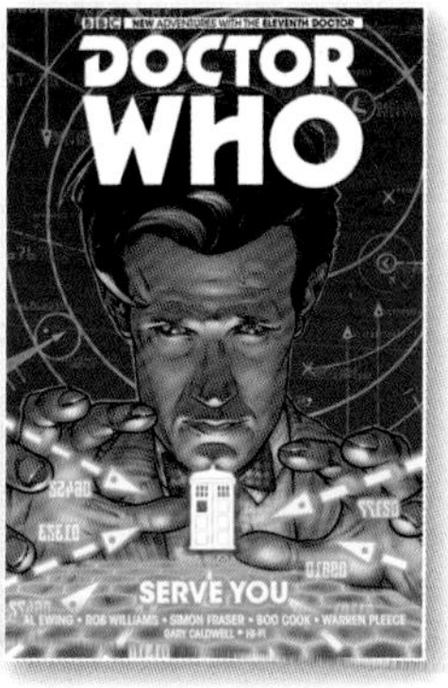
DOCTOR WHO
SERVE YOU

ISBN: 9781782761754
ON SALE NOW - $19.99 / $25.99 CAN / £10.99
(UK EDITION ISBN: 9781782766582)

DOCTOR WHO: THE ELEVENTH DOCTOR VOL. 3: CONVERSION

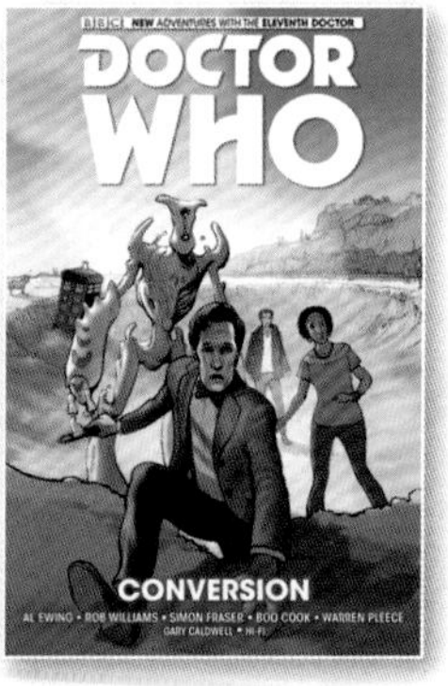
DOCTOR WHO
CONVERSION

ISBN: 9781782763024
ON SALE NOW - $19.99 / $25.99 CAN / £10.99
(UK EDITION ISBN: 9781782767435)

DOCTOR WHO: THE ELEVENTH DOCTOR VOL. 4: THE THEN AND THE NOW

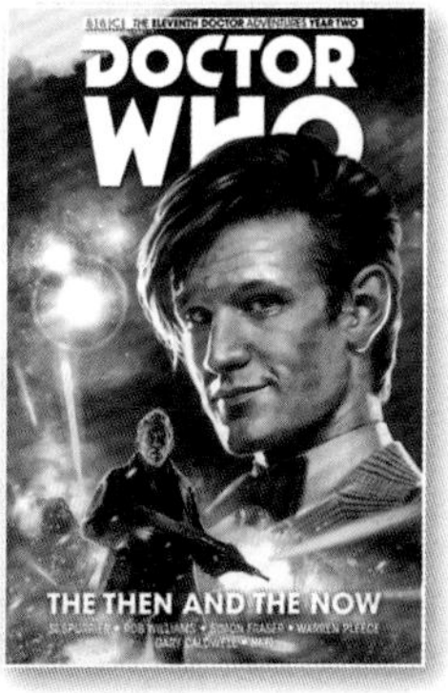
DOCTOR WHO
THE THEN AND THE NOW

ISBN: 9781782767466
ON SALE NOW - $19.99 / $25.99 CAN / £10.99
(UK EDITION ISBN: 9781722767428)

For information on how to subscribe to our great Doctor Who titles, or to purchase them digitally for your favorite device, visit:

WWW.TITAN-COMICS.COM

TITAN COMICS

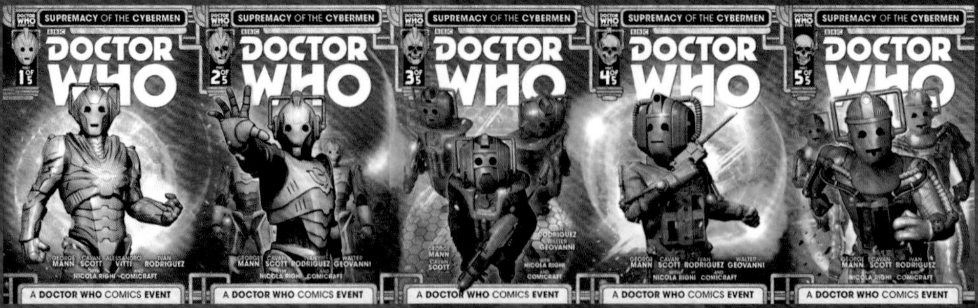
SUPREMACY OF THE CYBERMEN
DOCTOR WHO
A DOCTOR WHO COMICS EVENT
SUPREMACY OF THE CYBERMEN
DOCTOR WHO
A DOCTOR WHO COMICS EVENT
SUPREMACY OF THE CYBERMEN
DOCTOR WHO
A DOCTOR WHO COMICS EVENT
SUPREMACY OF THE CYBERMEN
DOCTOR WHO
A DOCTOR WHO COMICS EVENT
SUPREMACY OF THE CYBERMEN
DOCTOR WHO
A DOCTOR WHO COMICS EVENT

Collect all 5 covers!

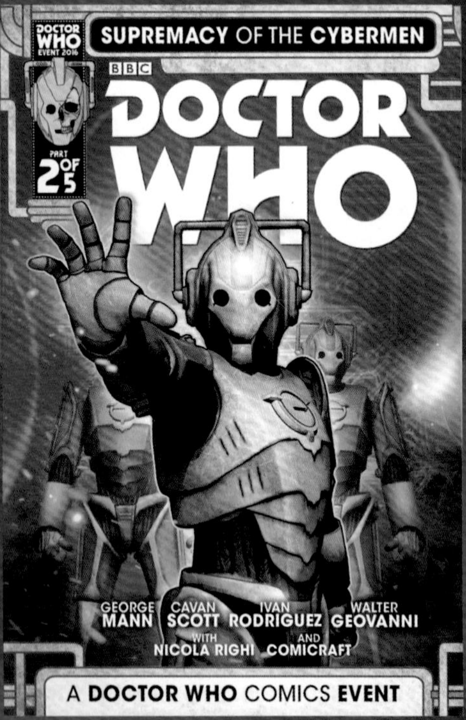
DOCTOR WHO EVENT 2016
SUPREMACY OF THE CYBERMEN
BBC
DOCTOR WHO
PART 2 OF 5
GEORGE MANN
CAVAN SCOTT
IVAN RODRIGUEZ
WALTER GEOVANNI
WITH NICOLA RIGHI AND COMICRAFT
A DOCTOR WHO COMICS EVENT

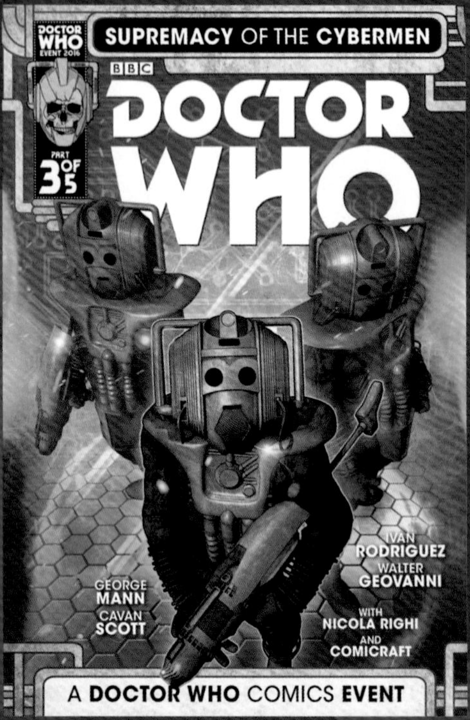
DOCTOR WHO EVENT 2016
SUPREMACY OF THE CYBERMEN
BBC
DOCTOR WHO
PART 3 OF 5
IVAN RODRIGUEZ
WALTER GEOVANNI
GEORGE MANN
CAVAN SCOTT
WITH NICOLA RIGHI AND COMICRAFT
A DOCTOR WHO COMICS EVENT

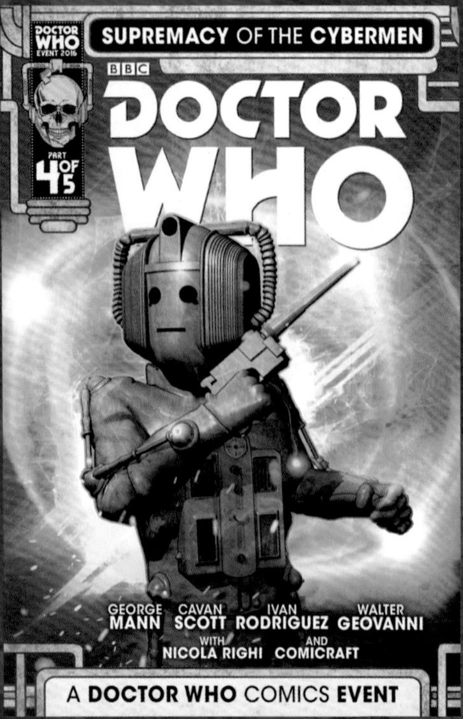
DOCTOR WHO EVENT 2016
SUPREMACY OF THE CYBERMEN
BBC
DOCTOR WHO
PART 4 OF 5
GEORGE MANN
CAVAN SCOTT
IVAN RODRIGUEZ
WALTER GEOVANNI
WITH NICOLA RIGHI AND COMICRAFT
A DOCTOR WHO COMICS EVENT

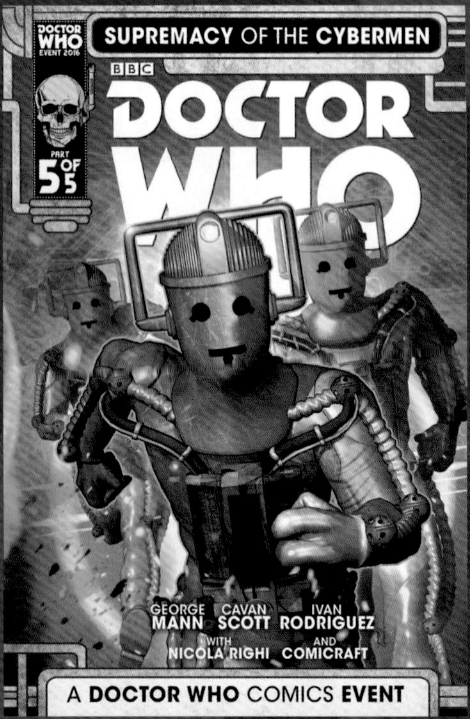
DOCTOR WHO EVENT 2016
SUPREMACY OF THE CYBERMEN
BBC
DOCTOR WHO
PART 5 OF 5
GEORGE MANN
CAVAN SCOTT
IVAN RODRIGUEZ
WITH NICOLA RIGHI AND COMICRAFT
A DOCTOR WHO COMICS EVENT

COMPLETE YOUR COLLECTION!

DOCTOR WHO: THE TENTH DOCTOR VOL. 1: REVOLUTIONS OF TERROR

DOCTOR WHO: THE TENTH DOCTOR VOL. 2: THE WEEPING ANGELS OF MONS

DOCTOR WHO: THE TENTH DOCTOR VOL. 3: THE FOUNTAINS OF FOREVER

DOCTOR WHO: THE TENTH DOCTOR VOL. 4: THE ENDLESS SONG

ISBN: 9781782761747
ON SALE NOW - $19.99 / $22.95 CAN / £10.99
(UK EDITION ISBN: 9781782763840)

ISBN: 9781782761754
ON SALE NOW - $19.99 / $25.99 CAN / £10.99
(UK EDITION ISBN: 9781782766575)

ISBN: 9781782763024
ON SALE NOW - $19.99 / $25.99 CAN / £10.99
(UK EDITION ISBN: 9781782767435)

ISBN: 9781785854286
ON SALE NOW - $19.99 / $25.99 CAN / £10.99
(SC ISBN: 9781785853227)

DOCTOR WHO: THE NINTH DOCTOR VOL. 1: WEAPONS OF PAST DESTRUCTION

DOCTOR WHO EVENT 2015 FOUR DOCTORS

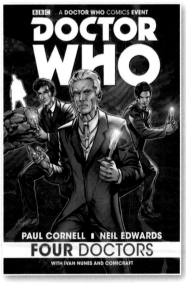

ISBN: 9781782763369
ON SALE NOW - $19.99 / $25.99 CAN / £10.99
(UK EDITION ISBN: 9781782761056)

ISBN: 9781782765967
ON SALE NOW - $19.99 / $25.99 CAN / £10.99
(UK EDITION ISBN: 9781785851063)

AVAILABLE IN ALL GOOD COMIC STORES, BOOK STORES, AND DIGITAL PROVIDERS!

BBC

DOCTOR WHO

SUPREMACY OF THE CYBERMEN

BIOGRAPHIES

George Mann is the writer of *Dark Souls, Warhammer 40,000, Doctor Who: The Eighth Doctor* and *The Twelfth Doctor* and *Newbury & Hobbes*, as well as numerous short stories, novellas, and *Doctor Who* audiobooks. He lives near Grantham, UK, with his wife and children.

Cavan Scott is a writer, editor and journalist, best known for his comics writing on *Doctor Who: The Ninth Doctor* and *Vikings,* as well as many novels, including *Star Wars: Adventures in Wild Space*. He co-wrote the bestselling *Who-Ology*. He lives in Bristol with his wife, two daughters, and an inflatable Dalek named Desmond.

Ivan Rodriguez is a Brazilian artist whose past works have included *The Shadow*.

Walter Geovanni is a comics artist, known for his many issues of *Red Sonja*.

Nicola Righi is an Italian illustrator and colorist who has worked in France and Italy for many years, with recent US titles such as *Spider-Man: Breed of Terror* and *Iron Man*.

Alessandro Vitti is an Italian comics artist who has worked on numerous titles such as *Secret Warriors, Red Lanterns* and *Captain America and Hawkeye*.

Tazio Bettin is an Italian rising star artist who has worked on *Warhammer 40,000* and *Sally and the Wasteland*.

Enrica Eren Angiolini is a colorist whose credits include *Warhammer 40,000* and *The Order of the Forge*.

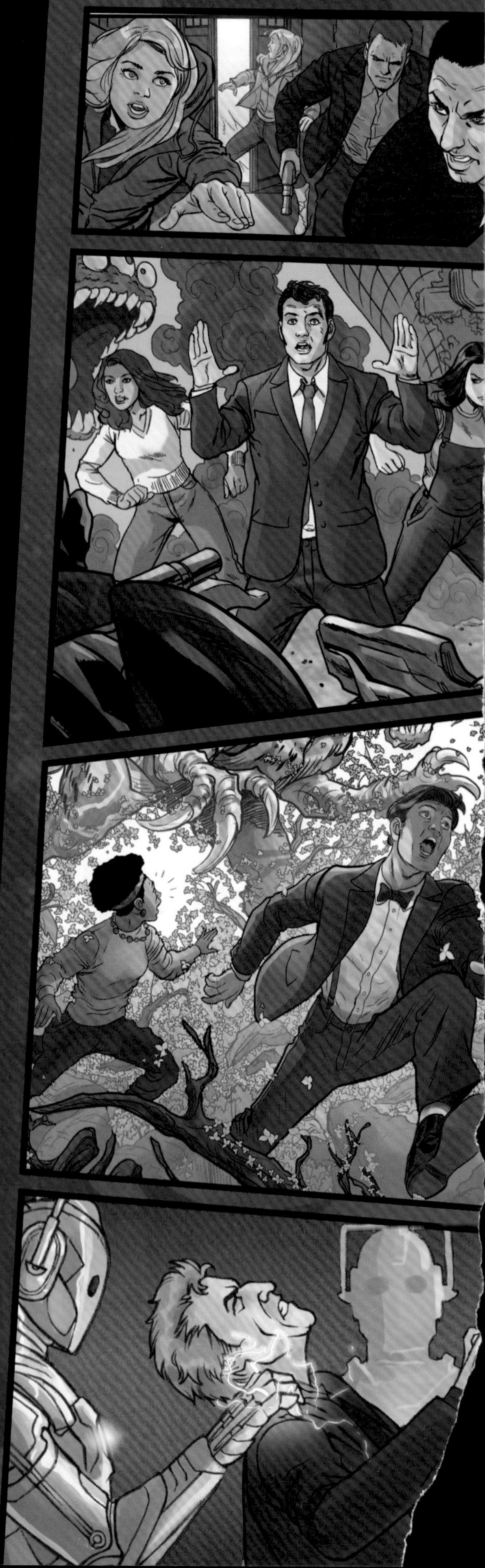